Race & Crime

Race & Crime

The *Key Approaches to Criminology* series is intended to help readers make intellectual connections between subjects and disciplines, and to understand the importance of studying crime and criminal justice within a broader context. There are surprisingly few books that synthesize concepts, theories and research concerning race and crime and in criminology 'race' is a subject that is frequently overlooked or is one that, at best, is confined to a single chapter in a textbook, as if issues of diversity and discrimination do not permeate all aspects of crime and justice. As someone who has researched topics as varied as the inner-city riots of the 1980s and 1990s, policing post-Macpherson, and youth perspectives on race and the criminal justice system, as well as establishing himself as a leading expert in the field of race and crime more broadly, Mike Rowe is ideally placed to write this volume. *Race and Crime* demonstrates the breadth, depth and richness of the field, encompassing social constructions and historical perspectives, representations and (mis)perceptions. Capturing some of the most controversial and pressing issues of our time, Rowe sheds new light on disproportionality in sentencing, racial biases in punishment, the challenges of policing a multi-racial society and the failures of criminology to adequately interrogate these issues or to problematize a concept that is, he argues, fundamentally flawed. This book is, then, the most up-to-date and comprehensive of its kind. Using contemporary and international examples throughout and providing vivid historical context, Rowe addresses topics ranging from colonialism and imperialism to human rights, and from eugenics and the Holocaust to terrorism and fears around security in the 21st Century. The scope, range and depth of this book is truly impressive and it is a welcome addition to the *Key Approaches* series.

Yvonne Jewkes
Series Editor

Race & Crime

A Critical Engagement

Michael Rowe

Los Angeles | London | New Delhi
Singapore | Washington DC

First published 2012

SAGE Publications Ltd
1 Oliver's Yard
55 City Road
London EC1Y 1SP

SAGE Publications Inc.
2455 Teller Road
Thousand Oaks, California 91320

SAGE Publications India Pvt Ltd
B 1/I 1 Mohan Cooperative Industrial Area
Mathura Road
New Delhi 110 044

SAGE Publications Asia-Pacific Pte Ltd
3 Church Street
#10-04 Samsung Hub
Singapore 049483

Library of Congress Control Number: 2011936824

British Library Cataloguing in Publication data

A catalogue record for this book is available from the British Library

ISBN   978-1-84920-726-3
ISBN   978-1-84920-727-0

Typeset by C&M Digitals (P) Ltd, Chennai, India
Printed and bound by CPI Group (UK) Ltd, Croydon, CR0 4YY
Printed on paper from sustainable resources

Contents

Acknowledgements

There are many people that I would like to thank for helping me to shape ideas discussed in this book. Current and former colleagues at Northumbria University, Victoria University Wellington and at the University of Leicester – at each of which I have taught modules covering topics addressed here – have always provided a supportive and collegiate environment. Other colleagues have also contributed ideas and discussion. In particular I would like to thank Adrian Beck, Neil Chakraborti, Bankole Cole, Adam Edwards, Jon Garland, Jamie Harding, Fiona Hutton, Nasar Meer, Michael Shiner, Matt Smith, Sarah Soppitt, Lizzie Stanley and Colin Webster.

Particular thanks are due to Yvonne Jewkes, who is not responsible for the content of what follows but is largely responsible for the fact that the book came into existence. Sarah-Jayne Boyd and Natalie Aguilera, at Sage, have been supportive and tolerant in equal measure and I am grateful to the anonymous reviewers who helped improve chapters along the way.

As always, the most significant debt is owed to Anna, Derry, Maggie and Niall, and the book is dedicated to them with love and thanks.

1

'Race', 'Crime' and Society

OVERVIEW

This chapter provides:

- critical consideration of the ways in which 'race' and 'crime' are socially constructed concepts that have no inherent ontological validity and so do not exist as 'natural' phenomena with independent properties;
- an outline of the nature of the 'critical engagement' between 'race' and 'crime' that forms the central theme of this book;
- an overview of the structure and chapters of the book.

KEY TERMS

- Crime
- Criminalization
- Race

- Scientific racism
- Sociological approaches to 'race'
- Racialization

Introduction

So pervasive and long-standing are the associations between 'race' and 'crime' that it might seem unnecessary to begin by critically examining the fundamental terms and concepts that form the backbone of the book. It has become axiomatic that issues of 'race' are central to the criminological cannon. Unquantifiable intellectual effort and research grant expenditure has been focused over many decades and across many societies in a vast array of studies that have sought to measure associations between 'race' and 'crime' in terms of patterns of offending, experiences of victimization, treatment by the criminal justice system and the impact and status that these have had in terms of social and political debates and media representation. A reasonable working definition of criminology is that it is a discipline concerned with the study of crime and social responses to crime (Mannheim, 1965): as the rest of this book demonstrates, debates relating to 'race' have been recurrent themes in relation to both of these dimensions of the discipline of criminology since it emerged in the nineteenth century. The relationship between 'race' and 'crime' is a near ubiquitous feature of undergraduate and postgraduate degree programmes in criminology and criminal justice in many parts of the world. Official statistics relating to 'race' and 'crime' are collated, analyzed and debated in many societies. Even in those countries that do not provide apparently authoritative profiles of the 'racial' component of criminal justice activity, the status of minority groups, indigenous peoples, asylum-seekers and migrants is often subject to intense political and social debate. Recently, Bowling (in Gabbidon, 2007) referred to 'criminology's quiet obsession with race and crime'. While the implication that the concept of 'race' has surreptitiously informed broad swathes of the discipline is apposite, the content of this book further illustrates that criminology's interest in 'race' has often not been clandestine, marginal or softly-spoken.

The Social Construction of 'Race'

Analysis based on sorting and classifying humanity into distinct 'races', and that these racial differences explained cultural, political, social and economic development, emerged in the eighteenth and nineteenth centuries. The emergence of the concept of race during this period is associated with the development of modern scientific approaches to the natural and social world that sought to develop rational epistemological models that replaced pre-modern or classical traditions (Banton, 1987). Goldberg (1993: 3) described 'race' as 'one of the central conceptual inventions of modernity' and the methodological and philosophical approach of key progenitors of nineteenth-century scientific racism reflected intellectual currents of the period. Anthropologists, zoologists, medical scientists and biologists in learned societies and universities, at the height of European imperial dominance, developed theories of 'racial difference' that categorized humanity into racial types organized hierarchically in ways that served both to explain and to justify the ascendant position of the white race. The Scottish medical scientist Robert Knox was among the first to develop a general biological theory of race and racial difference, claiming in his 1850 book *The Races of Men* that 'race, or hereditary descent is everything; it stamps the man' (Banton, 1967: 29). Solomos and Back (1996: 42–43) argued that nineteenth century 'scientific racism' comprised of four elements: (a) that physical appearances reflected discrete and permanent biological types, (b) that these determined cultural variations between groups, (c) that biological variations were the source of group conflict, and (d) that 'races' were differently endowed and could be organized hierarchically. On this basis, 'race' explained all of human civilization and shaped the course of history. The fundamental role of 'race' in human affairs was expressed strongly in a book published in 1854, *Types of Mankind*, in which Nott and Gliddon argued (1854, cited in Banton, 1967: 31–32):

> Human progress has arisen mainly from the war of the races. All the great impulses which have been given to it from time to time have been the results of

> conquests and colonizations ... those groups of races heretofore compre-
> hended under the generic term Caucasian, have in all ages been the rulers; and
> it requires no prophet's eye to see that they are destined eventually to conquer
> and hold every foot of the globe ... the superior races ought to be kept free
> from all adulterations, otherwise the world will retrograde, instead of advancing,
> in civilization.

Racial traits and typologies, discoverable through the application of scientific methods, formed a framework for explaining the human condition – this was reflected in early criminological studies of delinquency and offenders that also sought to identify biological bases for criminality, as is shown in Chapter Two. In relation to both 'race' and 'crime', the biological scientific certainties sought by scholars in the mid-nineteenth century were gradually eroded as anthropological, cultural and sociological perspectives focused instead on the social contexts in which the concepts developed. In relation to the notion of 'race', sociological approaches developed from the early twentieth century and concentrated on the social circumstances in which racial attributes came to assume significance. In the aftermath of the Second World War, UNESCO commissioned biologists and sociologists to study the scientific basis of the concept of race. Extended deliberations by panels of experts concluded that 'race' had no biological basis in the terms envisaged a century earlier during the zenith of scientific racism (Rex, 1970). The UNESCO studies arrived at a definition of 'race' that significantly departed from nineteenth-century racist orthodoxy, concluding that 'for all practical social purposes "race" is not so much a biological phenomenon as a social myth' (Montagu, 1972, cited in Malik, 1996: 15). Rex (1970: 3–4) outlined six key findings of the UNESCO study in relation to the biological status of 'race': (i) that human populations represent a continuum and that the genetic diversity within groups is as great as that between them; (ii) that observable human characteristics are the result of biology and environment rather than inheritance; (iii) the various characteristics grouped together as racial and said to be transmitted *en bloc* are in fact transmitted individually; (iv) human beings belong to a single species and are derived from common stock; (v) although different human groups may be loosely referred to as 'races', it is not justifiable to attribute cultural characteristics to genetic inheritance; (vi) human evolution has been greatly affected by migration and cultural evolution and the capacity to advance is shared by all *homo sapiens*.

After this period, sociological perspectives on race eclipsed biological and genetic approaches. As has been noted, 'race' became a social phenomenon worthy of study not because it had any inherent status in genetic or biological terms but because human beings so often acted upon the basis that it was meaningful: a concept real not in itself but in its consequences. This raises a fundamental problem that recurs throughout this book and is returned to in more detail in the final chapter; namely, the need to 'take race seriously' as a social phenomenon while at the same time not affording it spurious credibility or reinforcing its legitimacy. In Britain, the sociology of race relations often focused on social, economic and political relationships between white communities and the first generations of migrants from the Caribbean, who arrived in the 'mother country' during a period of labour shortages and post-war reconstruction. Studies such as those by Banton (1959), Glass (1960), and Rex and Moore (1967) examined conflicts and tensions between host and migrant communities in relation to competition for employment, housing, and various social and cultural issues. Crucially, in contrast to earlier approaches, the concept of race is not understood to be an independent causal factor such that social conflicts of these kinds are a result of innate, inevitable, determining characteristics of 'racial' types. Theoretically, sociological approaches to race relations focused on debates about the extent to which the concept of race was a form of 'status' in Weberian terms, acted to increase social solidarity in Durkheimian traditions, or represented 'false consciousness' that distracted from the fundamental dynamics of class struggle, as Marxist perspectives might suggest (Rex, 1986).

However, critics of these sociological approaches argue that by taking race seriously as a concept 'real in its consequences', such studies replicate dominant racist assumptions and fail to challenge structural and ideological relations of power that marginalize and criminalize oppressed communities. Miles (1989, 1993) offered a strong critique of the sociology of race relations on the grounds that they continue to grant the concept analytical validity, albeit in terms other than biology and genetics. For Miles, 'race' is an ideological construction that is intimately bound up in structural and economic foundations of capitalist society. Retaining 'race', even if understood in sociological terms, affords the concept a status it does not warrant and is a barrier to the development of progressive political action. On this basis, the focus ought instead to be on the ways in which the idea of 'race' is constructed in particular social and ideological contexts. Small (1994: 34) develops this perspective by arguing that the key challenge is not to explore the realities of race, but instead to consider processes of racialization that make the concept a powerful determinant of social relations. Small argues that (1994: 34):

> When we examine the process of 'racialisation' we find that our beliefs about 'races' and 'race relations' have more to do with the attitudes, actions, motivations and interests of powerful groups in society; and less to do with the characteristics, attitudes and actions of those who are defined as belonging to 'inferior' races ... we must also acknowledge that definitions, ideas and images once begun can vary and endure in ways that are complex.

As is elaborated further in the final chapter of this book, the approach adopted in this text is one that emphasizes the problematic social construction of the concept of race. The analysis of the various points of critical engagement between race and crime that is developed in the following chapters focuses attention on the particular ways in which crime, disorder, deviance, law, security, and terrorism have been racialized in different times and places. Four related features characterize the racialization approach (Murji and Solomos, 2005):

1   Race is a problematic concept that is socially constructed in particular spatial and temporal contexts;
2   Racialized debates that develop in local contexts draw upon and further contribute to historical discourse and understanding of 'race';
3   Racialization is an inconsistent and contradictory process that may not explicitly refer to biological, genetic or cultural themes;
4   Racialized discourse articulates with other socially constructed concepts, including those relating to gender, youth and crime.

It is to indicate recognition that the concept is fundamentally flawed and socially constructed that many authors use quotation marks, such that race becomes 'race'. Although this book seeks to further develop a critical analysis of processes of racialization and is based on the same theoretical standpoint that problematizes the concept, it does not continue to place the term in quotation marks. Although race is used, without quotation marks, in the remainder of the book, the entire theme of the analysis is to critically examine the social, political, cultural and intellectual contexts in which the term develops and has been deployed. Given that race has no inherent validity, the task becomes to explain the circumstances in which it comes to form a compelling way of understanding and organizing social relations.

The Social Construction of 'Crime'

As the concept of racialization draws attention to the ways in which 'race' is a socially constructed phenomenon, so too the term 'criminalization' suggests that analysis ought to be concentrated on the circumstances in which some forms of behaviour come to be understood as problems that require some form of state-sanctioned response. Focusing on the process of criminalization recognizes that 'crime' is a problematic term that cannot be understood as an independent category defined by its own inherent properties. Crime, and the appropriate responses to it, has dominated political and media debate in many countries for many decades. Serious, violent and dramatic cases are given a high priority on news agendas, political parties promise ever 'tougher' sanctions, and citizens consume infotainment shows, movies and computer games that offer thrilling opportunities to enjoy crime vicariously. For all that crime is easy to recognize in contemporary mass-mediated society, it remains difficult to define. A traditional approach to defining crime adopts a legalistic framework: crime is that category of activity that is subject to the criminal law. Clearly this circular definition – a crime is a crime because the law defines it so – has some merit. In applied terms it provides an operational framework that shapes the actions of the agencies of the criminal justice system. As much of the criminological literature has noted over many decades though, it is an unsatisfactory basis for understanding crime for a number of reasons. In the 1930s, Michael and Adler (1933, cited in Muncie, 1996: 8) noted that a logical consequence of the 'black letter law' definition of crime is that no action can be considered criminal unless it is proscribed by the law, which means that the criminal law is the formal cause of crime. Relatedly, no individual can be considered to have committed a crime unless they have been apprehended, prosecuted and convicted by the criminal justice system (Muncie, 1996: 8).

That the scope of the law varies across time and between different societies directs attention to the social, economic, political and cultural context against which certain actions come to be defined as criminal. Reiner (2007: 21–43) suggests that the construction of certain actions or behaviour as 'criminal' can be understood in five dimensions:

- *the legal*, representing the contingent outcome of centuries of legislation and case-law, united by the formal characteristics of criminal process, not the substantive nature of the multifarious behaviours subject to prosecution;
- *moral views* about what *should* be punished, varying between different cultures;
- *socially/culturally sanctioned* behaviour, stigmatized in everyday practice;
- *the criminal justice system* labelled pattern of offences and offenders;
- *mass media/public policy* representations, following a 'law of opposites' focusing on the rarest cases of homicide, violence and sex crimes.

While some actions and behaviour might be understood as criminal in terms of any and all of the dimensions identified by Reiner, others might not. Two examples that are examined at greater length later in this book illustrate the partial and differential ways in which activities come to be identified as criminal. The practice of lynching, a form of racist violence prevalent in the United States from the mid-nineteenth to mid-twentieth centuries, was clearly prohibited in legal and moral terms but, as is shown at greater length in Chapter Five, often was not sanctioned socially or culturally, or in sections of the mass media. Similarly, environmental damage that disproportionally harms marginalized ethnic groups in some developing societies might constitute a breach of international human rights law but has often not been addressed by criminal justice systems. Moreover, the practices of multinational corporations and governments that contribute to environmental degradation have tended not to be identified as a form of crime in mass media or public policy debate. The status of such problems as criminal practices is discussed in more detail in Chapter Six.

Although an emphasis on social processes of criminalization is preferred, it does not follow that crime is understood only as a category created through labelling and stigmatization. The concept of crime cannot be conceptualized in terms isolated from the spatial and temporal context in which it develops, but it contains an essential reality in terms of the harm and damage wrought. Reiner (2007) suggests that for all that crime needs to be understood along the five dimensions identified above, it retains a central characteristic related to the notion of 'trespass': the physical intrusion into a property or person. While the attention of criminology and criminal justice might be disproportionally focused on forms of trespass associated with the disadvantaged and the powerless and only rarely notice those forms of state and corporate crime that pose the most significant threat to humanity, the crimes of the powerful can also be considered as forms of trespass. The need to focus critical attention on such crimes is a core theme returned to at various points in the discussion that follows.

Race and Crime: a Critical Engagement

Although 'race' and 'crime' have come to form a natural association, reinforced by research, policy and political agendas, a central theme of this book is that these two core concepts ought to be understood in terms of a 'critical engagement'. Although that phrase forms a sub-title of the text, it is intended as the fundamental basis for the discussion and analysis that follows. The critical engagement between 'race' and 'crime' is considered along two dimensions. First, the analysis presented in the chapters that follow demonstrates the diverse and enduring ways in which the concepts of race and crime have been conjoined and mutually reinforcing. 'Race' has come to be seen as a significant independent variable that informs much contemporary debate about 'crime' in the context of urban society, for example. As Keith (1993) has argued, the racialization of contemporary debates about crime mirrors ways in which 'racial' identities have become increasingly constructed in terms of crime and disorder. The social construction of 'race' has continued in close relation to parallel processes of criminalization, in that they are mutually referential and conceptually co-dependent. The two concepts have been critically engaged for many decades, in various contexts and in diverse societies.

The argument and analysis that follows also provides a critical engagement with race and crime in a second sense; by foregrounding that both concepts are problematic and cannot be taken for granted. A critical approach recognizes that both race and crime are, independently and together, concepts that provide powerful and enduring ways in which people negotiate and narrate the social world and so neither can be dismissed as mere imagined constructions and so not valid units of analysis. As has been noted, both are real in so far as they are real in their consequences. Recognizing this while retaining a critical perspective is the challenge that the book seeks to meet.

Structure of the Book

In developing these core themes the book comprises nine subsequent chapters, each addressing distinct dimensions of the critical engagement between race and crime. Chapter Two considers the troubling relationship between academic and 'scientific' studies of race and the development of criminology. The discipline of criminology emerged in Europe in the mid-nineteenth century when 'scientific' race-thinking was ascendant. Early criminological thought often mirrored such efforts. While scientific racism has largely been discredited, elements of biological determinism continue to resound within criminological thought, and the prospect of genetic explanations of offending behaviour also suggest that debates about race and crime continue to converge.

Chapter Three examines media representation and popular discourse that have often signified 'strangers' and foreigners as threatening alien others with the potential to undermine consensual communities. The historical and contemporary criminalization and racialization of minority ethnic groups in media and popular culture are reviewed, including in news and infotainment and in emerging media forms. Popular cultural representations of ethnic organized crime, terrorism, and street crime are used as mini-case studies to explore wider themes as they apply in respect of the various types of media considered.

Disproportionality in offending is examined in Chapter Four. The chapter explores, in broad terms, arguments about the supposed over-involvement of minorities in criminal activity from the late nineteenth through to the twenty-first century. Deviancy has been associated with migrant groups of many kinds in Britain, the United States, Australasia, and elsewhere. Evidence relating to disproportionality is critically reviewed and key explanations of the apparent over-involvement of minority ethnic groups in offending are outlined and assessed. The chapter also considers disproportionality in victimization and representation in the criminal justice system and the extent to which this is linked to socio-economic, geographic and demographic factors and to institutional and system bias – arguments considered in greater detail in Chapter Seven.

Chapter Five considers evidence developed from victimization surveys, indicating that many minority communities are more likely to experience 'general' crime than other groups. The extent to which victimization rates are associated with wider processes of social marginalization are considered. The chapter continues with a review of the nature and prevalence of racist crime and considers reasons why often it has not been effectively investigated or prosecuted. Debates about the hate crime legislation, considered in terms of ethics and efficacy, are considered as part of a broader critique of efforts to strengthen the response to racist victimization.

Chapter Six begins by establishing that, globally, some of the most serious criminal episodes of the modern era have been closely linked with processes of racial and ethnic conflict. Slavery, racial segregation in the USA, apartheid in South Africa, the Holocaust, the 'ethnic cleansing' of Bosnian Muslims in the 1990s, and the genocide in Rwanda are among the most familiar episodes in contemporary world history and have involved death and injury on a scale far beyond most other criminal activity. Despite this scope and profile, such events have received little attention in the criminological literature. This chapter considers why this might be, and the implications that this has for reconceptualizing the discipline of criminology.

Disproportionality in the criminal justice system is analyzed in Chapter Seven. Minority ethnic groups are treated disproportionately, in comparison to the population in general, at every stage of the criminal justice system: from the 'entry' point of police stop and search and arrest, through the courts system, and to 'disposals' in the form of prisons and offender management services. Although some explanations of these patterns regard it as an inevitable consequence of disproportionate offending patterns outlined in Chapter Four, the chapter suggests that claims of discrimination and racism remain convincing even though establishing the ways in which they intervene at particular points of the system remains problematic.

Chapter Eight critically explores diversity and representation among the personnel of the criminal justice system. The 'normative whiteness' of criminal justice systems in many jurisdictions, closely associated with the under-representation of minority ethnic groups in the workforce, has been widely associated with the disproportionality discussed in the previous chapter. Chapter Eight considers why minority ethnic groups have been under-represented in criminal justice agencies, the impact of efforts to increase recruitment, and the impact that such strategies might have on institutional performance. Other efforts to promote diversity, for example, through training, community engagement and the promotion of ethical and professional standards, are critically reviewed.

Chapter Nine outlines ways in which racial, ethnic and religious differences have provided a powerful framework for understanding and responding to contemporary terrorism. Much of the military, security and law enforcement response to terrorism reflects wider processes of racialization and criminalization. Technologies and strategies of security management have consequences in terms of the fear of crime and have developed iteratively with racialized social relations. This chapter explores what Garland (2001) described as the 'criminology of the other', and concludes by critically assessing arguments that Muslim people have come to form a 'suspect community' in the twenty-first century.

The book ends with a chapter that summarizes the key debates and reiterates that race and crime debates have been closely intertwined since criminology emerged in the mid-nineteenth century. While biological and genetic determinism of the crude reductionist types associated with early 'race thinking' and explanations of criminal behaviour have become less influential, the two concepts continue to engage in uneasy dialogue. The conclusion questions whether contemporary criminological focus on 'race' – in the form of ethnic monitoring, for example – affords spurious legitimacy to a concept that is fundamentally flawed and ought not to be granted 'master status' with explanatory power. It is argued that the critical engagement between race and crime ought to be challenged, but that greater attention should be paid to the combined impact of racism, racialization and criminalization.

SUMMARY

The chapter has shown that the concepts at the heart of this book – race and crime – are both socially constructed. As such they have no core objective content that can be understood outside the social context in which the terms are used. In the nineteenth century, scientific approaches to race, and crime, sought to establish an empirical biological basis on which human beings could be categorized into distinct racial groups. Often, it has been shown, these groups were organized hierarchically in ways that reflected broader relationships of domination and subordination relating to European imperialism. Scientific approaches to race during that period suggested that biological genetic characteristics explained the different stages of development of distinct human groups. The scientific basis of race has been discredited, partially due to a comprehensive study by biologists and sociologists completed on behalf of UNESCO. Sociological perspectives focused instead on the social, economic, political and cultural circumstances in which 'race relations' developed. While these approaches recognized that 'race' was not an objective scientific fact but one that was an important object of enquiry, since it informed social practices and relations,

(Continued)

(Continued)

these approaches have themselves been critically challenged on the basis that they continue to give credence to the concept of race. A more important task is to examine processes of racialization that explain why 'race' has assumed such significant, though unwarranted, explanatory power.

The concept of crime also needs to be understood as a socially constructed concept, excavated of inherent properties. While the criminal law remains an important starting point for defining crime, it is insufficient. Reiner (2007) argued that moral, social, and cultural values as well as the practices of the criminal justice system and public policy also determine the definition of certain actions and behaviour as 'crimes'.

The critical engagement between 'race' and 'crime' that forms a core theme of this book can be understood in two dimensions. First, that the two have been conjoined and mutually reinforcing for many decades and, second, the analysis itself foregrounds a critical engagement focused upon the context in which debates about race and crime have continued since the mid-nineteenth century.

STUDY QUESTIONS

1   What were the core components of scientific racism developed in the mid-nineteenth century? How do they contrast with the sociology of race relations that emerged in the post-Second World War period?

2   Explain how the four elements of racialization outlined in the chapter seek to refocus analysis of the concept of 'race'.

3   What are the key weaknesses of 'black letter law' approaches to defining crime?

4   What are the two dimensions of the critical engagement between 'race' and 'crime' that are developed throughout this text?

FURTHER READING

Unsurprisingly, there is a huge volume of literature on both concepts introduced in this chapter. Back and Solomos (2000, Routledge) have edited a reader *Theories of Race and Racism* that provides a substantive overview of changing approaches to the analysis of 'race'. Murji and Solomos (2005, Oxford University Press) have edited a collection that explores the central idea of racialization in theoretical and applied terms. Reiner's (2007, Polity Press) *Law and Order: An Honest Citizen's Guide to Crime and Control* provides a compelling analysis of recent developments relating to crime and the concept of crime in Britain and the USA. Part 2 of Newburn's (2007, Willan Publishing) *Criminology* offers a clear exposition of different theoretical approaches to the concept of crime. An excellent collection of pieces relating to both core concepts of this book is Gabbidon and Taylor Greene's (2011, Sage) *Race and Crime: A Text/Reader*.

2

Race, Crime and the Criminological Imagination

CONTENTS

OVERVIEW

This chapter considers the troubling relationship between academic and 'scientific' studies of race and the development of criminology. The discipline of criminology emerged in Europe in the mid-nineteenth century when 'scientific' race-thinking was ascendant. Early criminological thought often mirrored such efforts. While scientific racism has largely been discredited, elements of biological determinism continue to resound within criminological thought, and the prospect of genetic explanations of offending behaviour also suggest that debates about race and crime continue to converge. The chapter will:

- critically evaluate the development of modern criminology and its relation to theories of race in colonial nineteenth-century Europe;
- examine the development of early sociological perspectives on crime, race and ethnicity;
- consider how critical perspectives on crime and race emphasize the socially constructed nature of both concepts.

KEY TERMS

- Biosocial theories of crime
- Classical criminology
- Criminological positivism
- Eugenics
- Holocaust
- Labelling theory
- Scientific racism
- Sociological approaches to 'race'

Introduction

This chapter explores the complex and enduring relationship between criminological theory and the concept of race. It shows that while much early criminological enquiry shared explanatory frameworks with scientific racism of the mid-nineteenth century, links between criminological theory and race have not always been clearly articulated. Since the middle of the twentieth century, a range of criminological perspectives has sought to challenge dominant understandings of crime and deviance in ways that echo contemporaneous efforts to deconstruct the concept of race and to explore its discursive knowledge and power relations. The converging and diverging relationship between criminological theory and ideas about race are explored in linear terms throughout this chapter, which ends by reviewing the extent to which resurgent arguments about the socio-biology of crime might resurrect racialized explanations of offending.

The chapter explores criminological theory in broadly sequential terms from the eighteenth to the twenty-first century, but it is clear that for all this approach makes presentational sense it risks obscuring the considerable similarities and messy boundaries that span the criminological perspectives reviewed here. Clearly, criminological thought has not developed in teleological form such that each new theoretical position has refined and improved on what went before; nor should it be assumed that the crude scientific racism evident in some early theory has been gradually 'weeded out'. 'Presentism' – whereby the assumptions and values of earlier periods are judged (and inevitably found wanting) when considered from the perspective of current norms and mores – is also important to avoid, to which end this chapter will seek to set perspectives on race and crime in their social, political and intellectual context. The central theme of the chapter is that criminological theory emerged concomitantly with 'race-thinking' and imperialism in the eighteenth and nineteenth centuries and that the two shared much intellectual ground. In the early decades of the twentieth century, genetic and biological perspectives on crime informed, and were in turn developed by, the rise of fascism in Europe. Through much of this period, theories that explained crime in sociological terms competed with biological perspectives. Those sociological accounts conceptualized race in different terms, as will be shown. More recently, biosocial criminology has refocused attention on genetic and biological paradigms, and only sometimes in ways that avoid earlier attempts to understand crime patterns in racial terms. These too are reviewed below. Post-Second World War, sociological and criminological perspectives associated with labelling theory engaged critically with the notion of race. The chapter concludes with an overview of emerging socio-biological approaches to offending and the implications that these have in terms of race and ethnicity.

This review cannot provide a general account of the history of criminology but instead seeks to explore how criminological thought and enquiry has reflected developing understanding of 'race' and racism. It is recognized that any effort to write a history of criminology reflects theoretical and intellectual preferences of the author and inevitably involves processes of selection, inclusion and exclusion that render any historical account incomplete and subjective (Garland, 1994).

Race and the Development of Classical Criminology

Modern criminology[1] formed in Europe in the nineteenth century during a period in which scientific developments across a range of human and natural

---

[1]Although the developments outlined here influenced what is now an academic discipline, efforts at intellectual archaeology of the kind attempted here are made more difficult since the term 'criminology' was not much used until the twentieth century. These progenitors of the discipline were neither trained nor educated as 'criminologists' (how could they be?) and did not tend to use the word: Rock (1994) has described their work as 'proto-criminology'.

fields was underpinned by, and in turn reinforced, innovations in methods and the philosophy of enquiry. Earlier pre-modern frameworks had understood criminality in fundamentally non-scientific terms that invoked metaphysical concepts such as original sin, evil and 'demonology'. From these perspectives, problems of crime were understood in conceptual terms derived from theology and philosophy and, as such, were not amenable to experimental method or scientific analysis. Enlightenment thought that developed in the seventeenth and eighteenth century conceived of human relations in terms of a tacit or imputed social contract, whereby rational human beings freely consent to forms of government that guarantee some basic levels of individual freedom, security and justice, and in turn have legitimate authority to enforce laws and punish transgressors. On the basis of the social contract, order was maintained by Hobbes' all-powerful Leviathan state, or Machiavelli's absolutist Prince (Melossi, 2008). John Locke conceived of the social contract in terms of a means to preserve 'natural' rights of life, liberty and property that exist beyond society and are God-given. In order to protect these rights, human beings chose, he argued, to pool their resources and to delegate power to state institutions able to enforce laws consistent with inalienable rights (Sabine, 1960). Classical criminology, most usually attributed to Cesare Beccaria and his 1764 publication *Essays on Crime and Punishment*, used the concept of the social contract as a means of defending individuals from harsh and arbitrary punishments of previous epochs. Instead of excessive corporeal punishment, the law ought to be based on the principle that the punishment fit the crime, and so be standardized according to the properties, quality and gravity of the act. The character, status or family background of the offender ought to have no bearing on the punishment imposed. From a classical perspective, the law reflected the consensus of the social contract and punishment was a form of social control that ought to be applied only to the extent necessary to deter others.

Classical criminology made little reference to emerging ideas about race that were developing alongside European imperialism of the era, although Locke's theory of property rights (whereby he suggested that proprietary rights were legitimate if human labour had been expended to create value in land over which all human kind might otherwise have equal claim) were used to defend exploitation of subject peoples and lands, and Locke himself was involved in the slave trade and the colonial administration of South Carolina (Glausser, 1990). Moreover, despite the language of universalism and equality, liberal arguments that society, government and law were a result of the free collective will of rational individuals belied the fact that those subjected to imperial domination by Europeans were often not seen as rational actors, and so were regarded as incapable of the judgement seen as integral to the foundation of social contract (Goldberg, 1993). In more general terms, liberal Enlightenment thinking drew boundaries such that rational subjects were afforded claims to equality and autonomy, but understanding of what constituted 'rationality' was

heavily racialized such that black people subject to slavery and imperial domination were defined out of the social contract and as such were regarded as the
legitimate property of superior European people. Rattansi and Westwood (1994:
3) argued that the Enlightenment values of Western modernity have been incul-
pated in some of the most appalling criminal episodes of the last two centuries,
since 'the other side of this modernity has been its close involvement with,
indeed its legitimation of, Western genocide against Aboriginal peoples, slavery,
colonial domination and exploitation, and the Holocaust'. As is examined in
greater detail in Chapter Six, it might be that contemporary debates within
environmental criminology or twenty-first-century globalization and neo-
colonialism add to the catalogue of crime that can be associated with Western
modernity. Given that criminology emerged during this era, it is remarkable
that the discipline has paid such little analytic attention to systematic and
organized crimes that have had terrible impact on minorities and marginalized
ethnic communities in a range of times and places. Reasons for this disciplinary
lacuna are also considered further in Chapter Six. Fundamentally, the social,
cultural and intellectual milieu in which criminology began to be developed
was deeply engrained with European colonialism and racism (Young, 1995).

One of the limitations of classical approaches emerged from its crude conceptualization of motivation. Offending was understood as the rational choice of individuals keen to maximize their pleasure and minimize their pain. The principle
that individual characteristics of offenders should not enter calculations of punishment was difficult to apply to offenders who were children, mentally ill in some
way, or if the offence involved some factor that might have affected the 'balance
of the mind' of the accused. Human rationality, it became clear, was more complex
than the classical school allowed. The development of neo-classicism, Taylor et al.
(1973: 8) argued, did not wholly transform models of offending or the basis of
punishment but they 'took the solitary rational man of classicist criminology and
gave him a past and a future ... they ... sketched in the structures which might blur
or marginally affect the exercise of voluntarism' and in doing so laid theoretical
foundations for the positivist school that emerged in the mid-nineteenth century.

Criminology as Science: Race and the Emergence of the Positivist School

Explanations of crime and criminality that emerged from the middle of the
nineteenth century were distinct from earlier approaches in that they adopted
positivist forms that couched offending in terms of social, biological and
physical factors that were held to be objective and discoverable through the
application of scientific methods of the kinds that originated in the natural

sciences. Through the development and application of scientific experiments, statistical analysis and so on, criminologists could formulate laws that explained offending and patterns of crime in ways akin to scientific explanations of phenomena observable in the natural world. Discovery of these objective laws of crime offered the possibility of intervention to reduce, or even remove, crime from society. Explanations of crime that developed were embedded in the intellectual context of the period and drew upon 'scientific' studies of race and racial typology that informed other emerging social sciences, such as anthropology and psychology (Richards, 1997; Armelagos and Goodman, 1998). The development of criminological theory along positivist lines in the nineteenth century meant that moral philosophical arguments about government and regulation of society were joined with scientific enquiry that imitated natural scientific method in an effort to explain human behaviour, including deviance and crime.

Pre-eminent among these approaches is the work of Caesare Lombroso, the Italian anthropologist widely regarded as the founder of modern criminology. Lombroso's work – particularly his 1875 book *L'Uomo Delinquente* – was significant in Europe and in the USA in terms of both his method and his explanation of criminal behaviour. In relation to the former, he adopted a positivist scientific method based upon measuring the physical cranial characteristics of offenders, which informed his theory that criminals were physically different from non-criminals and that offending was rooted in physiology rather than the innate evil or wickedness referred to in earlier religious accounts. Garland (1988) argued that Lombroso and criminal anthropology had little impact on the development of criminology in Britain, which emerged instead from medico-legal approaches associated with the penal system. These approaches were positivist but did not rely on ideas of atavism or share the aim of identifying predictable distinct criminal types. Similarly, Rock (2007) suggests that interest in crime and deviance in Britain had a particularly applied character that eschewed the pursuit of general theoretical models of offending in favour of responding to particular individuals in need of treatment. Moreover, he suggested, Lombroso's tendency to write 'in the overblown manner of a popular foreign novelist' put him at odds with Anglo-Saxon approaches (Rock, 2007: 123). Davie (2005: 144) notes, on the other hand, that while Lombroso's criminal anthropology was rejected in terms of both its tone and its conclusions by many British commentators, it is also clear that many prison doctors in the late nineteenth century measured the physical characteristics of offenders and the *British Medical Journal* offered qualified endorsement of Lombroso's position in 1889.

Methodologically, Lombroso's approach mirrored that used in the development of scientific racism of the period by Europeans who argued that human beings could be categorized into discreet biological types, that their biological character explained their behaviour, and that the various types could be arranged in hierarchical order (Miles, 1993). Moreover, Lombroso explicitly argued that criminal behaviour was associated with 'inferior' racial types: he explained, for example, that homicide rates were higher in southern Italy because of the preponderance of 'African and Oriental elements' (Gabbidon, 2007). Similar perspectives were articulated in the United States by, for example, Benedikt (1881), whose cranial analysis of offenders led him to the view that 'the brains of criminals exhibit a deviation from the normal type, and criminals are to be viewed as an anthropological variety of their species, at least among the cultured races' (in Rafter, 1992: 528). Lombroso's collaborator Enrico Ferri and his student Alfredo Niceforo made similar arguments about the biologically-determined violence of African people and suggested that these characteristics showed that these 'races' were less developed than their European counterparts, who had moved through similar patterns at an earlier stage of their racial evolution (Gabbidon, 2007). In these terms, criminal offending among the 'higher' European races was atavistic; among the 'lesser' races, however, crime was a normal result of biological character. Racist typologies of the period were also evident in the arguments of those who opposed a biological perspective on crime. For example, Lacassagne, a proponent of the late nineteenth-century French 'milieu social' school, argued that social factors were key but that these had an iterative relation with organic predispositions associated with different racial types. Lacassagne adopted a three-fold classification of human types based upon skull type: *races frontales*, *races pariétales* and *races occipitales*. These groups corresponded, respectively, to whites, Mongolians and Blacks, and to each was accorded a particular type of offending. The *races frontales* were associated with cerebral offending, and were the truly insane; the *races parietales* were 'occasional' criminals; and the *races occipitales* were instinctive, incorrigible offenders (Davie, 2005: 163). Lacassagne was not a biological reductionist, though, and argued that interventions to alter social conditions could ameliorate the negative potential of these innate characteristics. That competing sides in early arguments about nature and nurture, hereditary and environmental influences could effectively share the racist typologies of the period reveals much about the intellectual and material context of the time.

It is clear, even from this brief review, that biological approaches to crime in the nineteenth century were often racist, either in intention or implication, or sometimes both. Gabbidon (2007: 18) noted that Lombroso's work 'with its pungent racism, began the linkage of biology, race and crime, which has persisted until modern times – a fact that ... has resulted in misery for countless peoples of colour'. However, some caveats can be introduced, not in defence of Lombroso's methods or conclusions, but in an effort to demonstrate that these perspectives require nuanced evaluation. First, as Rafter (2008a) noted, in his later career Lombroso repudiated as simplistic some of the features of his early work that are often held to represent the whole of his contribution to criminology. Vold and Bernard (1986) noted that in later editions of *L'Uomo Delinquente* Lombroso devoted much more attention to environmental, rather than biological, causes of crime and that his final work (1911), *Crime: Its Causes and Remedies*, similarly focused more on environmental than biological factors. Furthermore, some of the early biological positivism of the mid-nineteenth century was developed as a basis on which to defend criminals from excessive and arbitrary punishment on the basis that their offending behaviour was not, as the classical school suggested, freely chosen, but was based on factors beyond individual rationality. From this perspective, Ferri, for example, proposed social reforms in housing and recreation facilities as a method of reducing crime (Hopkins-Burke, 2001). While nineteenth-century biological perspectives on crime clearly influenced early twentieth-century eugenics, which, in turn, were influential in the development of Nazism, it is simplistic to assume that these movements developed one after another in a natural or inevitable manner. Rafter (2008b) has noted that the criminology in Nazi Germany developed along very different lines from that in Italy under Mussolini: even though both can be traced back to biological approaches of the previous century, the political, social and institutional dynamics of each country also had significant influence.

While those early forms of criminology that developed in Western European societies at the height of their colonial powers shared an intellectual paradigm with scientific racism of the period, there were also other important associations between colonialism and the emerging discipline. In terms of policy and institutional developments, various forms of crime control and criminal justice systems were developed and refined within imperial networks. Models of public order policing, for example, that were developed in Ireland, were deployed in England and re-exported on, in varied forms, to India, Australia and elsewhere in response to local economic and political developments in the middle of the nineteenth century (Brogden, 1987; Cole, 1999). Technologies to investigate crime, for example fingerprinting and photographic techniques, were developed in imperial India, in an effort to strengthen administrative capacity to profile and survey the subject population (Anderson, 2004). The role of the law itself, and its relation to forms of governance and the state, were also perfected and refined throughout European empires (Godfrey and Dunstall, 2005). The colonial context was important to the development of criminology in theoretical terms, but also to emerging institutions of criminal justice, law enforcement, and regulation more widely. As Agozino (2003) pointed out, this contribution was even more extensive, since the wealth expropriated from colonial subjects provided the material necessities – the universities, laboratories, learned societies, and even subjects for scientific analysis – that enabled the development of modern criminology.

Eugenics

The direct intellectual and material links between emerging 'scientific racism' and early criminology are clearly apparent, if sometimes overstated, in some of the work of the 'founding fathers' of European criminology. While this may have been less influential in the development of British criminology than in other countries, it is clear that notions of heredity, atavism and biological determinism formed a compelling explanation for apparently intertwined social problems identified in late nineteenth- and early twentieth-century British society. Crime and disorderly behaviour were, then as now, regarded as representative of a broader crisis in society that included issues of alcoholism, poverty, poor education, disease, and urban decay. Combined concerns around these issues, Morris (1994: 22) argued, were expressed in terms of the apparent 'degeneracy' of the British 'race' and 'struck fear into the heart of the secure and respectable population in the latter half of the nineteenth century, and fuelled the fire of the eugenics movement'. Anthropological approaches developed in the imperial periphery were 'brought home' and applied to the new urban underclass emerging in British cities of the nineteenth century. The language of racial and biological superiority that had been used to justify imperial expansion was also employed to account for problems at the European centre in a process Miles (1993) described as the 'racialisation of the interior'. In Britain and in France, Miles (1993: 94) argued, the impoverished surplus population of the industrial cities were 'the dangerous classes *par excellence*, a population that was seen to lack a work ethic, to be without morals: in sum, this class was thought to be degenerate, uncivilized or uncivilizable. As a result of involvement in criminal activity or forms of political protest, or both, it was potentially a source of disorder'. The notion of the 'lesser breeds without the law' was applied to colonial subjects in the wider nexus of the British Empire and to the domestic *lumpen proletariat*. Radzinowicz (1966, in Taylor et al. (1973: 40)) argued that biological perspectives on crime reinforced the domestic interests of the ruling class: 'it served the interests and relieved the conscience of those at the top to look upon the dangerous classes as an independent category, detached from the prevailing social conditions. They were portrayed as a race apart, morally depraved and vicious, living by violating the fundamental law of orderly society, which was that a man should maintain himself by honest, steady work'.

Against this background, eugenics offered to cleanse the genetic stock through selective breeding programmes. While this approach culminated in the sterilization programmes associated with the Nazis in the mid-twentieth century, earlier advocates of eugenics were, in Britain, mainstream (even progressive) social reformers. The impact of eugenics on debates about crime was considerable in the USA in the early twentieth century. Among the first criminology courses taught in the United States was 'criminal anthropology and race mixture', established at Harvard University in 1916 by Ernest Hooton, a committed eugenicist and one of the leading American criminologists of the period (Rafter, 2004: 744). Rafter (2004: 743) argued that Hooton shared the perspective of many that social decay had to be arrested by a combination of invasive biological engineering and policy reform: 'the only hope seemed to be eugenics – birth control, sterilization of morons and criminals, and (less directly) a curtailment of welfare programs that encouraged the unfit to breed'. Criminology in the USA in the first decades of the twentieth century was often developing in the shadow of Lombroso and his followers, and these debates transferred into law, policy and practice. During the same period several US states passed laws allowing for the sterilization of the 'feeble-minded' and criminals. The categories of people liable to sterilization varied from state to state; one contemporary source (Hunter, 1914/15) suggested that Iowa had the most extensive provisions for sterilization covering:

> the inmates of public institutions for criminals, rapists, idiots, feeble-minded, imbeciles, lunatics, drunkards, drug-fiends, epileptics, syphilitics, moral and sexual perverts, and diseased and degenerate persons. In that state, sterilization was compulsory for persons twice-convicted of felony or of a sexual offence other than 'white slavery', for which offense one conviction made sterilization mandatory.

Even though eugenic ideas that human behaviour was biologically determined and heritable were influential in early twentieth-century criminology and criminal justice (and continued to find advocates for several decades), they were controversial and contested in that period. The state laws mentioned above were challenged and in several cases, including that of Iowa, were found to be unconstitutional; in other states, the laws were not applied in practice (Emory Lyon, 1914/15). Even some of those who advocated eugenics did not necessarily argue that genetic inheritance was the direct cause of criminal behaviour, but instead that it caused mental and physical conditions ('feeble-mindedness' or alcoholism) that were criminogenic in turn (Goddard, 1914). Neither did all advocates of eugenics support sterilization: for ethical and practical reasons, for example, Battaglini (1914/15) suggested that rehabilitation within prisons could 're-adapt' offenders to society in ways that would be eugenically beneficial. Moreover, even those who argued for a biological approach to human behaviour also tended to recognize that environmental factors played a vital role as mechanisms that could unleash problematic behaviour that was pre-determined by genetics. The extent to which eugenic explanations are racist is also somewhat contestable, as Rafter (2004) noted that the eugenic tradition in the USA comprised different approaches, which makes generalization difficult. Much of the discussion in the USA about the genetic stock was carried on using the word 'race', but this was sometimes used as a synonym for national population or humanity as a whole; often there is no apparent suggestion that supposed racial groups exist in hierarchical relation to one another. While Hooton might have maintained that his work did not suggest that different racial groups were subordinate and others superordinate, his research was organized in ways that reflected and sustained ethnic typologies of the era. His 1939 study *Crime and the Man* presented an analysis of the physical characteristics of criminals with different chapters allocated to Old Americans, New Americans (those of 'foreign stock'), Negroes ('pure blood'), and Negroids (mixed blood, 'mulattos') (Gabbidon, 2007).

Criminology, Nazism and the Holocaust

Eugenic and biological explanations of crime were integral to the development of Nazi criminology in Germany from the mid-1930s and provided theoretical and material foundations for the Holocaust. Perspectives on the relation between the Holocaust, modernity and Enlightenment thought extend from those that regard the 'final solution', highly rationalistic, mechanized and 'scientific' as the epitome of modernity, through to arguments insistent that the Holocaust was the abrogation of ideals of individualism, equality and freedom that were central to Enlightenment thought. These 'master narratives' have been applied in consideration of the relation between other scientific disciplines, and have been characterized by Wetzell (2000: 11) in the following terms:

> The first of [the narratives] assumes that science is fundamentally progressive and argues that science and medicine were 'perverted' by the Nazis. The second narrative, by contrast, portrays modern science and medicine as major contributors to the Holocaust and sometimes come close to presenting the Holocaust as a logical outcome of certain strands of modern science.

Wetzell's account of criminology in Germany from the mid-nineteenth to the mid-twentieth century focuses on the contextual features of that society that led to programmes of 'scientific' experiments, sterilization, and the murder of populations held to be genetically criminal. Clearly, these practices drew upon wider theoretical perspectives in criminology, of the kind associated with the biological determinism outlined earlier in this chapter. Lombrosian criminology was influential in Germany – as it was in other European societies and the USA – but was subject to critical debate, refinement and reformulation as the tension between environmental and sociological influences on criminal behaviour and those attributed to biological and genetic factors were played out. When the Nazi party took power in Germany in 1933, Wetzell suggests that various perspectives on crime and justice competed, such that it was not inevitable that the new regime would develop policies that reflected biological criminology. Siemens (2009) has shown that German newspapers in the Weimar Republic wrote about crime in general and individual cases in terms that presented offenders as victims of circumstances, social deprivation, or extreme momentary psychological pressure. Furthermore, some early Nazi jurists were critical of biological determinism which sought to deny individual responsibility for offending. Even those who pursued biological scientific approaches to crime were not necessarily doing so to further racist ends; indeed, Wetzell (2000) noted that Aschaffenburg, a leading biological scientist, who lost his post because he was Jewish, did not recognize that his work would become linked to eugenics until the mid-1930s. By the end of 1937 the Criminal Biological Service had taken on a national role in measuring the 'genetic traits' of prisoners through the use of medical examination and questionnaire, and the service was assigned specific roles in identifying criminals to be targeted for eugenic measures (Wetzell, 2000: 184–185). The application of biologically-determined approaches to criminality took two distinct, though related, forms in Nazi Germany, Rafter (2008b) noted. First was a broad programme of eugenics that sought to encourage the genetically healthy to procreate through positive inducements while discouraging those (of all races) who were 'defective' through prohibitions on marriage, through exile, through sterilization and, ultimately, through extinction. Distinct from that was a broad programme of 'racial hygiene' that was intended to rid Germany of 'inferior' groups, such as Jews and Gypsies, and so to redevelop the purity of the superior Aryan race.

Clearly, the policies and programmes that resulted from Nazi biological science led to the systematic brutalization and murder of groups and individuals on a scale that remains difficult to comprehend. Criminologists have paid relatively little attention to explaining the Holocaust, and other forms of state-sponsored genocide, and even historians of the Third Reich have not paid attention to the ways in which criminals were treated by Hitler's regime (Rafter, 2008b). Reasons for these disciplinary gaps are considered more fully in Chapter Six, which questions why the discipline of criminology has often been somewhat mute in the face of some of the most serious and extensive crimes of the modern era. In terms of considering links between race and criminological theory, though, it is clear that the atrocities of the Third Reich can be traced back to biological science and ultimately to the first forms of criminological positivism that emerged in the mid-nineteenth century. To suggest, though, that those perspectives inevitably led to the gas chambers is clearly overstating the case. After all, biological accounts that informed eugenic approaches were influential in many countries, including fascist Italy (Rafter, 2008b), which did not develop policies of racial purification or genetic manipulation. Nevertheless, the experience of the Holocaust contributed significantly to post-war shifts in criminological thinking that were much more interested in sociological and environmental paradigms: clearly these did not simply 'take over' from biological science and can be identified also in earlier approaches to criminology. That debates about crime and criminality were 'vacated' by biological positivism left the stage open to competing perspectives and these came to dominate criminological theory in the decades that follow. The chapter turns to these perspectives in its final sections, but before that, we consider socio-biological accounts developed in the last two decades or so that revisit earlier approaches.

Biosocial Theories of Crime

Biological perspectives on criminal offending remerged in the 1970s and 1980s and to integrate older biological approaches with social, psychological and environmental factors. Few, if any, of the recent contributions to this field suggest that biological or genetic factors can explain offending without some reference to external factors associated with culture, socio-economic circumstances, family patterns, and so on. Not only do recent variations seek to integrate biological perspectives with other paradigms, they also (important exceptions notwithstanding) eschew attempts to identify 'racial typologies' of crime. Biosocial approaches to crime were particularly developed by James Q. Wilson and Richard Herrnstein in their 1985 study, *Crime and Human Nature*, in which they argued that crime was best explained by a combination of biological, environmental and social factors. They argued, for example, that the general over-representation of young males in crime could be explained in biological terms, (for example, aggression could be attributed to high testosterone levels), but that these interacted with conditioned behaviour learnt from the environment, and individual conscience, which also derives from the environment and will shape decisions to commit or desist from crime. These approaches need not entail any return to earlier debates suggesting that human kind could be categorized into hierarchical racial groups, and much of the recent biosocial criminology literature self-consciously seeks to disassociate itself from crude reductionism and to insist it should not form the basis of repressive techniques of penal control (Walsh and Beaver, 2009). The huge programmes of research, such as that associated with efforts to map the human genome, have meant that Western societies are now 'saturated with biological concerns and solutions' to a wide-range of social, educational and health issues that in the mid-twentieth century were largely the preserve of sociological and environmental paradigms (Rafter, 2008a: 200).

Clearly, though, some have sought to use biosocial theories to explain apparent differences in the offending rates of racial groups. Significant claims have been made that link low IQ scores to poverty and crime, and many of these have posited inherited genetic factors to explain lower scores among black groups compared to whites (Bowling and Phillips, 2002: 59). Often these studies proceed on the basis of apparent 'scientific' neutrality, claiming, as Wright (2009) does, that 'inconvenient truths' ought not deter the objective scientist from investigating contentious matters. It is argued below that this claim to the scientific high ground is often deeply flawed. A key recent attempt to associate race, genetics and crime was *The Bell Curve*, which explicitly argued that black people and Latinos in the USA had lower intelligence levels, that these were inherited, and that they were predicative of criminal activity (Herrnstein and Murray, 1994). Similarly, Philippe Rushton (1990) argued that different crime rates associated with 'mongoloid', 'caucasoid', and 'negroid' races could be attributed to distinctions in the genetic character of these groups. Using international crime data, he argued that societies that were predominantly Negroid had much higher rates of homicide, rape and serious assault than Caucasoid societies, which in turn had higher rates than Mongoloid countries. These differences, he argued, were influenced to a considerable extent (he did not say they were 'determined') by genetic factors. Wright (2009) cites compelling evidence showing that black people are over-represented at various stages in the criminal justice systems of many societies – as is explored at greater length in Chapters Four and Seven of this book – and argues that these trends are related to genetic differences that have evolved between racial groups. These biological differences relate, he argues, to various forms of executive functioning in the brain, such as 'self control' and 'intelligence' (measured by IQ), which he claims are less developed among black races than whites. The other broad category Wright identities relates to racial differences in the 'ability to organise socially', by which he means maintain collective norms and values and stable family patterns. A final example of recent biosocial explanations of crime is the attribution of high levels of Māori imprisonment in New Zealand to (what is sometimes referred to as) 'the warrior gene' (Raumati Hook, 2009). Research studies have found that Māori are more likely than other groups to have forms of monoamine oxidase genes, enzymes which breakdown neurotransmitters such as serotonin and dopamine and are associated with various mental health issues, such as depression and alcoholism. Lea and Chambers (2007) suggested that Māori who had this genetic blueprint might have had some evolutionary advantage in terms of seafaring, courage and capacity for war and violence as they travelled to

Aoteroa/New Zealand from the Pacific Islands; that those who survived these epic journeys subsequently became involved in conflict, war and violence, they speculated, might explain the contemporary over-representation of Māori in the criminal justice system.

These biosocial approaches raise a series of concerns in terms of ethics, concepts and methods. Ethical debates continue about the extent to which scientific researchers should be obliged to consider the policy implications of their work or should feel a great duty to pursue 'truth' and scientific knowledge regardless of any impact that this might have. Clearly, these complex debates cannot be properly explored here, but there are sufficient concerns about the scientific validity of some forms of biosocial accounts of crime to suggest that even those who argue that they are engaged in the pursuit of scientific progress might have to reconsider links between crime and biology. First, the conceptual frameworks of 'race' and 'crime' are often underdeveloped. Scientific efforts to establish the genetic profile of human populations are highly technical and it is difficult for those without particular training and expertise to comment upon them, but some general problems remain, for example, relating to the extent to which human beings can be organized into distinct groups. Those who are labelled 'black' in the USA, for example, are reasonably likely to have ancestors who were white, and, of course, the opposite is also true (Roberts and Gabor, 1990). Furthermore, while there might be considerable genetic difference between ethnic groups, it is also the case that there is considerable biological difference within them: talking about 'caucasians' becomes a fairly meaningless exercise on that basis. Moreover, it is not clear that the biological differences between groups necessarily have much explanatory reach in terms of the extent to which they can account for differences in human behaviour. While few would argue that factors such as brain chemistry, for example, might shape an individuals behaviour, it is less clear how some other forms of genetic difference (hair structure, for example) has any influence.

Criminologically, there are often significant concerns about the hugely uncritical manner in which crime data is used by those who claim to find differences between racial groups. Fundamentally, there is a failure to consider the problems of using contact with the criminal justice system as a proxy for criminal activity. Simply put, processes of over-policing and criminalization in broader terms need to be scrutinized alongside studies of the personal characteristics of offenders. Even if it is assumed that the criminal justice system is relatively even-handed in these terms, it remains the case that most offenders are not apprehended and processed such that they become available to the type of analysis reviewed above. Reiner (2007: 54) calculated that as little as 3 per cent of offences result in a conviction or a custodial sentence, so any analysis of the characteristics of criminals caught and detained by the criminal justice system effectively excludes the majority of offenders about whom no corresponding data can be analyzed. This caveat can also apply to sociological or environmental analysis of the characteristics of offenders that are reviewed further below.

Race, Ethnicity and Sociological Positivism

As has been noted, opponents of biological perspectives sought alternative explanations of crime in sociological, environmental and cultural terms. Broadly, these perspectives shared the positivist approach of the biological determinists and eugenicists that they opposed, but sought to locate the problem of crime in mutable sociological terms. These perspectives reflect theorizing of race that moved away from biological determinism towards a sociological approach. This section of the chapter explores the early development of sociological positivist explanations of crime and the ways in which the concepts of race and ethnicity informed these perspectives.

Ecological or environmental explanations of human behaviour are widely associated, in their early incarnations, with the Chicago School that emerged in the 1920s, predominantly in the work of Robert Park and Ernest Burgess. Park had been a newspaper journalist in Chicago and adapted those investigative skills to research social and urban conditions more widely. The work of the Chicago School was not focused specifically on crime, but the nature and causes of delinquency is explained in terms of the urban environment held to shape all manner of human behaviour. Park and Burgess (1925/1967) conceptualized the city as akin to a natural organism, an interconnected set of relationships such that changes and transition in one part ecologically influenced the behaviour of inhabitants. Their analysis of Chicago suggested that the city was divided into concentric zones moving outwards from the central business district, through residential zones, to an outer 'commuter zone'. The border areas surrounding one type of space from the next were 'zones in transition' in which social change and migration created criminogenic conditions as inhabitants were challenged to adapt to a shifting environment. Reflecting earlier analysis by W.B. du Bois (1899) of urban patterns in Philadelphia at the end of the nineteenth century, Park and Burgess (1925/1967: 108) argued that the problem of delinquency among the black population was attributable to migration to the North following emancipation: while migration might lead to greater freedom and economic opportunities, it is 'none the less disorganizing to the communities they have left behind and to the communities into which they are now moving'. Du Bois (1899) had also noted that the deprivation and marginalization that underpinned social disorganization and crime in Philadelphia was exacerbated by the discrimination experienced by the black population. Du Bois noted that blacks were arrested for less cause than whites and tended to serve longer sentences (cited in Gabbidon, 2007: 51), and so he prefigured debates and arguments that reverberated in criminology through-out the twentieth century and beyond. This urban sociological framework of analysis was adopted and adapted to British cities, in which a number of stud-ies situated problems of crime and deviance in the context of the local urban ecology (Downes and Rock, 2003: 75). Prominent among more general British studies that developed the Chicago School model was Rex and Moore's (1967) *Race, Community and Conflict*, which argued that tense 'race relations' in Sparkbrook in the mid-1960s were best understood in terms of competition for scarce jobs in the district and competition for housing. In these accounts, eth-nicity and/or race tend to be understood as a sociological variable, along with housing tenure, socio-economic circumstances, and demographic factors relat-ing to age or family structure, that correlates with crime patterns. Shaw and Mackay (1942), for example, found in their mid-twentieth-century study of crime in Chicago that reported crime rates were high in areas characterized by high infant mortality, fluctuating population, high truancy rates and a hetero-geneous ethnic profile. The latter was not conceptualized as a strong determi-nant of crime, though, as Shaw and Mackay (1942) also noted that crime rates remained high over time, even as the particular ethnic profile of the areas changed: it was the diversity and mix of groups, rather than the cultural or biological characteristics of particular groups, that seemed to be associated with high crime rates.

Critics of these perspectives have noted that ecological explanations of crime often pay little attention to the mechanisms and circumstances that influence individuals in these urban contexts to engage, or not, in criminal or delinquent activity. Cultural and subcultural theories of offending contributed a model for understanding the link between the broad macro-level social context and micro-level individual behaviour. Key among these is Edwin Sutherland's (1949) concept of 'differential association', which suggested that criminal and deviant behaviour was more pronounced among some groups in some circum-stances because individuals were more likely to associate with other deviants and criminals. Criminal behaviour is understood as a culturally transmitted phenomenon, which explains the persistence of problematic deviant behav-iour within certain groups and that this can continue over generations. Studies of various 'ethnic gangs' in mid-twentieth century US cities suggested not that race is a fixed biological determinant of deviant or criminal behaviour, but rather that socially constructed forms of ethnicity can shape problematic cul-tural patterns that themselves become criminogenic. Cultural factors were cited in studies that sought to explain different crime levels among ethnic groups, and these cultural variables tended to be conceptualized in ethnic terms. One example of this approach is found in Hayner's (1938) explanation of lower crime levels among 'Oriental' groups in the USA: Japanese migrants, he argued, had strong family patterns and were a well-integrated community which explained low levels of criminality among that group. In contrast, the cultural values and demographic characteristics of Filipino migrants explained their higher involvement in crime and delinquency. In various forms, arguments about cultural and ecological causes of crime continue. While ethnicity has been associated, in research and popular cultural representations, with delinquent and criminal gangs, much of the focus of subcultural studies has been on gender and class. Albert Cohen (1955), for example, found that young males engaged with deviant subcultures in an effort to secure or develop status that was not otherwise available to those in marginalized neighbourhoods. Another important contribution from the period was Cloward and Ohlin's (1960) study, which identified social and economic factors that might push lower-class adolescent males into illegitimate routes to status and success as legitimate opportunities are denied to them (Vold and Bernard, 1986). As will be outlined at various stages later in this book, subcultural perspectives that associate culture, ethnicity and crime continue to be applied in contemporary debates, particularly in Britain to those relating to street crime, drugs, and gang-related offending among black and Asian youth (Hallsworth, 2005).

One of the most influential models of crime and policing, although one much misunderstood (Tilley, 2008), has been the 'broken windows' theory developed in the 1980s by Wilson and Kelling (1982). The model adapts ecological approaches by suggesting that neglected neighbourhoods in which manifest social problems remain unchecked become subject to spirals of decline as law-abiding residents migrate from the area as criminal and antisocial behaviour flourishes. Sampson and Wilson (1995) also drew upon ecological models of offending to develop a theory of race and crime that rejected suggestions that the persistence of a threatening criminal underclass, disproportionally comprising minority ethnic groups, was a problem rooted in dysfunctional culture – a persistent theme of New Right critics in the 1980s (Murray, 1984). Instead, Sampson and Wilson (1995) argued, following Wilson's (1987) book *The Truly Disadvantaged*, that cultural problems were themselves adaptations to ecological conditions faced by excluded communities. They attributed higher crime rates among the black population of the USA to 'macrosocial patterns of residential inequality [that] give rise to the social isolation and ecological concentration of the truly disadvantaged, which in turn leads to structural barriers and cultural adaptations that undermine social organization and hence the control of crime' (Sampson and Wilson, 1995: 38). This argument had been used in Britain in Ken Pryce's (1979) study *Endless Pressure*, which suggested that black youth crime was one adaptation to marginalization and experiences of racism. More recently, other studies of the spatial distribution of crime data have also suggested that the apparent high crime levels in areas with high minority populations reflects social and economic structural features of those districts rather than the ethnic or cultural features of residents (Shihadeh and Shrum, 2004). A recent study of links between offending, victimization and racial differences in Britain has similarly argued that 'headline' differences showing that black youth are more involved in some types of crime compared to their presence in the population as a whole – evidence reviewed in more detail in Chapter Four – largely disappear when other factors, including those related to the environmental character of neighbourhoods involved, are taken into account (House of Commons Home Affairs Committee, 2007).

Notwithstanding that there are important differences between the various perspectives reviewed in this chapter so far, the various biological, eugenic, sociological and cultural perspectives on the causes of crime share a framework that broadly accepts that 'racial differences' are ontological realities that have some causal relation with offending. In the final section of this chapter, criminological theories based on the premise that social realities are constructed phenomenon are considered.

'Empiricism' to 'Social Constructionism'

As has been noted in Chapter One, the two key concepts – crime and race – considered in this chapter increasingly came to be recognized, during later decades of the twentieth century, as socially constructed concepts. In criminological terms, the notion that crime was itself a problematic concept, open to different interpretations and definitions such that it changes over time and between places, represented a significant break with much of the theory reviewed thus far in this chapter. One of the key authors who outlined new perspectives on the nature of crime and deviance was Howard S. Becker in his 1963 study *The Outsiders*, in which he noted that deviant activity could only be understood in its particular context and needed to be understood as an outcome, the result of the successful application of the label 'criminal' to an individual engaged in activity that is understood as criminal. Actions are not criminal in and of themselves, but rather because they are understood and labelled as such, and these processes are determined, to a large extent, by dominant powerful voices. Becker (1963: 9) argued that 'the deviant is one to whom that label has been successfully applied; deviant behaviour is behaviour that people so label'. Becker's study included analysis of the different arrest rates for white and black young males, which showed that the latter were more likely to be formally arrested and charged by police, while the former were treated more leniently. Clearly, Becker's work significantly disrupts much of the analysis presented in earlier sections of this chapter, since one implication of his study is that arrest rates do not act as a reliable indicator of crime levels in any absolute sense. If police and other agencies act on the basis of 'labels' disproportionately applied to black rather than white people, then this suggests that the over-representation of minorities in the criminal justice system might be an artefact of racism within the criminal justice system and society more widely. Subsequent variations of this approach emphasized that the attribution of labels produced not only primary deviance and criminality, but also second-ary deviance – that is deviance that occurs as a result of the initial label. After individuals are labelled as deviant they subsequently find it harder to secure a job or access higher education, while it becomes more likely that they will be suspected of subsequent offences as they become subject to greater levels of police attention. Labelling establishes deviance in the first place, since it is not a property of actions themselves, but causes deviance 'amplification' in that it denies other identities and opportunities and so encourages those labelled into further behaviour regarded as problematic (Wilkins, 1964). This framework of explaining crime as a process of social construction informed theories of moral panic (Cohen, 1973), which have been widely applied to debates about minor-ity ethnic communities and crime (Hall et al. (1978), as will be explored at greater length in Chapter Three and elsewhere in this book. A number of criti-cisms have been made of labelling theory, relating to the difficulty of under-standing what 'deviance' might mean in relation to different forms of activity: while it may be that some forms of 'deviant' activity are best understood as emerging from a social reaction, this approach is more difficult to apply to more serious harm associated with some other forms of deviance (Hall et al., 2008). Furthermore, criticism has been levelled that labelling approaches pay too much attention to the experiences of the offender and do not do enough to focus on the impact of offending on victims and that the notion of primary and secondary deviance is not empirically tested and cannot explain the processes by which some individuals do not engage in long-term or 'career' deviance even after they have been labelled (Taylor et al., 1973).

While the implications of labelling and related theories continue to be influ-ential and are applied and examined at later stages of this book, the discussion here continues by considering how social construction approaches have also been applied to the concept of 'race'. While debates about race and crime in the nineteenth and twentieth centuries reflected different emphasis on the extent and nature of any relation between the two concepts, the fundamental nature of 'race', like that of 'crime', was broadly accepted. The extent to which 'race' biologically determined human behaviour was keenly debated, as has been shown here, but there was, even among those who preferred an ecological or sociological perspective, a general understanding that human beings could be conceived in 'racial' terms as distinct groups with fixed differences between them. Just as the concept of crime has been unsettled by criminological analy-sis and theorizing over the twentieth century, so too has that of 'race'. As Solomos and Back (1996) argued, the general trajectory of these debates has led to a position such that there is widespread recognition that 'race' does not exist in the sense that many, even most, of those included in the discussion in this chapter have used the concept. However, the concept of 'race' as a socially constructed phenomenon remains central to debates across a very wide range of the humanities, arts and social sciences, as the rest of this book attests. An important consequence of recognition that race is an 'essentially contestable concept' is that the terms and phrases used vary considerably in time and space. This chapter has reflected some of these changes and has used terminology in the context of older discussions of 'race' and 'racial difference' that would not be considered appropriate, or be useful, in more recent discussions. Terms such as 'black' are of relevance to debates about race and criminal justice in twenty-first-century Britain, but the extent to which this might be a generic term, inclusive of, for example, those of Indian, Pakistani or Bangladeshi background, is open to debate. Sometimes in contemporary Britain, these groups are referred to as Asian, but that is misleading in geographic terms, and does not transfer to US debates or to other parts of the world where that label is used to denote people from China, Japan, Korea. Comparing data and debates from different jurisdictions becomes problematic, as analysis of over-representation in different parts of the world that are reviewed in Chapter Seven demonstrate. The final chapter of the book also considers the problematic categorization and labelling of ethnic and racial groups within criminal justice.

SUMMARY

Criminological theory emerged concomitantly with 'race-thinking' and imperialism in the eighteenth and nineteenth centuries and the two shared much intellectual ground. Positivist criminological theory developed in the nineteenth century, and sought to adopt natural scientific method to explain human behaviour. Biological and genetic explanations of criminal behaviour were applied to 'lesser races' and atavistic Europeans. Into the twentieth century, eugenics offered to cleanse the genetic stock through selective breeding programmes and so to eliminate criminal behaviour. In the shadow of the Holocaust such explanatory frameworks were scientifically discredited. Recent biosocial criminology need not entail any return to earlier debates suggesting that human kind could be categorized into hierarchical racial groups, and much of the literature self-consciously seeks to disassociate itself from crude reductionism and to insist it should not form the basis of repressive techniques of penal control. Clearly though, some have sought to use biosocial theories to explain apparent differences in the offending rates of racial groups. These biosocial approaches raise a series of concerns in terms of ethics, concepts and methods.

(Continued)

(Continued)

Ecological or environmental explanations of human behaviour explained the nature and causes of delinquency in terms of the urban environment and its capacity to shape human behaviour. In these accounts, ethnicity and/or race tend to be understood as a sociological variable correlated to crime. Cultural and subcultural theories of offending contributed a model for understanding the link between the broad macro-level social context and micro-level individual behaviour.

The notion that crime was itself a problematic concept, open to different interpretations and definitions such that it changes over time and between places, represented a significant break. For Becker, deviant activity should be conceived as an outcome, the result of the successful application of the label of 'criminal', rather than something inherent to an action. Labelling theory has been applied to many aspects of the 'race–crime' debate addressed in this book: from media coverage to a host of issues relating to disparities in the criminal justice system.

STUDY QUESTIONS

1 How do positivist accounts of criminal behaviour differ from classical perspectives? What are the implications for debates about race and crime?
2 Are biological theories of crime inevitably racist?
3 How might labelling theory be applied to contemporary debates about street and gang crime?

FURTHER READING

Rock's (1994) edited collection, *History of Criminology*, is a comprehensive account of the development of the discipline; a historical perspective that Agozino (2003, *Counter-Colonial Criminology: A Critique of Imperialist Reason*) locates in the context of the development of European imperialism and colonialism. Rafter (2008, *The Criminal Brain*) re-assesses biological perspectives on criminal behaviour from the nineteenth century to the present and provides a compelling account of criminology in Nazi Germany. For a broad overview of theoretical perspectives on race and racism see the collection edited by Back and Solomos (2000): *Theories of Race and Racism*. Gabbidon (2007, *Criminological Perspectives on Race and Crime*) offers the most comprehensive analysis of theoretical and applied debates in this field.

3

Race, Crime and Popular Culture

OVERVIEW

The aim of this chapter is to review the historical and contemporary criminaliza-tion and racialization of minority ethnic groups in media and popular culture. It is argued that some of the racist news coverage of crime evident in Britain in the 1970s and 1980s has subsided, but that factual, fictional and 'infotainment' cov-erage of crime continues to be racialized. The chapter concludes by considering the ways in which digital gaming media reflect race and ethnicity in their repre-sentation of urban crime. To this end, the chapter:

- outlines why contemporary debates about subjective fear of crime means that media representation is an important constitutive component of debates about lawlessness and antisocial behaviour;
- critically reviews the ways in which news media reporting of race and crime has developed since the early 1970s;
- examines the content and implications of 'infotainment' representations of race and crime;
- evaluates the ways in which race, ethnicity and organized crime have been portrayed in movies and TV series;
- considers new forms of interactive digital media – using the *Grand Theft Auto* series as an exemplar – and the ways in which they represent race and ethnicity.

KEY TERMS

- Cinema
- Digital media
- Fiction
- Infotainment

- Newsmedia
- Television
- Visual representation

Introduction

The previous chapter explored the complex and enduring ways in which theo-ries of racial difference and explanations of criminal behaviour have co-existed and mutually reinforced one another. In recent decades there has been increasing recognition that both 'crime' and 'race' are socially constructed concepts, intimately bound up with normative and cultural processes associ-ated with the particular contexts in which they emerge. Concerns about con-temporary crime problems, such as, for example, paedophilia or street robbery, cannot be understood as straightforward responses to emerging objective prob-lems. Instead, they reveal something about broader trends and tensions associated with social and cultural change in late modern societies characterized by an increasing social dislocation, changing family patterns, and wider insecurities associated with the fear of crime (Coleman, 2004; Lee, 2007). Similarly, the problematization of different ethnic groups across different historical periods, as will be demonstrated below, often reveals more about broader social relations than it does about the inherent properties and features of migration or population change. From the late 1940s onwards, sociological approaches to race effectively replaced biological perspectives that had previously assumed that differences and tensions between groups were the immutable result of fixed biological difference. Race and racism, then, came to be understood in particular social contexts that revealed more about, for example, tensions around local housing or competition for employment (Rex and Moore, 1967). Subsequent critiques of the sociology of race relations argued further that the concept of race itself ought to be confronted and that a more critical perspective developed that interrogated the circumstances in which ideas of race came to influence debates about social problems, including that of crime (Gilroy, 1987; Solomos, 1988; Keith, 1993).

The more that the socially constructed nature of crime and race is understood, the more important it becomes to recognize that both are inherently mediated concepts. For the most part, the population have little direct personal experience of crime, especially serious crime, and it is clear that much public perception of trends and problems in antisocial behaviour, drug-related offending and violence, to name three current examples, is shaped by mediated information. The most obvious form that this takes is the media itself, but this chapter seeks to develop a comprehensive and complex approach to 'the media' and to explore how ideas about crime, and race, are communicated and represented across a broad range of formats, including traditional news media, popular cultural fictional and 'infotainment' formats, as well as digital games and interactive platforms. Consideration of some of these later forms of new media demonstrate that crime continues to provide narrative and visual images in digital formats as it has done in print, cinema, radio and TV since the mid-nineteenth century.

Much sociological and criminological analysis of race, crime and media has been focused on the ways in which news media, newspapers in particular, have (mis)represented marginalized groups and constituted them as criminal threats to orderly society (Hartmann and Husband, 1974; Chibnall, 1977; Law, 2002). The nature of news media crime coverage and the explanations that surround it are reviewed in the first part of this chapter, which then moves on to analyze fictional media representations and the ways in which race and crime co-join in entertainment genres and new forms of digital media. Consideration of fictional and visual media representations of race and crime is particularly important in a society increasingly reliant on visual images in relation to many aspects of contemporary social problems (Jencks, 1995). The importance of visual images to media coverage of crime has been widely noted, for example by studies that suggest that the availability of dramatic photographs or video footage is an important determinant of whether an event becomes part of the news agenda (Van Dijk, 1991). The availability of new media forms, many of which use the collective technological capacity of 'citizen journalists' who supply material from the frontline of current affairs, has further entrenched the importance of the visual, as Greer et al. (2007: 5) have argued:

> ... today the visual constitutes perhaps the central medium through which the meanings and emotions of crime are captured and conveyed to audiences. Indeed, we would suggest that it is the visual that increasingly shapes our engagement with and understanding of, key issues of crime, control and social order.

The broad approach to understanding race, crime, media and popular culture adopted in this review reflects developments in cultural criminology that emphasize the centrality of reflexive mediated images to contemporary debates about crime and disorder. Clearly, traditional formats, such as newspapers, cinema and TV documentaries, communicate important images and perspectives, but new forms of media, many of which are interactive, grassroots and relatively unregulated, also provide sites in which crime is imagined, sometimes in racialized formats. Ferrell et al. (2008: 130) argued that 'a useful criminology of contemporary life must be, if nothing else, culturally reflexive – that is self-attuned to image, symbol, and meaning as dimensions that define and redefine transgression and social control'. The symbiotic nature of new media forms is considered further towards the end of this chapter.

Race and Crime in the News Media

Much analysis of race and racism in British society during the 1960s, 1970s and 1980s drew upon newspaper reports that exhibited racial stereotypes and prejudice that would now – in the twenty-first century – seem out of place in anything other than fringe publications associated with extreme right groups. Ferguson (1998: 180) argued that TV representation of race has moved away from the crude racism evident in previous periods and that news media is 'much more careful about the surface of its discourse'. He also noted, however, that the apparent retreat from racist stereotyping does not extend beneath the surface. Law (2002: 36) similarly warned that the apparent 'death' of racism in the media has been greatly exaggerated and that coverage of crime, and other social problems, shows that 'the capacity for the renewal of hostile news messages about groups who are positioned outside the white nation ... is regularly demonstrated year after year'.

An extensive body of research in the UK and elsewhere has catalogued both that media representation of black and minority ethnic communities is heavily skewed towards crime and lawlessness and that coverage of crime and lawlessness disproportionally feature black and minority ethnic communities. From the early 1970s onwards, studies have shown how street crime, drugs, urban unrest and violent crime were represented in the news media as aspects of Britain's 'black crime problem'. Husband and Hartman (1974) found that crime stories were the third most frequent topic of newspaper stories of Britain's black and Asian communities and that readers cited crime stories above any other topic associated with reporting minority populations. News media coverage of street crime in the 1970s and 1980s often explicitly identified the problem with the black community. In 1982 the Metropolitan Police released statistics that purported to show that the majority of 'muggings' in the capital were committed by black people, a claim reinforced in a TV programme in which a Deputy Assistant Commissioner stated that 80 per cent of 'muggings' were carried out by black people. Newspapers reflected this primary definition of the problem, linking street crime to lax immigration policies, urban decay and the metropolitan socialism of the 'race relations' industry (Gordon and Rosenberg, 1989). Headlines included 'Black Crime: the Alarming Figures' (*Daily Mail*) and 'The Yard Blames Black Muggers' (*The Sun*), and failed to acknowledge that such statistics were hugely problematic (Gordon and Rosenberg, 1989). Sim (1982) argued that engagement in racist stereotyping of street crime formed part of a response to criticisms of the policing of urban unrest contained in the 1981 Scarman Report and concerns relating to police racism and violence. Contriving the criminal threat of the black community drew upon dominant media themes established in the 'mugging' panic that emerged in the early 1970s, and with a longer historical perspective, which had associated migrant communities with various crime threats for generations.

The racialization of street crime has been widely noted in relation to press coverage of the 'mugging' panic in early 1970s Britain. Chibnall (1977) noted that the first instances of 'mugging' reported in 1972 were couched in terms of an alien form of crime imported into British society from the United States. That mugging was presented in the press as a frightening new form of violent crime was not only historically inaccurate, since Britain had a long history of this type of offence (Pearson, 1983; King, 2003; Hallsworth, 2005), but it also implied that the urban unrest and racial conflict around the civil rights movement and Black Power in the USA were prefigured by what was regarded as a

'racial' crime. As Hall et al. (1978) – in one of the most influential criminological and cultural studies texts – have shown, the newspapers quickly established shorthand ways of presenting the 'mugging' epidemic, such that the
archetypal victim was an elderly white female preyed upon by a frightening
young black man. The representation of mugging as a 'black crime problem'
was often done explicitly, although newspapers often tended to legitimize such
perspectives with comments from authoritative figures such as judges or black
youth workers (Chibnall, 1977). In other instances, the moral panic surrounding mugging that developed in the mid-1970s did not explicitly portray it as a
black crime problem, although the same effect was gained by identifying certain localities as particularly prone to such offences. Kennington, Brixton and
Notting Hill, Chibnall (1977: 123) noted, were reported as districts with particular problems of street crime, venues that, even in the early 1970s, were
spatial representations of the ethnic geography of London. Hall et al. (1978)
noted that once locations such as Brixton were effectively racialized in media
and political discourses they became loaded synonyms in barely coded racialized discussion of street crime.

The preponderance of racialized crime stories can be partly understood
in historical terms. Successive groups of migrants into British society, from
the Jews and the Irish of the nineteenth century, to Arab and African seafaring communities of the early decades of the twentieth century and the
Maltese communities who migrated in the immediate post-Second World
War era, have been subject to racist newspaper reporting that associated
them with various problems relating to crime, immorality and disease.
Gang-related offending and street robbery, apparently key components of
'broken Britain' in the early twenty-first century, were often portrayed by
nineteenth-century media as being associated with minority ethnic communities who did not share national virtues of law-abidance and respect for
property (Davies, 1989).

In this way, newspaper coverage of crime, as with other issues, relies upon
primary definers: court officials, police spokespeople, politicians, academic
experts and the like, who establish a narrative framework that continues to
shape stories even as it comes to be challenged by secondary definers who
later might seek to challenge dominant perspectives. Gilroy (1987) noted
how press and TV coverage that presented Rastafarians as a religio-political
threat to orderly British society developed symbiotically with police discourse: the press drew upon the authoritative commentary of senior police
officers to provide racialized accounts of a crime threat which in turn looped
into demands for greater police powers and increased resources. Similarly,
Hall et al. (1978) showed that primary definers shape media narratives
because they are organizationally and culturally well placed to do so: police
have media liaison teams and journalists have long-standing contacts with

expert commentators, neither of which extend to those engaged in crime, protest or disorder. Once established as primary definers of news, established voices enter into 'reciprocal relations' with the media, such that the media coverage of crime issues is then used as evidence of policing and crime problems. Hall et al. (1978) showed that exaggerated media coverage of 'mugging' included reported comments made by judges, for example, who noted that this amorphous type of crime was increasingly prevalent but that, in turn, the judiciary began to cite newspaper coverage of the problem as evidence that warranted exemplary sentences for some offenders. The iterative relations between media and the criminal justice system has also been indentified in regard to infotainment and fictional genres – Ferrell et al. (2008) described the relationship between cultural representations and material practices of crime and criminal justice as 'looping' – as is discussed further below.

This process of narrative establishment and challenge was also apparent in the urban unrest of the 1980s, which was widely presented in the media in heavily racialized terms that themselves drew upon themes of racial conflict and problems established since the early 1970s. Van Dijk's (1991) analysis of British press stories relating to ethnic affairs during the six months from August 1985 to January 1986 found that the four most common words used in headlines were 'police', 'riot', 'black', and 'race'. He argued that the lexicon of newspaper headlines is significant for a number of reasons, not least that they are often the part of a story most often recalled by both consumers and producers of news. During the period Van Dijk examined there were a series of urban disorders, newspaper coverage of which was heavily racialized, but his analysis demonstrated that the use of key words and phrases cannot be explained in terms of the properties of events themselves; they are always selective and interpretative. *The Daily Telegraph*, for example, headlined reports of court cases arising from the disorders in ways that foregrounded the ethnicity of participants ('Second Black on Murder Charge' and 'Black Brixton Looters Jailed', both from December 1985, in Van Dijk, 1991: 64). Highlighting ethnicity in this way signifies it as a salient factor: the gender or age of those involved in the disturbances might be of greater explanatory interest but it was the imputed ethnic characteristics of participants that were constructed as significant by much of the media. As with street crime, such racialized media representation had considerable historical precedent. Urban unrest was similarly attributed to migrant communities in the period after the First World War and again in the 'race riots' in Notting Hill and Nottingham in the late 1950s (Jenkinson, 1993; Rowe, 1998).

These trends have been identified in other Western societies, which might reflect the globalization of media forms and formats, which extends to news and current affairs as well as entertainment genres. In Canada, for example, a recent analysis of research into crime reporting on TV news programmes noted that:

> racial minorities and new immigrants to Canada from minority racialized groups in particular, are often presented as threats to the nation-state, and non-White groups are portrayed consistently as mysterious or inscrutable, or linked invariably to crime and deviant patterns of behaviour. (Tamang, 2009: 196)

Analysis of US TV news showed not that black people were over-represented as suspects when compared to their presence in arrest data, but that they tended to be presented as more threatening than white suspects (Chiricos and Eschholz, 2002). In Britain, research has suggested that television news coverage of crime has been heavily racialized, such that urban disorder, for example, since the 1980s has portrayed minority ethnic communities – initially Britain's black population but more recently Asian people too – as problematic threats to the social order. Malik (2002) has argued that the disproportional nature of racialized crime reporting on British TV is made more significant by the relative absence of minority ethnic groups in other news and current affairs coverage: the problem is not that just crime stories tend to focus on black and Asian people, but that these communities are heavily under-represented in relation to other themes and topics. Moreover, Malik (2002) also noted that problems facing minority communities – whether racial violence, health or social exclusion – are barely mentioned in mainstream news stories. Malik's (2002) analysis of the portrayal of black and Asian people in British comedy has also tended to portray them as troublesome, with cultural values and norms that present problems to established British society. Any racism that then stems from white society, it is implied, is presented as an understandable, if unfortunate, response to challenges emanating from the presence of minorities in British society.

Much of the analysis of news media coverage of crime and minority groups in Britain in the 1970s, 1980s and 1990s has tended to focus on the portrayal of black communities as problematic and crime-prone. While the crude racism of earlier periods might have become somewhat tempered in more recent coverage, portrayal of Asian people in the news media has – if anything – tended to move in the opposite direction. In coverage of the urban disorders of the early and mid-1980s, for example, sections of the media argued that racism could not explain events, since Asian communities, who faced racism, had not been involved in the unrest. Indeed, press and political commentary often held British Asians up as a model migrant population: demonstrating strong family values and a commitment to hard work that other groups might imitate (Rowe, 1998). Stereotypical though this perspective might have been, it was relatively benign in contrast to subsequent coverage that has often equated British Asians, and the Muslim community in particular, as criminogenic and a threat to law and order. Media criminalization of British Asian communities was particularly apparent in the aftermath of the 'milltown' disorders of 2001. Arguments that second-generation Asian youths were culturally alienated from both older generations and from mainstream British society formed one explanation of the disorders, while others related to economic deprivation, poor police engagement with the community, and growing drug problems. Alexander's (2004) analysis of the response to the 2001 disorders notes that the media often represented young Asian men in terms of 'gangs'; prototypical criminal organizations engaged in drug dealing and racist violence against white people. Although other explanations of the disorders were presented in the news media, Alexander's (2004: 531) study found that:

> At the forefront of these portraits of cultural dysfunction and social breakdown stand Muslim young men, encapsulated in the image of 'the gang'. Reports up to, during and after the riots weave a picture of angry young men, alienated from society and their own communities, entangled in a life of crime and violence.

Such perspectives have increasingly been presented through a prism of terrorism, an approach which has suggested that Muslim communities are primarily loyal to networks and movements beyond the nation state. Modood and Ahmad (2007: 188) suggested that popular media conjoined with political commentary have identified British Muslims as a categorical problem:

> Many politicians, commentators, letter-writers and phone-callers to the media from across the political spectrum, not to mention Home Secretaries, have blamed the fact that these questions have had to be asked on the alleged cultural separatism and self-imposed segregation of Muslim migrants, and on a 'politically correct' concept of multiculturalism that fostered fragmentation rather than integration and 'Britishness'.

Given that 'active citizenship' has been promoted as a key component of effective responses to crime and disorder, problematizing their status as separate from the mainstream establishes the Muslim community as a prospective security threat (Spalek et al., 2009). The impact of security and threats of terrorism on governance and multiculturalism are considered further in Chapter Nine, but it is clear that media coverage has been vital to the criminalization and racialization of the Muslim community.

Infotainment

Traditionally, criminological and sociological analysis has concentrated on the representation of crime in news media, which apparently purports to represent objective reality. What much media analysis has demonstrated is that for cultural, technical and operational reasons, media coverage of news events selects and constructs stories according to established discourse and narratives. As has been shown, the problem of street robbery, for example, is not explicitly defined in racialized terms, but the ways in which such stories have been framed over a period of decades means that they are effectively racialized as they are articulated in terms that are synonymous with minority ethnic communities. As Hall et al. (1978), Keith (1993) and Van Dijk (1991) showed, place names associated with minority communities (Brixton in south London during the 1980s being an obvious example) could be referred to in ways that associated stories with established racialized frameworks while not mentioning race or ethnicity in direct terms. While it is important to recognize that objective news coverage is actually shaped by editorial and professional norms, a relatively recent media format throws much greater doubt on the boundaries between news, documentary and entertainment genres. 'Reality television' has come to dominate schedules in many forms, but crime-based shows have been an early, persistent and widespread sub-genre, co-representing the brutal realism and mundane inanity of crime and antisocial behaviour in the contemporary urban landscape. A pre-eminent example of the format on British TV is *Crimewatch*, the programme that seeks public information in response to crimes reconstructed for the viewing public. The 'public interest' defence for these formats might be somewhat thin, although clearly they have elicited important information relating to some cases, and it is clear that they focus disproportionally on dramatic and violent incidents in the same way that the regular news media also tends to do. The editorial maxim 'if it bleeds, it leads' seems to apply to the TV reality shows as to more traditional newsrooms. Analysis of the representation of offenders and victims in terms of race and ethnicity also suggests some distortion of reality. Jewkes' (2004) analysis of *Crimewatch*, for example, concluded that the show over-represented crimes involving black offenders and under-represented those where a black person was the victim.

Not only is it clear that the apparent veracity of these 'reality shows' is the result of selective representation and manipulation, sometimes engineered by police gatekeepers granting access to broadcasters and sometimes by editors and directors themselves, there is also evidence of 'looping', such that the realist content presented onscreen serves to constitute practices of criminal justice (Doyle, 2003). Ferrell et al. (2008) noted a number of problematic examples whereby procedures and practices normalized by infotainment and *verité*-based formats such as the *CSI* series have informed real-world criminal justice decisions. For this reason alone, it becomes increasingly important that analysis of media portrayal of crime pays attention to themes and narratives that transcend fictional, documentary and news media genres, the boundaries between which are increasingly blurred. Doyle (2003) found that the narrative demands of 'fly on the wall' documentary makers influenced the conduct of police investigations and the ways in which officer participants in reality shows behaved. Reality-based TV shows, like news media and cinema, tend to concentrate disproportionally on violent crime and to over-represent minorities as offenders and to under-represent them as police officers (Oliver, 1994). The prevailing tendency of academic analysis has been to consider each format in isolation, but it seems increasingly important to consider the cross-format representations.

Screen Fiction

The association of organized crime with ethnic groups has been a recurring feature of many popular cultural forms. Early cinema continued narratives evident in nineteenth-century popular fiction that presented outsider ethnic groups as exotic and dangerous (Rafter, 2006). Fritz Lang's 1931 movie *M* depicts the hunt for a paedophiliac serial killer. The movie starred Peter Lorre as Hans Beckerts, the murderer, which allowed the Nazis to claim the movie depicted Jewish perversity (Kaes, 2000). Hitchcock's 1934 *The Man Who Knew Too Much* portrayed a gang of East European assassins thwarted by the determined ingenuity of the plucky British heroes. Among the most enduring representations of the ethnic crime gang has been that of Italian Americans as Mafia, which developed in the 1930s and continued through *The Godfather* (1972, 1974, 1990) movies to *Goodfellas* (1990) and, more recently, transferred to television in the *Sopranos* series (1999–2007). Movies such as *Little Caesar* (1931) and *Scarface* (1932) are early examples of the organized crime genre and both featured Italian Americans in a period in which the wider status of that community and its fidelity to the USA was under scrutiny (Cavallero and Plasketes, 2004; Rafter, 2006). Not only did cinematic representation of Italian Americans as gangsters reflect stereotypes of that ethnic community and more general concerns about organized crime, the association between crime and ethnicity effectively distanced emerging social problems from mainstream American values. Cavallero and Plasketes (2004) argued that:

> by depicting [1930s gangsters] as different, as not quite American, the challenges the films post to American ideals are made less threatening to 'average Americans'. That is to say, because ethnic gangsters instigate a corruption of American ideals, non-ethnic Americans are afforded the opportunity to blame the failure of [American] myths during the Great Depression on the individual ethnic characters and their respective ethnic groups rather than the failure of the myths themselves.

Similar critical perspectives have been applied to more recent depictions of Italian Americans in film and television. In 2001, the Italian American Defense Association unsuccessfully sued broadcaster HBO for defamation in *The Sopranos*. The show engendered considerable debate about the nature of stereotyping and the place of Italian Americans in contemporary US society. For all that the lead character, Tony Soprano, disturbed conventions of the genre by displaying a fundamental moral ambiguity that led him to seek psychiatric help, it was equally apparent that the programme revisited many established stereotypes of Italian American life (Wynn, 2004). It also continues to present organized crime as a specialist ethnic business, and so one separated from mainstream American society (Larke, 2003).

Ethnic gangs also form the central dramatic structure of *The Wire*, another HBO show that ran for five seasons between 2002 and 2008 and, in addition to huge popular and critical acclaim, has become subject to burgeoning academic analysis. *The Wire* portrays Baltimore Police Department surveillance strategies to gather evidence against a series of major drug gangs. The cultural and organizational dynamics of the gangs and the police form the central storylines as different characters promote their favoured strategies to tackle the city's drug problem or, conversely, to seek new alliances among criminal networks that will endure political and law enforcement attention. One reason why the show has been subjected to considerable critical attention is that it conveys a strong sociological imagination dealing with questions such as the intergenerational transmission of the underclass and the role of education and the media in relation to crime. *The Wire* offers an apparently authentic account of urban crime that locates the violent and criminal behaviour of its characters in terms of the broader social, cultural, economic and educational structures that shape their lives. Using narrative structures unconventional by the standards of contemporary TV drama, Potter and Marshall (2009: 17) noted that 'its stories scream of verisimilitude, and the authentic dialogue draws the viewer into a sympathetic consideration of characters who live the sort of lives many viewers will not ever have examined with careful, concerned, critical awareness'. On these grounds alone, it is evident that *The Wire* provided fertile ground for criminologists, sociologists and those interested in cultural studies.

Moreover, though, *The Wire*'s storylines subverted traditional stereotypes and boundaries of class, gender, race and ethnicity often associated with crime genres. *The Wire* questioned and challenged much conventional portrayal of law and order in television and cinema. Deviance, corruption and unethical behaviour are properties of police departments and City Hall just as much as they are associated with murderous street gangs. The violence and machismo of the crime gangs is leavened by the strong moral and ethical code – albeit an unconventional one – of a key character, Omar Little, who has been construed as a twenty-first-century equivalent of Robin Hood since he violently steals from drug dealers and claims to abhor the targeting of 'civilians'. If Little is a parasite on the misery perpetuated by the drug trade, then so too are the lawyers, politicians and police officers who seek to build their reputations off the back of criminal gangs. One of the 'chief executives' of the central drug dealing operations is Stringer Bell, who works hard at evening classes in business studies and applies conventional marketing techniques to his local supply of heroin. Conferences with representatives of competitor narcotics enterprises are held in the boardrooms of local hotels as deals and agreements are struck over supply arrangements and territory rights: these are only marginally more sinister meetings than those that might be held by rotary clubs or in Masonic Lodges.

Race and ethnicity feature heavily in *The Wire*, although, as the above might suggest, not in straightforward ways. Many of the gangs are presented as relatively ethnically homogeneous. The drug gangs are predominantly African American, the importation of heroin is largely controlled by 'the Greeks', and the dock workers who smuggle contraband are 'Polacks'. The police department appears to be more ethnically mixed than the other gangs – certainly the normative whiteness of most onscreen police departments is not apparent (Rafter, 2006). Nevertheless, the officers' informal socialization revolves around an Irish American identity that is embodied in their unofficial anthem 'Body of an American' which celebrates migration and assimilation into US society.

For all that *The Wire* transgressed stereotypes of genre and representation of crime, it could only do so within a dominant racialized framework. Just as 'secondary definers' in news media respond to a primary account already established and so reproduce dominant frameworks they wish to challenge, so too *The Wire* often only works dramatically by recalling established racialized accounts. Although the show offered complex and nuanced renditions of African American masculinity (Petersen, 2009), these representations often only worked because they invoked older narratives. One of the most subversive episodes in respect to established presentations of race and crime occurred in Season 2, which, of all five seasons of the show, focused the least on the activities of the African American drug gangs. The dominant story of the season was the efforts of the dockworkers' union to resist the decline of their industry and threat to their livelihoods. For some, economic hard times led them to explore illicit opportunities by trading goods stolen from the dockside and by importing chemicals and narcotics. In episode 5, the Serious Crimes Unit of the Baltimore Police Department is developing an undercover operation to gather evidence about the street corner drug dealing associated with some of this organized crime. Captain Daniels details three of his officers – Herc, Greggs and Carver – to stake out a street drug market 'operating the corners'. The officers' experience in covert surveillance is underlined by Daniels' entreaty to 'do what you do best'. The operation differs from the usual deployment though since it is in a predominantly white neighbourhood. Herc – the only white officer of the three – points out to his boss and his colleagues: 'A lot of these port guys are white, right? So that means you're going to need a white boy to go down to some of these south eastern corners, right? So, Keema [Greggs] and Carver on the roof house; it's my turn to front out: let me show you how it's done homes ...'

The next scene shows Greggs and Carver setting up surveillance equipment and peering out at the street from within the stakeout property. As they do so, they, and the audience, overhear an angry tirade from the street:

> I'm saying, Dirt, you wanna be my nigger, you got to be with me for real. All the time I be telling you 'be on the post', but damn, homes, you all the time up in some damn crib, trying to play house with them bitches. You all be fucked up because I'm out here, getting done what needs done. Feel me, nigga?'

Cautiously the officers peek out of the window at the street scene. 'Well, I'll be ...', Greggs exclaims in disbelief. The shot reveals the reason for her surprise: dressed in urban sports chic with low-slung jeans exposing designer underwear, the two targets in conversation on the side of the street are white. Shaking his head, Carver mutters 'thieving motherfuckers take everything don't they?' Out on the street the rant concludes: 'You know what I'm saying, Dirts, you wanna be my nigger, you gots to deliver'.

While the episode consciously subverts expectations and undermines the usual portrayal of street drug dealers as African American, it only works in dramatic terms by invoking the very associations it apparently questions. The comedy of these scenes is that the white drug dealers seek to pass as black, in a reversal of the long-standing process whereby black people posed as whites in an effort to escape the racial identity imposed upon them in a racist segregated society. Moreover, the authoritative commentary on the scene is provided by two black officers who share the viewers' surprise as the white ethnicity of the dealers is revealed. The denouement only works, though, by reinforcing dominant motifs of drug dealing and the street subculture of African Americans. As Carver rues the appropriation of African American culture by white youth he reminds the viewer that 'thieving motherfuckers' are more commonly presented as black than white.

Digital Media

Relative to other media formats, little criminological attention has been paid to digital media and gaming culture, and most of the research effort has focused upon the potential imitative capacity such formats might have in reproducing violent behaviour among viewers, participants and consumers. The focus of the discussion below will be somewhat different although the 'audience effect' debate is also important to a consideration of the impact that racialized representations of crime in digital media might have. Instead of considering the violent properties of these environments, this discussion focuses instead upon the ways in which they tend to appropriate, commodify, reinforce and reproduce racist discourse about crime (particularly violent crime) in contemporary society. There may be several reasons why media and communication studies have tended to overlook these formats, apart from their novelty. The scope and scale of digital environments makes it more difficult to operationalize conventional research methods and the audiences and consumers of such formats are not easy to access. Further, the ephemeral nature of much of the content found in such environments also makes analysis difficult. All of these caveats apply to the discussion that follows, and it is for these reasons that there is no suggestion that the analysis applies across the whole spectrum of media types loosely corralled together under the sub-heading of 'digital media'. Instead the discussion is based upon a loose 'reading' of the *Grand Theft Auto* (GTA) digital gaming series. While GTA cannot be considered as 'representative' of the wider sector, it has been one of the most high-profile games, one of the biggest selling, and one that has attracted considerable controversy for its apparent celebration of violent crime, hyper-consumerism and sexual content.

GTA was first published in 1997 and has undergone various changes in format in subsequent iterations, most significantly perhaps when GTA III moved the game into full 3D. All versions operate a similar format such that the player operates a central character located in a particular environment, time and space with the objective of developing their criminal career while avoiding various organized criminal opponents and cops. While the player responds to a broad narrative, there are multiple opportunities to deviate from the central story to explore marginal territories, interact with characters on the sidelines or just to cruise the streets of the various fictional cityscapes. In later versions of the game, the player has many opportunities to select vehicles, clothing, food, musical and other tastes such that their character is moulded and developed as the player chooses. The latitude afforded to players to explore the virtual world of GTA is often cited as fundamental to the series' success. Miller (2007) suggested that the first versions of GTA eschewed the cultural politics of race and identity although the game's various 'radio stations' were programmed such that the rap and hip-hop soundtrack to the bleak crime-ridden urban districts contrasted with the country music playing in rural areas. Several gamers cited in Miller's study note that they select music appropriate to the places and activities they are immersed in. Even when deliberately subverting these aural relationships, they reinforce the implied association of black music forms with urban violence, as one player's reflection illustrated: 'Sometimes I like to use the country station on San Andreas when I am doing a drive-by because it's so surreal' (Miller, 2007: 425).

Apart from the technical changes that enhanced the gaming experience offered by GTA III, it also featured a stronger central character, CJ: a young black man who must return to West Coast Los Santos (a virtual Los Angeles) from Liberty City (as New York) for his mother's funeral. While there he is set up by corrupt cops and becomes embroiled in gang activity in his old neighbourhood, Ganton (Compton). The game is set in 1992 during the aftermath of the Los Angeles riots. Clearly, then, the game provided an opportunity for players to enjoy the 'virtual ghettocentric spectacle' of crime and violence in the cultural geography of early 1990s USA (Leonard, 2006). That this carnival of crime represented the celebration and wholesale commodification of violent conflict is apparent from more than 45 million sales of the game, sufficient to make it the best-selling game in the USA in the year it was released and in the top ten sold in the UK.

The publication of GTA III in 2004 led to considerable political and media panic about the impact of the game and to efforts to censor and restrict the availability of the game to adults ('to protect our children'). The game was banned in Australia and subject to 18+ adult ratings in many countries; a number of European countries required cuts to the more controversial content (Finn, 2006; Kerr, 2006). Much of the concern in the USA was articulated in terms of the risks that the violent and sexual content of the game posed to young people. Leonard (2006) noted, though, that many previous games that were equally violent had not been subject to such high-profile or prolonged concern and argues that games in which the violence is perpetrated by state officials against third world terrorists or urban criminals seemed to be culturally acceptable and was not subject to the moral and political opprobrium afforded to GTA III. What distinguished GTA III was that the violence was directed outwards from the black urban underclass and '... pose[d] a threat to the national fabric, just as those who inhabit those real-life communities pose an equal danger. In each case, policing and regulation are needed to protect those who live outside South Central and San Andreas from the physical and cultural dangers facilitated by potential contact with blackness' (Leonard, 2006: 55).

On the other side of this cultural war were many who celebrated GTA III, and argued that it afforded a degree of creative freedom to players and exposure to a range of experiences not safely available in the real world (Murray, 2005). A frequent defence of the game was that the violence it portrayed was the reality of the ghetto: violence there might be a cause for concern, but the game itself is only a mirror of that and so should not itself be criticized. If the game portrays black criminals, well that too is realistic; although the verisimilitude is questionable. Leonard (2006: 59) pointed out that 'GTA erases much of what happens daily within America's ghettos, from mothers and fathers working and sons and daughters playing and going to school to families eating dinner ... to claim realism is to accept the idea that America's ghetto is nothing more than war zones inhabited by lawless gangstas in need of policing, surveillance and state control'.

SUMMARY

The socially constructed nature of crime and race makes it important to explore how ideas about crime, and race, are communicated and represented across a broad range of formats, including traditional news media, popular cultural fictional and 'infotainment' formats, as well as digital games and interactive platforms. While racial stereotyping might be less apparent in media reporting than it once was, it is clear that news agendas continue to be heavily racialized. In addition to examining developments in media representation in terms of news agendas, the chapter has also focused on infotainment formats, cinema and television coverage.

An under-researched aspect of media coverage of crime relates to emerging forms of digital media, such as gaming environments and the ways in which they tend to appropriate, commodify, reinforce and reproduce racist discourse about crime (particularly violent crime) in contemporary society. It has been argued that games such as *Grand Theft Auto* rely upon audio and visual representations of urban black culture and associate these with law and order problems.

STUDY QUESTIONS

1 What did Hall, and others, mean when describing 'reciprocal relations' between media and authority spokespeople?

2 In relation to examples of your choosing, what similarities are there in fictional, infotainment and non-fiction representations of race and crime?

3 Does it matter if fictional media representations distort and exaggerate the role of minorities in crime?

(Continued)

(Continued)

FURTHER READING

One of the most influential criminological, socoiological and media studies texts of recent decades is *Policing the Crisis* (1978, Macmillan) by Hall, Critcher, Jefferson, Clarke and Roberts, which provides a compelling analysis of racialized media coverage of crime in the 1970s and relates this to political and ideological developments of the period. A strong analysis of the media coverage of crime in more general terms can be obtained in Jewkes' (2011, Sage) *Media and Crime,* and Law's (2002, Palgrave) *Race in the News* is a very useful source on race and racism in news media. The primary journal for scholarly analysis relating to the themes addressed in this chapter remains *Crime, Media and Culture,* http://cmc. sagepub.com/

4

Disproportionality in Offending

OVERVIEW

Claims that minority ethnic communities commit more crimes than other groups have been among the most controversial public, policy and academic debates about offending and justice in Britain and many other countries for many decades. Since the late nineteenth century a range of ethnic groups migrating to Britain have been associated with a variety of criminal activities and subject to related processes of criminalization and racialization that have defined them as inherently problematic and antithetical to a law-abiding British society. Both of the preceding chapters have explored ways in which criminological theory and popular cultural representations have focused upon the criminality of minority ethnic communities. This chapter will develop those debates by considering specific examples of crime problems associated with minority groups and assess the evidential basis relating to disproportionality in offending. Theoretical criminological perspectives relating to these issues are assessed towards the end of the chapter.

The aims of the chapter are to:

- consider the limited statistical evidence relating to differences in offending across and within ethnic groups;
- briefly outline historical concerns about the criminality of migrant and minority ethnic communities;
- critically consider contemporary concerns and explanations about minority ethnic over-involvement in street, gang, and gun crime.

KEY TERMS

- Disproportionality
- Gun and gang crime
- History of crime
- Moral panic
- Victim surveys

- 'Mugging' and street crime
- Offending, Crime and Justice Survey
- Racial profiling
- Urban unrest

Introduction

As is explained at greater length in Chapter Seven, minority ethnic groups are generally over-represented, compared to their presence in the population, at many stages of the criminal justice system, from police stop and search, through arrest, prosecution and sentencing. While much policy and research attention has been focused on the extent to which institutional racism within the criminal justice system and society more generally explains these patterns, differences in the nature and extent of criminal activity might also influence differential engagement with the system. A conservative and traditional perspective suggests that the agencies of the criminal justice system play a relatively neutral role in terms of crime trends and problems, such that the police, courts and penal system responds to developing incidents and issues rooted externally in social, biological, demographic, cultural, economic and political contexts. Right realist perspectives maintain that minority ethnic groups are over-represented in the criminal justice system because they commit more offences. In contrast, left realists maintain that the over-representation results from a combination of disproportionate policing practices, political and media concerns about crime, and the impact of social and economic deprivation and racism on offending. These theoretical perspectives are critically reviewed in more detail later in the chapter. Prior to that, the extent of disproportionality is assessed, both in terms of the statistical evidence and in relation to historical and contemporary debates about disproportionality in the context of particular crime problems and trends.

Statistical Evidence of Disproportionality

The two key concepts at the heart of this book – race and crime – are essentially socially constructed; with no substantive inherent property that can be understood without reference to the social context in which they have developed. In addition to significant methodological challenges, this remains a central reason why finding wholly convincing statistical evidence of disproportionality in offending patterns between ethnic groups is impossible. Arrest data provide one measure of offending and demonstrate apparently clear differences between ethnic groups: in 2008/09, 30 people in 1,000 were arrested in England and Wales. The rates for white people and for the 'Chinese and other' group were lower than the average at 27 and 29 per 1,000 of the population respectively. For black, Asian and mixed groups, the rates were higher: at 89 per 1,000 of black people, 31 of Asians, and 65 for the mixed group (Ministry of Justice, 2010: 29).

Taken as a crude indicator of offending, this data seem to suggest that black people and those of mixed ethnic origin engage in crime at greater rates than other groups. However, further analysis demonstrates that these general patterns appear more complex when examined in greater detail. One complication is that the aggregation of the data into broad ethnic categories effectively denies wide disparities between groups. Within the ethnic category 'black', for example, the sub-category of 'black African' has a rate of 68 per 1,000, 'black Caribbean' has a rate of 88 per 1,000, and 'other Black' a rate of 239 per 1,000. While all of these rates are higher than that for the population as a whole, and so there remains some indication of disproportionality, they are clearly of a very different magnitude in terms of these smaller sub-ethnic groups. The issue of disproportionality in arrest data becomes even more complex, however, when considered in relation to different police force areas. Black people across England and Wales might have a rate of 89 per 1,000, and all sub-groups have a higher rate than the average for the population as a whole, but in some police force areas the picture appears very different. Broken down by police force area, black Africans have a rate as low as 23 per 1,000 in Lancashire (below the national average for that ethnic cohort) and as high as 123 per 1,000 in Gwent. The statistical evidence varies even more considerably for the 'other black' category: across England and Wales as a whole this group has an arrest rate of 239 per 1,000, but across the 43 police force areas this rate varies from the lowest in South Yorkshire – at 95 per 1,000 – to the highest in the neighbouring area of North Yorkshire, which has a rate of 804 per 1,000. Unless 'other black' people in North Yorkshire are offending more than eight times as much as their ethnic counterparts a few miles away in South Yorkshire, then it must be that some of these apparently authoritative statistical differences are artefacts of the data collection and collation process and do not reflect 'real' differences in offending levels.

While some of the statistical evidence might reflect different levels of offending, they share a general weakness of police crime data in that they relate only to the relatively small proportion of offences that come to the attention of officers. Methodological innovations in the measurement of the extent and trends in crime have, since the early 1970s, provided a wealth of data relating to offending and victimization. To overcome limitations with Uniform Crime Reports, that only include incidents that are reported to and recorded by the police, the US National Crime Victimization Survey (NCVS) was instigated in 1972 as a survey 'to produce national estimates of the levels and characteristics of criminal victimization. ... The NCVS constitutes a key component of our nation's system to measure the extent and nature of crime [and] is the primary US source of information on criminal victimization' (Bureau of Justice Statistics). In Britain, a similar household survey of the experiences of crime was developed in the early 1980s in the form of the British Crime Survey, which also forms a useful complementary measure to police-recorded crime statistics. The BCS was first run in 1982 but since 2001/02 it has been a continuous study: the 'sweep' commenced in 2009 included 51,000 respondents. In some years, the BCS has included a booster sample of minority ethnic respondents. Both the NCVS and the BCS, and other crime surveys, reveal a great deal in terms of the social, economic and demographic profile of crime victims, including information about their ethnicity. The British Crime Survey (Home Office, 2010a: 46) found that only 43 per cent of crimes were reported to the police, and that is only the first step required for the identification and apprehension of an offender. An earlier study (Barclay and Tavares, 1999) found that only in 5.5 per cent of cases was the crime 'cleared up' by the police, such that an offender was identified, and only in 2.9 per cent of cases was an offender found guilty at court or subjected to a caution. While arrest data does not necessarily arise solely from cases reported to the police, and it is clear that individuals who are arrested might not be guilty of any offence, it is apparent that arrest data – and other similar evidence – serves as a very poor measure of actual levels of offending.

Self-reported Offending

An alternative measure of offending can be found in the Offending, Crime and Justice Survey (OCJS), which asks respondents about their own level of criminal activity and involvement in various forms of antisocial behaviour. The 2003 OCJS included 12,000 respondents aged between 10 and 65 years of age from across England and Wales. The survey included a booster sample of 1,882 minority ethnic respondents and almost half of the sample was aged between 10 and 25 years (Sharp and Budd, 2005). Since the survey sampled people living in private residents, it excluded the homeless, those in institutions and prisoners, all of whom might have higher rates of offending. The OCJS asked respondents about crime in relation to 20 types of offence, among which theft of a vehicle, burglary, robbery, theft from a person, assault resulting in injury, and selling Class A drugs were categorized as serious offences. Clear differences emerged between ethnic groups in terms of offences committed at any time during the respondent's lifetime. As Figure 4.1 indicates, 42 per cent of

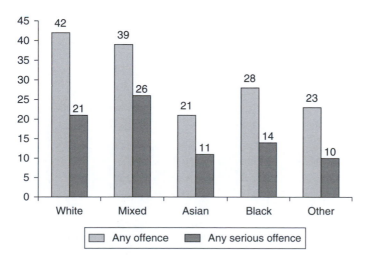

Figure 4.1   Percentage committing any offence and any serious offence in their life-time, by ethnic group (2003 OCJS)

Source: Sharp and Budd (2005: 8)

white respondents admitted to any offence during their lifetime, a higher proportion than any other ethnic group; for Asians and 'others', the respective rates were 21 and 23 per cent. In terms of serious offending, the 'mixed' ethnic group had the highest level, at 26 per cent, while Asians and 'others' were again the lowest, at 11 and 10 per cent respectively.

The survey found similar patterns, in terms of ethnicity, in respect to offending that had taken place during the previous 12 months, as Figure 4.2 indicates. Again, the white and 'mixed' categories reported the highest level in terms of any offence and any serious offence, and other ethnic groups were lower in respect of both broad categories of offending.

The OCJS also asked respondents about their participation in antisocial behaviour, which included being noisy or rude in a public place, behaviour that led to a neighbour complaint, graffiti, joy-riding, carrying a weapon, and racial harassment. Figure 4.3 indicates that young people were more likely to admit such behaviour than all respondents reported offending. While white and 'mixed' groups were again the highest, the differences appear less marked in respect to antisocial behaviour than for crime. The figure for Asians, at 22 per cent the lowest rate, was statistically significant from that of the highest group, whites, but differences were otherwise not statistically significant.

OCJS data suggested that black respondents who reported that they had offended in their lifetime were more likely to have been arrested and to have been to court than offenders from other ethnic groups. Thirty-five per cent of lifetime black offenders had been arrested and 29 per cent had been to court; comparable figures for white offenders were 25 and 19 per cent respectively

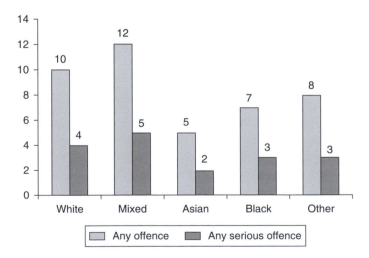

Figure 4.2   Percentage committing any offence and any serious offence in the last year, by ethnic group (2003 OCJS)

Source: Sharp and Budd (2005: 10)

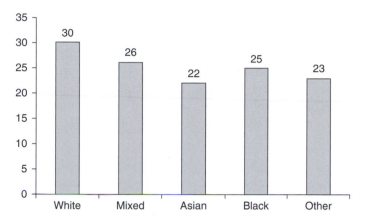

Figure 4.3 Percentage committing antisocial and other problem behaviours in the last year, by ethnic group (10–25 year-olds only) (2003 OCJS)

Source: Sharp and Budd (2005: 14)

(Sharp and Budd, 2005: 24). This suggests that the higher arrest rates for black people that were identified earlier in this chapter might not be related to the over-involvement of black people in offending in absolute terms but might be linked to the types of offending, disproportionate policing activity or the social and economic context that might make black people more 'available' to the attention of the criminal justice system. The 'availability thesis' is discussed at greater length in relation to stop and search in Chapter Seven.

Analysis of the OCJS suggests that minority groups are under-involved in crime and antisocial behaviour relative to white communities – a finding sharply at odds with a mass of data demonstrating over-involvement in the criminal justice system. However, Sharp and Budd's analysis shows that ethnic disproportionalities might be strongly influenced by age, gender, socio-economic and demographic factors. Their analysis of one survey, albeit a large-scale study, notes that the statistical data gathered were not sufficient to conduct regression analysis that would indicate the relative strength of multiple variables that might influence offending.

A study of successive 'sweeps' of the OCJS, from 2003–2006, focused upon the offending and antisocial behaviour of young people and sought to identify, through statistical analysis, factors that put respondents at greatest risk of engaging in such problematic behaviour (Hales et al., 2009). Among the variables considered was the ethnicity of the respondent. Whereas Sharp and Budd's (2005) analysis suggested that ethnicity appeared to be related to lower levels of offending and antisocial behaviour, the longitudinal study suggested that ethnicity was not a strong determinant of these risks. Instead, social and demographic factors were of greater importance. Having a sibling or peer group member who was engaged in offending behaviour or belonging to a single-parent family meant greater risk of offending, while ethnicity, religion or social class had no influence. As the authors' noted, this finding indicates that ethnicity does not influence offending behaviour. While this is contrary to Sharp and Budd's (2005) analysis of a single survey, both offer important challenges to predominant social, media, policy and political representations of crime that have, for many decades, tended to suggest that minority ethnic communities are more likely to offend. It is to these debates that the chapter now turns.

Other Evidence of Disproportionality

For all that the statistical evidence does not suggest that minority ethnic groups commit crime at higher rates than majority ethnic people – and that age, gender and area of residence do have some influence on offending rates – other sources of information sometimes suggest otherwise. Even if minorities do not commit more crime than others, it might be that they engage in types of offending that have greater visibility and are more likely to be subjected to criminal justice sanctions. This section of the chapter considers these trends and patterns in their historical and contemporary forms.

Historical Perspectives

Migrants to British society have been associated with a range of crime (and other) problems since at least the middle of the eighteenth century. During that period, for example, Irish migrants were widely associated with drunkeness and disorderly behaviour, and Jewish migrants with other offending behaviour, as Emsley (1987: 86–87) noted:

> The Irish were notorious for alleged criminality, though their offences were primarily of the public order variety as is evidenced by a cursory glance at the headlines of any nineteenth-century urban newspaper ... as well as court records. Jews were singled out as criminal in late eighteenth and early nineteenth-century London. There was particular outrage in the 1770s following the murder of a servant who tried to resist a gang of Jewish burglars in Chelsea in 1771. Jews appear to have played prominent roles as coiners and receivers in Georgian London; Dicken's Fagin had at least one well-known original in Ikey Solomons. The Jewish community had its share of pickpockets and petty thieves, and the poorer members were known to fight and riot in the same kinds of ways as the poorer classes of London; however, they were never as closely identified with drink as the Irish.

Emsley demonstrates that criminal problems posed by different migrant groups drew upon wider racist discourses – the Irish were violent and drunk and Jews were financially untrustworthy – but it is also apparent that the criminality of the dangerous classes in Victorian London was itself explained with reference to genetic and bodily characteristics. Henry Mayhew's 1861 survey of *London Labour and London Poor*, for example, identified the rootless nature of Jewish migrants as a particular challenge to an orderly society, but saw them as part of an underclass that was feckless, transient and outside civilized society. The 'wandering' population was not defined in ethnic terms, but was identified as a 'race apart': biologically identifiable and distinct (Morris, 1994: 17). The depravity and deprivation associated with migrant groups extended to the lower orders more generally. As Colls (2002: 285) observed: '... if the Catholic Irish were seen as stupid and feckless, so were the English poor. And if they were distrusted for their religion, so were many English non-conformists.' Miles (1993) argued that the development of racism in the colonial periphery was mirrored domestically in the 'racialisation of the interior' that was applied to the subordinate underclass; as was demonstrated in Chapter Two, biological approaches were used in relation to 'race' and other social issues, including crime. The criminalization of migration in terms of security and terrorist threats is explored in its contemporary forms in Chapter Nine. Antecedents of twenty-first-century associations between migration and terror can be found in nineteenth-century concerns relating to Jews and the Irish, the former in relation to revolutionary activity experienced elsewhere in continental Europe, and the latter in respect of 'Fenianism'.

The nature and extent of disproportionality in offending between minority ethnic groups has been an extended debate in relation to various migrants to Britain in the period following the Second World War. Partly as a result of that conflict, British governments actively sought to recruit migrants from the Commonwealth to meet a growing labour shortage in the late 1940s. While there had been black people resident in Britain for many centuries – indeed since African soldiers accompanied the Roman army in the third century (Fryer, 1984) – it was not until the 1940s and 1950s that a significant and indigenous black population began to become established. The extent to which the black community has been disproportionally involved in offending has been a matter of highly contested debate for much of the subsequent period. Before considering the ways in which street crime became racialized during the 1970s, it is important to recognize that during the 1950s and 1960s a range of authoritative perspectives suggested that the black community was generally under-involved in crime. In the late 1950s, for example, a report of the Cabinet Committee on Colonial Immigration stated that black migrants conducted themselves well and posed no problem in terms of public order, although a minority were involved in crime (Whitfield, 2004: 145). In the early 1970s the Home Affairs Select Committee on Race Relations and Immigration took evidence from community groups, experts and police into the state of 'police/immigrant relations'. That this topic was considered sufficiently significant for parliamentary attention indicates that there was some level of concern that the 'golden age' of policing was becoming tarnished, although it is notable that many submissions to the Committee stated that black people were not disproportionally involved in offending. The Police Federation, for example, noted that offending patterns among black people were similar to whites, and motivated by the same factors. The Chief Constable of Sheffield stated that 'the crime ratio is far less with the immigrant people than it is with white people, a view reflected in a Metropolitan Police survey of Notting Hill and Notting Dale that also showed a lower crime rate among immigrants than indigenous people (Gilroy, 1987: 89). The Select Committee's report summarized that:

> The conclusions remain beyond doubt: coloured immigrants are no more involved in crime than others; nor are they generally more concerned in violence, prostitution, and drugs. The West Indian crime rate is much the same as that of the indigenous population. The Asian crime rate is very much lower. (Solomos, 1988: 96)

While the authoritative perspective was that minorities were not overly represented in offending behaviour, it is clear that at other levels stereotypes and prejudices associating black people with crime were having considerable impact. Whitfield demonstrates that at street level, many police officers acted upon racist assumptions that migrants were engaged in crime. This informal racial profiling was applied particularly to offences related to the vice trade, especially prostitution, drugs and unlicensed drinking dens. Although it might have been maintained that black people were not over-represented in terms of crime in general terms, concerns were expressed about forms of crime related to racialized stereotypes about black male sexuality, licentiousness and morality (Rowe, 1998). Much of the immediate post-war migration from the Caribbean had been driven by labour market demands in Britain such that most of the arrivals were men who might subsequently have formed relationships with white women. Racialized taboos about sexual relationships between white and black people were a recurring feature during British imperial expansion, and continued once migration patterns changed and commonwealth citizens arrived in the Mother Country (McClintock, 1995). In such a context, police officers reflected broader social prejudices against sexual relations between white women and black men in ways that resulted in the criminalization of the social lives of black migrants. Similar processes applied in the context of other forms of migrants' social behaviour, such as in relation to drinking in unlicensed premises or congregating on street corners. Official discourse might have held that black people were not especially engaged in criminal offending in general terms, but even during the 1950s and 1960s the perceptions and practices of police officers, magistrates, newspaper editors and some MPs effectively criminalized them.

This street-level criminalization was exacerbated during a few years in the early 1970s, however, when 'the definition of blacks as a low-crime group turned around 180 degrees' (Gilroy, 1987: 92). As shown in Chapter Three, during the 1970s media coverage of 'mugging' assumed the status of a racialized moral panic. Hall et al. (1978) described how the phenomenon developed in the early 1970s and served as a metaphor for a wide range of perceived social, economic and cultural concerns about law and order, urban decay, and declining national fortune. Central to this process was the establishment in popular discourse of the image of the black 'mugger', preying on white victims. As Hall et al. (1978) and others (for example, Gilroy, 1987) have made clear, there was no reliable basis on which it could have been argued that black youths were disproportionately involved in such crimes or that this type of offending tended to be directed at white victims.

Guns, Gangs and Street Crime: Mugging and Onwards

Since the 'mugging panics' of the 1970s, which created the folkloric image of the aggressive black mugger preying on white society, the racialization of crime in Britain has taken various forms and continues to unfold. Loader and Mulcahy (2003) have shown how the nostalgic reconstruction of the 'golden age' in which Britain was an orderly and low-crime society – when the bobby on the beat was more authoritative and effective than his contemporary counterpart – refers to a period prior to the development of a multiethnic society. Gilroy (2004) has described this nostalgia for a vanished age in terms of 'postcolonial melancholia' that harks back to a period mis-identified as peaceable and ethnically homogeneous. Such narratives fail to recognize contemporaneous evidence from the immediate post-war period that has highlighted police corruption, crime and violence during the 'golden age'. The corollary of this reading of recent British history is that the tarnishing of the golden era has accompanied the transition into a multicultural and multiethnic society.

Over the last few decades the 'race–crime' debate has incorporated various themes and ethnic groups. For much of the period, it has tended to focus on the alleged criminality of sections of the black community, initially in terms of street robbery, but also in respect of the urban unrest of the 1980s that was widely explained in terms of the cultural proclivities of the black community who were unable to exercise necessary control over youths predisposed to violence (Gilroy, 1987; Solomos, 1988; Keith, 1993). That this interpretation of public disorder could not explain the widespread involvement of white people in the unrest, nor recognize any formative role that policing or socio-economic factors might have played, did not prevent it from forming the dominant explanatory framework. One reason why this racialized discourse proved so resonant was that it spoke to a broader theme in the imagination of the nation, which is that a defining characteristic of the English people is respect for and obedience to the law (Colls, 2002). Collective violence of the sort witnessed in many inner cities in the 1980s assumed a wider symbolic importance during a period in which national identity was heavily contested between New Right attempts to reformulate and reassert former glories and those keen to establish a post-colonial multiculturalism. In such circumstances, the police embodied the 'thin blue line' protecting the mainstream law-abiding community from threatening interlopers.

Some of those who located the cause of the 1980s disturbances in the cultural dysfunctionalism of the black community contrasted the problem with imputed strengths in other minority ethnic groups, often doing so in order to claim that their analysis could not therefore be racist in nature. Along these lines, other minorities, most often Asian and Jewish communities, were held to be model additions to English society characterized by the value that they placed on the integrity of the family, the benefits of hard work and self-reliance, and respect for the law. That these groups did not resort to collective violence in response to social and economic privations reinforced the culpability of those – the black community – that did. Subsequent urban unrest in Bradford, Oldham, Burnley and elsewhere during the early 1990s and again in 2001 that did involve sections of the Asian community required the reformulation of connections between 'race' and national identity, but retained the theme that it was the cultural properties of those communities that led to violence. In particular, it was asserted that irreconcilable tensions between different generations of the Asian community placed Asian youth in a moral vacuum that pitched them into conflict (Rowe, 2004). The Chief Constable of West Yorkshire Police analyzed the disorders in terms that problematized the Asian community:

> What we are dealing with here is young men, Bradford-born, brought up and educated. They have lost in some way their ties with their old religion and their country, yet they feel themselves alienated within Western culture. Then you have this tremendous powder keg within them. The frustration and anger which they vent on the police, they are also venting on their own community. (*The Times*, 1995, cited in Rowe, 2004: 163)

Claims of a cultural crisis amid the Asian population have been supplemented by more recent concerns about Islamic fundamentalism and an apparent irreconcilability of British and Muslim identities. While these debates have not been primarily focused on the apparent criminality of the Asian community, although issues such as drug dealing have certainly featured, they do rely on the notion of a relatively homogeneous mainstream of society and a marginal but threatening danger: an emerging 'enemy within'. These debates are examined at greater length in Chapter Nine.

While processes of racializing crime, disorder and policing have broadened since the 1970s' and 1980s' focus on the black community, various concerns have reiterated these long-established themes. A variation on the problem of mugging emerged in 2001 when media, policing and political attention focused on 'taxing' and the theft of mobile phones. Although discussion of these problems may not have reflected the crude racist imagery of constructions of the 'race–crime' debate of earlier periods, such themes were often implicit. Hall et al. (1978) noted the discursive power of places associated with minority ethnic communities in the context of discussion of street crime, law and disorder. Mention of these symbolic locations invokes association with minority ethnic communities and reiterates images of criminality even in the absence of explicit labelling of the particular problem as one related to a certain ethnic group. Media coverage of mugging in the 1970s or urban unrest in the 1980s often explicitly identified the black community as responsible. Such connotations may have become less overt in response to more recent concerns about the theft of mobile phones, but a similar effect can be achieved more subtly by drawing upon the symbolic power of locations. A recent example of the discursive work done by referring to symbolic locations occurred in press reporting of gun crime, which suggested that the problem was developing to such proportions in urban Britain that 'some parts of London are now said to be more dangerous than Soweto [and] parts of Birmingham have acquired a sinister atmosphere reminiscent of the worst quarters of Los Angeles' (*The Sunday Telegraph*, 2003, cited in Rowe, 2004: 164). Invocations of locales that conjure up broader associations of black unrest and rebellion reinforce the relation, not explicitly stated in this article, between ethnicity, crime and disorder.

While debates surrounding street robberies in recent years have seen a continuation of well-established processes of racialization, an apparent rise in gun crime has led to unprecedented developments that have been explicitly related to an apparently 'new era' in police relations with minority ethnic communities brought about by the Macpherson Report (Macpherson, 1999). The shooting of two black teenagers in the early hours of New Year's Day 2003 in Birmingham was followed by intense media discussion about the apparently increasing prevalence of gun use in Britain and the role of garage music and gangsta rap in influencing a generation of black youth towards a ghetto culture centring on violence, machismo and drugs. In the wake of the shootings in Birmingham and official statistics that indicated a 35 per cent increase in gun-related crime in the preceding year, a 'summit' of senior police officers, prosecutors and the intelligence services was convened in January 2003 to develop a 'tougher' strategy.

An editorial in the *Mail on Sunday* (2003, cited in Rowe, 2004: 164) argued that research was needed to determine the link between violent computer games and other forms of media 'which may have played a potent role in spreading the toxic gangster culture that infects so many parts of Britain'. In addition, the paper argued, 'the police must understand that they need to re-establish themselves in ethnic minority areas. There need to be more black officers, not for public relations' purposes but to penetrate the unpoliced parts of society where armed disorder is rapidly becoming endemic'. A few years later these debates resurfaced in the wake of the fatal shooting of three non-white teenage boys in London. In an editorial, *The Independent* (2007) fused ethnicity with familial problems, crime and subculture:

> It is clear that there is a significant lack of positive role models for young Black boys. Black fathers often play too small a role in the lives of their children. There is also a shortage of Black male teachers. Gangsters and drug-dealers often fill the void in the lives of impressionable and angry young men. This dynamic is reinforced by a popular culture that often irresponsibly glorifies criminality, violence and misogyny. (cited in McMahon and Roberts, 2011: 20)

While the suggestion that aspects of popular culture are criminogenic, infectious and morally damaging frequently recurs, what has been noteworthy in the wake of these recent developments has been the voices from within the black community, and the music industry, that have argued that some aspects of youth cultures were having a damaging effect. Some suggested that the problem of gun crime within the black community could not simply be attributed to rap music but had more complex origins. Commentators and activists have responded positively to Prime Minister Blair's 2008 argument that 'the Black community need to be mobilised in denunciation of this gang culture that is killing innocent young Black kids' (cited in McMahon and Roberts, 2011: 20). In 2007 it was reported that the Mayor of London was investing £20 million into youth projects intended to divert young people away from gun and drug crime (Willetts, 2007). While this initiative was not targeted specifically at the black community, it was focused on London boroughs with a high minority ethnic population and reflected a wider perspective that the black community was particularly vulnerable to gun crime. *The Guardian* newspaper reported, for example, that 'there have been more than 3,500 gun incidents in London over the past 12 months; thousands of guns are said to be on the streets; the capital has more than 200 gangs; the average age of black Londoners murdered by a gun is 19; the average age of black Londoners charged with murder using a gun is also 19' (Willetts, 2007).

Recorded crime figures indicate that there was an increase in the number of firearms offences from the late 1990s onwards. In England and Wales in 1997/98, 12,805 offences involving a firearm were recorded by the police, a total that increased by 53 per cent by the peak year of 2003/04 in which 24,094 incidents were recorded (Hales et al., 2006). By 2008/09, 14,250 firearms related incidents were recorded, a total that had fallen for five consecutive years (Smith et al., 2010). A significant increase in the number of offences recorded might explain growing media and policy concern about gun crime, even though the number of crimes involving firearms was relatively small. Only 0.3 per cent of all recorded offences included a firearm in 2007/08 and only 3 per cent of incidents involving a firearm resulted in a serious or fatal injury. Moreover, firearm offences were heavily concentrated in Greater Manchester, Metropolitan and West Midlands police force areas that accounted for 60 per cent of incidents but are resident to only a quarter of the population of England and Wales (Smith et al., 2010). Roberts and Innes (2009) demonstrate that even within these cities, gun crime is a highly localized problem – in London, for example, between 2000 and 2005, just four boroughs (Lambeth, Hackney, Brent and Southwark) accounted for more incidents than all of the others combined. High-profile incidents, such as those noted above, during a period in which the number of recorded offences was increasing, have been followed by equally widely reported crimes that have taken place while the overall number has been in decline.

As has been suggested, the problem of gun crime in Britain during recent years has been racialized in various ways that echo earlier responses to street crime and mugging in the 1970s. Pitts (2008) has shown how debates about the extent and nature of gang-related crime in Britain has long been conducted in the shadow of the experience of the United States, in which 'ethnic gangs' have been a sustained feature of urban crime narratives. Along similar lines, debate about gun crime in Britain invokes racialized imagery by comparing problems with those from other countries in which offending is associated with particular minorities or with 'racial conflict' more generally. Suggestions that neighbourhoods experiencing gun crime in the UK are transforming into south central Los Angeles or Soweto perform the same ideological work that Hall et al. (1978) noted in 1970s media coverage of mugging that equated Handsworth with Harlem.

There is little evidence that recent media coverage of gun crime has explicitly associated problems with the black community to the extent that has been noted in earlier periods in relation to other crime problems. In a post-Macpherson environment, police officers have not tended to argue directly that gun crime is specifically associated with the black community in general terms and media commentary has also been more nuanced than was the case in coverage of crime in the 1970s. Law (2002) has cautioned, however, that the apparent 'death of media racism' might be exaggerated and there are several grounds for concern that gun crime has continued to be racialized in press and TV coverage. First, just as the names of certain symbolic locations are used as synonyms for ethnicity, so too reference to 'urban' problems, 'gangstas' and a range of youth subcultures effectively ascribes ethnicity such that specific ethnic labels become superfluous. Moreover, in a media environment that is increasingly driven by visual content, photographic representation of victims and perpetrators of gun, gang and drug crime become important 'signifiers' of race. Consideration of media representation of black youth needs to recognize that analysis of the coverage of any particular issue – such as gun crime – cannot be done in isolation. Explicit negative references continue to be apparent across a range of policy areas and are reinforced by a concomitant lack of positive coverage of minorities and their more general exclusion from the media. Law's (2010: 211) study of media representation of race identified:

> A continuing linkage between blackness, violence, masculinity and dangerous-ness and the ensuing high-profile misrepresentations of young black men in the media has been exacerbated by both government and media response to a series of shootings, stabbings and related violent incidents in the UK. ... National controversy over black male youth has focussed on the problems of gangs and gang-related violent crime, under-performance in education and the labour market, school exclusions, over-representation in the criminal justice system, absentee fathers and low aspirations.

Explanations of gun crime that identify cultural problems as a key determinant reflect a key component of the 'new racism' identified in the 1970s as accounts of black under-achievement increasingly switched from apparent biological inferiority to a new model predicated on alleged cultural dysfunction (Barker, 1981). The 'cultural dysfunction' associated with minority ethnic groups has been blamed for gang violence and gun crime in ways that transcend the par-ticular ethnicity of those who might be involved. Musical, linguistic and fashion associated initially with black youth have transcended that demographic group, but as they have become more widely adopted they have been seen to transfer cultural norms relating to materialism and consumption, gender and violence that are held to underpin dangerous street crime. Arguments that street crime and gang affiliation amount to an adaptive response to social deprivation and marginalization have been made in relation to sections of the black community in Britain – the 'endless pressure' that Pryce (1979) argued partially explained urban unrest. As some of the cultural styles of black youths have been appropri-ated and reworked by other groups also engaged in violent crime in contempo-rary Britain, then these racialized modes have continued to provide an authoritative perspective on gun crime, and related problems, even in circum-stances where perpetrators are from a different ethnic background.

Race and Crime: a Critical Realist Perspective

The racialization of gun crime in the twenty-first century has proceeded along lines less overt than have been identified in previous periods. Media and polit-ical commentary might not crudely suggest that black youth are disproportion-ally involved in gun, gang and street crime, but visual representation of offenders (and victims) and concern about the criminogenic nature of 'urban' culture effectively signifies the problem in racialized terms. Police and policy responses are developed in ways that do not necessarily target specific ethnic groups but do frame problems in ways that reinforce a racialized understanding of crime. The Metropolitan Police Operation Trident, specifically designed to tackle gun crime in London, has sometimes outlined its aim to respond to 'black on black' crime, although it has sought to do so through partnership work with local community groups and so to avoid replicating previous hard policing operations focused on minority groups (Murji, 2002; Roberts and Innes, 2009). Media coverage of 'black on black' gun crime might represent a partial representation of reality in so far as, in some districts, significant proportions of such offences are intra-ethnic in terms of perpetrator and offender. However, media and police framing of the problem in this context reifies the ethnicity of those involved and suggests that this has explanatory power, couched in terms of supposed cultural dysfunction. As Murji (2002: 33) has noted, other forms of offending might similarly involve people of the same ethnic background but very often these are not represented in such terms:

> ... the construction of black on black crime is deceitful. It draws on an idea of a bounded racial grouping that is shared by the police and 'community representatives'. In this sense the construction of black on black crime is ideological in a rather old-fashioned sense: it draws attention to some things while obscuring others, it mobilises law enforcement, and it provides the basis for moral enterprise. And it makes race meaningful as a supposedly obvious and natural way of comprehending social (dis)order.

Critical analysis of the ways in which minority ethnic communities are construed to be over-represented in some forms of criminal activity does not require a denial that there might be significant crime problems within those communities. As Hallsworth (2005) has argued, it is possible to remain critical of the various ways in which forms of crime are represented and explained in racialized terms while recognizing that minority communities might be disproportionally affected by some types of crime. While radical criminology might maintain that processes of criminalization and racialization aimed at minority groups need to be challenged, it does not then follow that any debate about differences in crime across and between communities is fundamentally racist. Left realist perspectives developed since the 1980s have provided a framework for analyzing crime that accounts for its grounding in social, economic and political marginalization while continuing to recognize that crime is socially constructed in ways that can be distorted and disproportionate. Hallsworth (2005: 90) identified four strengths of approaches that combine analysis of the 'real' causes and contours of crime problems, while recognizing that these are refracted through prisms of power, structure and processes that sustain social disadvantage and marginalization. The strengths of a left realist approach that Hallsworth noted are:

- that they highlight the relationship between social class, disadvantage and street crime;
- that they conceptualize street offending as an adaptation to the experience of deprivation in a class-divided society;

- that street crime is situated in an analysis of political economy;
- that the social response to street crime 'is never simply conditioned by the scale of its seriousness. There is always a politics at play in the attention it receives that needs to be recognized'.

A realist perspective, characterized by the above concerns, is borne out by research into gun, gang and street crime that tends to suggest that the ethnicity of those involved is highly contextual in terms of those areas particularly affected. A Home Office study interviewed 80 convicted firearms offenders and found that 45 per cent were white, 35 per cent were black, 13.8 per cent were 'mixed', 5 per cent were Asian, and 1.3 per cent were of 'other' ethnicity. The study identified a range of socio-economic and demographic features that characterized the offenders (Hales et al., 2006: 38):

> The men interviewed for this research typically (although not exclusively) grew up in disrupted family environments, had unsuccessful and adversarial relationships with education and have poor legitimate work histories. A majority had previous convictions and most had been the victims of crime, including some very serious offences involving firearms. Against this background their social lives provided an important focus and three broad 'social lifestyle' groups have been identified with individuals in all three having used crime to fund their leisure activities. These in turn often formed a significant dimension of their public identity, to be defended if challenged.

If minorities are over-represented in firearms offences and other forms of street crime when compared to their presence in the overall population, this is because they are concentrated in districts that broadly share the characteristics identified in the above quotation. Pitts' (2008) study of gang activity in three London boroughs found that there was a high proportion of African Caribbean, Asian and mixed ethnicity young people involved, but that this reflected the characteristics of the youth population of the districts. Pitts (2008) pointed out that gang-related crime in other cities (he cites Glasgow and Liverpool) that have a predominantly white population is mainly associated with white people. Similarly, Aldridge and Medina's (2008) research found that gang membership was ethnically mixed and tended to reflect the profile of the areas in which they were based. However, the study found that 'it was only the gangs from areas with a proportionally higher black minority that received media and policy attention' (Aldridge and Medina, 2008: 18). This raised strategic problems for community leaders who could seek empowerment and resources on the basis of this racialized policy response, but in so doing would contribute to the further criminalization of a suspect community and provide authorities with a culturalist account of crime problems that effectively exempted them from responsibility (Aldridge and Medina, 2008).

Ultimately, determining the ethnic composition of offenders (in relation to street, gang, gun or any other type of crime) is not possible. As is repeatedly demonstrated in this book, the terms 'ethnicity' and 'race' are conceptually problematic, are classified and recorded in ways that are often mutually incommensurate, and frequently obfuscate more than they clarify. Little is known about offending and the characteristics of offenders. Fundamentally, though, even in a hypothetical situation in which it were possible to design a methodology that overcame these problems, there would remain the foundational mistake that the ethnic identity of the offender was somehow a causal factor. While it might be that some minority ethnic communities are disproportionally impacted (as victims and offenders) by crime, it is clear that the causes of these problems remain complex and elusive and cannot be reduced to the skin colour, culture or ethnic identity of those involved. Many of those involved in the forms of 'black on black' crime discussed above also share other characteristics; most of them are male, most of them are young, most of them have little or no educational qualifications, and most of them have little or no role in the legitimate labour market. That, amidst all of these factors, their ethnicity often acts as the organizing concept around which the problem is analyzed and debated reveals more about the wider social context than the realities of offending. The need to critically engage with the coupling of race and crime is further explored in Chapter Ten. As Hallsworth and Young (2008: 184–185) suggested:

> The term gang does not designate a social problem in any neutral sense; it denotes and, in a tautological way, explains this problem simultaneously. ... The monstrousness of the group is certainly bound up with perennial fears the adult world has with its young, but there is an ethnic dimension to this fear in so far as the gang is always seen to wear a black or brown face. Thus the gang problem is always a problem of Jamaican 'Yardies', the African Caribbean Ghetto boys, the Muslim Boys, the Chinese Triads, the Turkish/Kurdish Baybasin Clan, the Asian Fiat Bravo Boys and so on. These are outsiders threatening the good society; outsiders unlike us, essentialized in their difference.

SUMMARY

The chapter has critically explored statistical data, historical perspectives and other research evidence relating to apparent disproportionalities in offending between and among different ethnic groups. Central to the difficulty of identifying patterns in disproportionality is the broader criminological problem of defining and measuring offending. Proxy measures, such as arrest data, victim survey results and self-reported offending were examined. Findings from self-report studies have tended to show that minority ethnic groups in England and Wales are involved in offending and antisocial behaviour at lower levels than 'white' and 'mixed' groups, although longitudinal study of the data suggested that ethnicity was not a determinant of offending risk and that other social and demographic factors were key.

(Continued)

(Continued)

Concerns associating types of offending with particular ethnic groups were also explored, such as media and political debates that associated post-war migrants to Britain with vice and related problems and contemporary debates about gang- and gun-related offending. Research evidence into firearm offences shows that such crimes are highly focused in particular localities and that media mis-represent 'the gun-crime problem' in terms of cultural dysfunction among young black males. A realist perspective was outlined that recognizes that there might be disproportionality in terms of offending patterns among some minority groups but that these are understood and represented in a distorted manner when they are explained in terms of ethnicity.

STUDY QUESTIONS

1 What are the key differences between right realist and left realist explanations of the disproportionate representation of minority ethnic groups in offending data?

2 In what ways do self-report offending surveys and victim surveys add to the measurement of crime rates?

3 What role have moral panics played in contemporary debates about street, gun and gang crime?

FURTHER READING

Statistical data relating to crime patterns, in terms of offending, victimization and many of the other issues addressed throughout this book can be found at the Ministry of Justice website at www.justice.gov.uk/publications/statistics-and-data/criminal-justice/race.htm. Data from the Offending, Crime and Justice Survey is analyzed in Sharp and Budd (2005, Home Office) and in Hales et al. (2009, Home Office).

Historical perspectives on crime and ethnicity in England are further developed in Emsley's (1987, Longman) *Crime and Society in England, 1750-1900* and in Morris's (1994, Routledge) *Dangerous Classes*. Debates about contemporary studies of gang crime can be explored in the work of Pitts' (2008, Willan Publishing) *Reluctant Gangsters* and in Hallsworth and Young's (2008) article 'Gang Talk and Gang Talkers: A Critique'.

5

Race and Victimization

OVERVIEW

This chapter considers:

- data relating to ethnic differences in terms of 'ordinary' criminal victimization;
- the extent to which victimization rates are associated with wider processes of social marginalization;
- the nature and prevalence of racist crime and the reasons why it has often not been effectively investigated or prosecuted;
- debates about the hate crime legislation – in terms of ethics and efficacy – as part of a broader critique of efforts to strengthen the response to racist victimization;
- different forms of racist hate crime and the motivations of perpetrators of such incidents;
- legal and policy developments that have been designed to improve criminal justice and other agencies' responses to racist victimization.

KEY TERMS

- Collective violence
- Hate crime
- Perceptions of crime
- Racially and religiously aggravated offences

- Perpetrators
- Reporting rates
- Victimization

Introduction

Patterns and processes of victimization remained largely neglected by criminology until the last decades of the twentieth century. Scholars such as van Hentig (1948) challenged the prevailing model of offender–victim relations that saw the latter playing only a passive role in the criminal incident. Instead, Van Hentig (1948) argued that victims might play a constitutive role in the commission of crime: their behaviour might precipitate victimization and certain groups might be particularly victim-prone. Although such approaches to victimization have been widely criticized on the grounds that they tend to blame victims for crime, an increased research focus on victimology has drawn attention to a broad range of cultural, social and economic factors that might explain why becoming a victim of crime is often not a random, unfortunate experience but one that disproportionately affects some groups more than others (Fattah, 1986). Related

to this academic research has been the development of a victims' rights movement within the criminal justice system that has sought, and achieved to some
extent, a greater voice for victims who have often been marginalized in adver-
sarial legal contest between prosecution and defence. Advocacy groups and
victim welfare groups, most notably in the UK Victim Support, have become
familiar agencies within the criminal justice system in the last few decades
(Davies et al., 2007). This combination of academic research work and the
activities of pressure groups explains Zedner's (2002: 419) observation that
'the victim has moved from being a "forgotten actor" to become a key player in
the criminal justice process'.

Alongside this interest in the nature and status of victims of crime in general
terms has developed a body of academic, policy and legal work relating to racist victimization and the broader concept of 'hate crime'. As is examined
below, racist violence has a long and varied history in Britain and key incidents and events have been widely documented. Only in the last few decades,
though, have more specific research studies into the nature and extent of racist crime been developed and contributed to legal and policy measures
designed to more accurately record such incidents and improve criminal justice and other responses to prosecute offenders and assist victims. Improving
criminal justice responses to racist hate crime has been a major component of
broader efforts to increase the trust and confidence of minority ethnic communities in the police and other agencies, a priority identified by the 1999
Macpherson Inquiry into the racist murder of Stephen Lawrence.

Minority Ethnic Groups and Criminal Victimization

The 2009/10 British Crime Survey (BCS) reported that the long-term downward trend in crimes identified in previous rounds of the survey had continued. The total number of crimes counted by the survey was 9,587,000 in
2009/10, which was a 9 per cent reduction on the previous year and fully 50
per cent lower than the 19,351,000 crimes recorded in the peak year of 1995.
In terms of ethnicity, the BCS suggests that minority ethnic groups tended to
have only marginal differences in the likelihood that they would become victims of household and property crimes, but that people of all ethnicities living
in multicultural areas had higher rates of victimization than those living in
other types of neighbourhood. Figure 5.1 indicates that non-white respondents
had very similar incidence of victimization to whites, in terms of both personal
crimes and all incidents counted by the BCS (including, that is, 'household'
offences such as burglary, vandalism and vehicle-related crimes). A higher

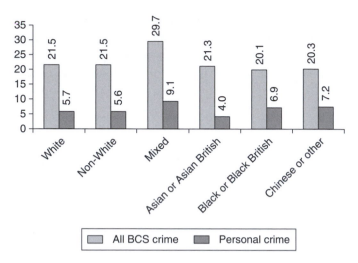

Figure 5.1   Proportion of adults who were victims of all BCS crime and personal crime by ethnicity, 2009/10

Source: Home Office (2010a)

proportion of respondents who were of mixed ethnicity experienced personal crimes and all BCS crime (29.7 per cent and 9.1 per cent respectively).

Earlier sweeps of the BCS, however, have shown greater disparities in terms of ethnicity and victimization and have suggested that some minority ethnic groups have experienced higher risks. In 1999, the survey found that Pakistani and Bangladeshi respondents were more likely to experience household crime (29 per cent compared to 25 per cent for whites, 25 per cent for blacks and 27 per cent for Indians). For burglary and vehicle theft, all minority ethnic groups were more at risk than white people and for personal crimes black people were at highest risk, although Indians, Pakistanis and Bangladeshis had similar rates to white people (Clancy et al., 2001: 11–12). The BCS has not always included respondents younger than 16 and so misses their experiences of crime victimization. Since minority ethnic groups often have a younger demographic profile, the omission of this cohort suggests that the BCS underestimates some of the crime experienced by minority ethnic communities. Local crime surveys have identified greater rates of victimization among minority ethnic communities than among the white community, and Webster (2007) has argued that the narrower focus of such studies means they are more able to identify geographical concentrations in offending and the uneven spread of crime across different social factors, such as age, class and ethnicity.

The 2009/10 BCS demonstrates that victimization rates also varied across different types of neighbourhood, and that those living in multicultural areas were at greater risk of experiencing crime than those in some other districts.

Although respondents from neighbourhoods characterized as 'blue collar' or 'city living' had higher rates of all BCS crime, those in 'multicultural' areas had higher rates than those in 'prospering suburbs' or 'countryside' districts. In terms of personal crime, those in 'multicultural areas' had the second-highest rate, behind those in 'city living' areas.

The data presented in Figure 5.2 makes no direct link between ethnicity and crime victimization but does indicate that the complex relationship between ethnicity, social and economic marginalization, and neighbourhood characteristics have some relationship with crime, as they are similarly related with health problems, educational under-achievement and other public policy issues. Just as Shaw and Mackay noted, in relation to mid-twentieth-century Chicago, that districts with high levels of migration were characterized by social transition, upheaval and dislocations that might be criminogenic, so too contemporary BCS data indicates that some minority ethnic communities might be more likely to reside in neighbourhoods that have relatively high rates of crime. That the relationship between crime victimization and ethnicity is complex and correlated with a host of other social, economic and demographic variables has been widely noted in the research literature. Clancy et al. (2001) ran a series of statistical tests on the 1999 BCS data and found that ethnicity had relatively

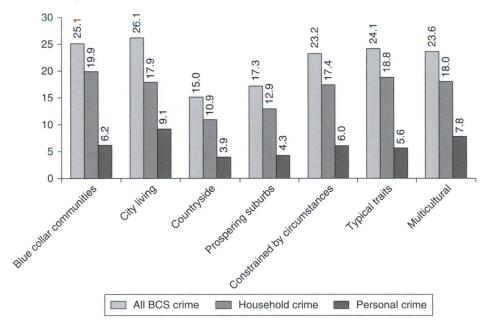

Figure 5.2   Proportion of adults who were victims of all BCS crime, household crime and personal crime by area characteristics

Source: Home Office (2010a)

weak explanatory power in relation to experience of victimization, and that other variables were of more significance. They noted that:

> the risks of crime run by different ethnic groups are largely accounted for by socio-economic and demographic factors other than ethnicity. On the whole, where people live and work are the strongest predictors of victimisation risk for all ethnic groups. The exception to this generalisation is burglary, where Indians are more at risk after taking other factors into account. All minority ethnic groups were less at risk of personal crime overall, after taking other factors into account. (Clancy et al., 2001: 13)

Distinct from actual experience of victimization, the BCS also measures perceptions of and worry about crime, phenomena that have come to be regarded as significant criminological problems that have affective emotional impacts independent of 'objective' victimization risks (Cromby et al., 2010). The perceptions of minority ethnic communities have remained largely overlooked in research terms, especially in the context of rural communities that include very small numbers of minority ethnic people, although this minority status might reinforce fear of victimization and enhance their isolation (Chakraborti and Garland, 2003). The 2009/10 BCS found little ethnic difference in terms of the perceived trend in crime nationally: 67 per cent of whites and 65 per cent of non-whites reported that crime had risen across the whole country. For all ethnic groups, the proportion that reported crime had risen locally was lower, although Asian and mixed ethnicity respondents were more likely to report a rise in their locality than were other ethnic groups (44 and 42 per cent respectively, compared to 30 per cent for whites and for blacks). Perceived levels of antisocial behaviour were also higher among minorities compared to whites. While 13 per cent of whites felt that antisocial behaviour was high in their locality, compared to 23 per cent of non-whites, the highest rate was for Asians, 25 per cent of whom reported high levels in their locality. Figure 5.3 demonstrates that minority ethnic groups were also more worried about crime than were white respondents to the BCS. Higher rates of worry were found in relation to burglary and car crime, but the discrepancy was greatest in relation to violent crime: while 11 per cent of whites were worried about that type of offence, the rate was at least double for minorities and was 32 per cent for Asian or Asian British people.

Quantitative data reveals little about the context in which perceptions of crime trends or worry about victimization develop. Moreover, they present ethnicity in an essentialized form that not only, as Webster (2007) noted, does not account for localized differences, but fails to provide for the particular experiences of crime and victimization that emerge within specific ethnic and cultural communities in the context of specific times and places. Ethnographic studies (for example, Loader and Mulchay, 2003; or Bolognani, 2009) indicate that public perceptions of crime and antisocial behaviour are best understood in their local context and aggregated statistics risk conveying a coherent

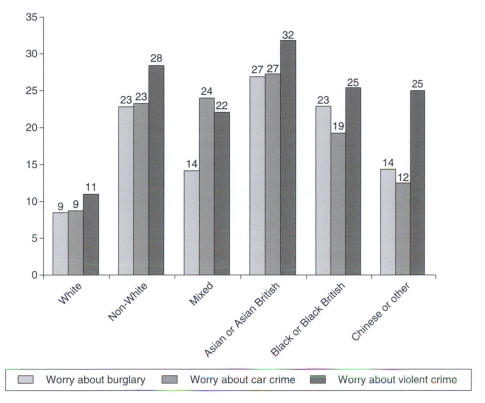

Figure 5.3   Worry about crime by personal characteristics

Source: Home Office (2010a)

ethnic experience of crime that might be misleading. The ethnic data represented in the above figures needs to be treated with caution for a number of reasons, including that it fails to differentiate the distinct experiences and perceptions within the various categories: 'white', for example, is an omnibus category that includes a range of groups, including Irish people and Eastern European migrants who might have different experiences and perceptions of crime. The mixed category is also a complex one that, by definition, will include considerable breadth of ethnic identities, and the experiences of Chinese people are collapsed with those of 'other' ethnicities, such that their particular circumstances are lost, which reinforces their marginalization within criminological research and criminal justice practice. Similar caveats apply to any presentation of ethnic data – including the data on racist hate crime presented below – and the BCS provides useful quantitative information of considerable importance. Another limitation of victim survey methods, also related to a limited explanatory reach, is that relations between experience and perceptions of crime and antisocial behaviour, in general terms and the more specific problem of racist crime and harassment, cannot be untangled within the data. In short, the extent to which general concerns about crime levels are shaped by experiences of racist hate crime cannot be determined from quantitative data. Some studies of the experience of victims of racist crime and harassment have added considerably to an understanding of the processes and dynamics of these problems by adopting qualitative methods, and many of these are drawn upon in the discussion below.

Racist Hate Crime: Victims and Perpetrators

The violent victimization of groups and individuals on the basis of their actual or perceived ethnicity or 'race' has a long and ignoble history, and has assumed many different forms. State-level crimes of genocide, slavery, the Nazi Holocaust, and a wide range of legally sanctioned racist practices in Jim Crow-era USA or apartheid South Africa are forms of racist hate crime considered in detail in the following chapter. Other manifestations of racist hate crime have been perpetrated by relatively large groups of individuals in circumstances that might have normalized racist violence. Various twentieth-century 'race riots' in Britain and the USA, for example, were collective forms of violence that can be understood as hate crimes, as can the racist murders of black people lynched in the late nineteenth and early twentieth centuries. Both forms of racist hate crime are analyzed in the discussion that follows, which also draws a distinction between racist hate crime perpetuated by individuals as part of neighbourhood or interpersonal disputes and those committed by individuals or small groups motivated by racism, fascism and white supremacism.

Racism as Group Violence

There is a huge catalogue of collective racist violence in British history. In addition to establishing principles of justice, the Magna Carta settlement of 1215 included clauses designed to restrict the role and power of Jewish financiers – legal provisions that followed decades of violent anti-Semitism that included the killing of 30 Jews during rioting in London in 1189 and pogroms the following year in York claimed 150 lives (Saggar, 1992: 24–25). Collective violence was directed at Irish migrants arriving in Liverpool in the nineteenth century, partly in response to fears that as travelling workers they were contributing to the spread of disease, as Scally (1995: 206–207) noted:

> When the cholera scare was at its peak, the Home Office was receiving con-
> stant reports of civil disturbances in the northern districts ... there had been
> incidents between English and Irish workers in which the mixture of wage com-
> petition and the fear of infection had produced a threat to the peace. Regular
> troops were needed to quell 'serious disturbances' in Wellington, where quar-
> rels broke out between English and Irish navvies and were 'made tranquil' only
> when the Irish were dismissed or 'sent to other parts of the line'.

Removing the apparent victims of violence implicitly reinforced perceptions
that their presence was the cause of the problem, and marginalized consideration of the racism of perpetrators. Similar official responses – in the form
of a programme of assisted repatriation, for example – to mass racist violence
were also evident in the aftermath of disturbances in Liverpool and other
port cities around England in 1919 and 1920. In Liverpool, soldiers returning
from the First World War faced high levels of unemployment and poor housing conditions that contrasted starkly with Lloyd George's promise of a 'land
fit for heroes' (Jenkinson, 1993). This context of competition for scarce
resources was coupled with racialized concerns that the local population of
African seamen threaten the health and sexual morality of the local white
women. Against this background, in June 1919, groups of local white people
engaged in 'an anti-black reign of terror' in Liverpool (Fryer, 1984: 301) that
led to the death of Charles Wootton, a young black sailor who was chased
through the streets and drowned in the dock. The Chief Constable of
Merseyside Police described how the violence escalated in the days after
Wootton's death:

> On the ninth and tenth [of June] a well-organised gang, consisting principally of
> youth and young men, soldiers and sailors, ages of most of them ranging from
> sixteen to thirty years and who split up into different gangs, savagely attacking,
> beating, and stabbing every Negro they could find in the street, many of the
> Negroes had to be removed under police escort to Great George Street fire sta-
> tion for their own safety. When no more Negroes were seen on the street these
> gangs began to attack the Negroes' houses ... and in some cases they com-
> pletely wrecked them. At times the crowds of rioters would number from 8,000
> to 10,000 people and they kept the disturbances going on for two days and
> nights, during which time the strength of the police was so severely taxed and
> they were so over-powered that no arrests could be effected. (Rowe, 1998: 52)

Other incidents of racist violence occurred during the same period, including
riots in Cardiff that led to the deaths of three black men and violent attacks on
Chinese and black communities in London (Fryer, 1984). Contemporary
responses to these disturbances tended to condemn the violence of the lower-
class perpetrators but in ways that served to also inculpate the black communities who were victims. Their behaviour, lifestyle and sexual promiscuity were

widely held to have provoked white youths, whose reaction was unacceptably violent but was conceived as an understandable response to the presence of alien groups (Jenkinson, 1993; Rowe, 1998). A similar combination of racialized social and economic competition for scarce resources provided the explanatory framework for the collective racist violence against black people that occurred in Nottingham and in Notting Hill, London, in the late 1950s. In both cases, media, political, policing and judicial responses to the violence tended to draw attention to the lifestyles and behaviour of 'West Indian' migrants that were held to have exacerbated difficult material circumstances in the neighbour-hoods concerned. Additionally, though, the violent response of white youths was condemned in terms of broader contemporary concerns relating to delin-quent subcultures and deviant youth.

Relatively little criminological attention has been paid to racist murder in the form of lynchings practised in the United States from the nineteenth to the mid-twentieth century, but much of the analysis also focuses attention on the social context in which this form of collective racist violence was practised. Clarke (1998) noted that in 14 former slave states between 1882 and 1962, 3,873 lynchings were recorded, and that in 84 per cent of cases (3,264) the victim was black. One of these incidents, in 1904, was described by the Vicksburg *Evening Post* as a lynching that attracted a mob of a thousand people in Doddsville, Mississippi:

> Luther Holbert and his wife, negroes ... were tied to trees and while the funeral pyres were being prepared, they were forced to hold out their hands while one finger at a time was chopped off. The fingers were distributed as souvenirs. The ears of the murderers were cut off. Holbert was beaten severely, his skull was fractured and one of his eyes, knocked out with a stick, hung by a shred from the socket. Some of the mob used a large corkscrew to bore into the flesh of the man and woman. It was applied to their arms, legs and body, then pulled out, the spirals tearing out big pieces of raw, quivering flesh every time it was withdrawn. (Oakley, 1976: 49)

The terrible phenomenon of lynching has been explained in terms of structural factors relating to economic fluctuations in cotton prices, the changing status of African Americans post-slavery, and a cultural propensity to violence in the southern states (Clarke, 1998; King et al., 2009). While much analysis of racist violence has focused on the characteristics and motivations of those who com-mit hate crimes, as is examined below, Garland (2005) focused attention on the cultural and normative context of the period that permitted lynching to con-tinue. He noted that this form of racist violence was conducted in an open, explicit manner and that the 'barbecue', as the popular euphemism had it, had the status of a family day-out, complete with souvenirs and picture postcard photographs of murdered 'negroes'. Lynchings cannot be dismissed as pre-modern barbarism: those who attended them travelled in cars, drank coca-cola and recorded events with Kodak cameras in the early decades of the twentieth century in the most advanced democracy in the world (Garland, 2005). Moreover, these were not incidents of random 'mob violence' or vigilantism, but were often planned and structured – sometimes advertised in advance – and occurred with the participation and sometimes the consent of the local criminal justice system, and attracted respectable viewers who sent postcards depicting the gruesome results of their day out. While the practices of lynching appear barbaric and distant to twenty-first-century sensibilities, continuities in the killing of African Americans are evident in rates of incarceration and the practice of capital punishment. Clarke (1998) noted that in the 14 states for which data relating to lynchings is available, between 1901 and 1982, 2,613 people were executed, 75 per cent (1,963) of whom were black, and others have similarly argued that contemporary penal policy in the USA continues as a practice for the social control of African Americans (Wacquant, 2000; Zimring, 2003).

Racism as Interpersonal Violence

Most of the research and policy agenda relating to racist crime has focused upon interpersonal incidents rather than the collective actions highlighted above. Since the 1980s, a considerable body of literature as accrued examining the extent, trends, dynamics and impact that racist incidents have had on specific victims and on minority ethnic communities in Britain more generally. As with other issues relating to crime, justice and minority ethnic communities, considerable policy attention has been focused on the development of more robust quantitative data measuring the extent of racist crime in Britain. This compliments qualitative records of the experiences of victims that catalogue a horrific picture of racism and violence affecting many communities in contemporary British society. While statistical analysis is central to understanding crime phenomena and to developing effective policy responses to assist victims and prosecute offenders, data such as that presented below fails to convey the lived experiences of racist violence. The recording of incidents as discrete events does not capture the cumulative impact arising from the continuing experience of racism as an ongoing process of victimization (Bowling, 1998). Adamson et al. (2009: 86) examined the extent and impact of racist harassment of the Chinese community in England, using both quantitative and qualitative data. One of their respondents described the psychological impact of such crime:

> Having experienced these racist incidents, I have a lot of psychological pressures. It's not too bad during the daytime, I don't feel too scared. ... But at night, it's dark. I'm worried. Sometimes I open the door for business in the morning, I am afraid that horrible incidents will happen at night.

Garland and Chakraborti's (2006) study found that the racist harassment experienced by minority ethnic people living in rural areas was often compounded by their wider isolation in communities that were predominantly white. A Pakistani Muslim respondent to their survey described how his living arrangements had been disrupted over a considerable period by the experience of racist harassment:

> [The racist harassment] wasn't over one day, it was spread over nearly two months, going on every night. We were mostly worried about petrol bombing, you know. That's the bit we were worried about. Especially as I've been sleeping here since then, I now sleep down here. (Garland and Chakraborti, 2006: 57)

The development of more accurate statistical counts of racist crime and harassment has been regarded as central to generating more effective responses from the police and the criminal justice system more widely. Among the first official reports into racist violence in Britain, the 1981 Home Office study Racial Attacks argued that the lack of robust information about the problem had been a major impediment to legal and policy responses (cited in Gordon, 1993: 169). The same year, Lord Scarman's report into the Brixton disorders also recommended that gathering more reliable information about the experiences and needs of minority ethnic communities was necessary for the development of more effective policy and practice (Scarman, 1981: 132). Efforts to develop better data were accelerated through legal and policy changes in the 1980s and 1990s, perhaps most significantly in the form of the 1991 Criminal Justice Act, which made ethnic monitoring in the criminal justice system a statutory requirement. More recently, it was the Macpherson Report into the racist murder of Stephen Lawrence in London in 1993 that has given greatest impetus to the collation of stronger data on racist crime and harassment. This was achieved through a series of policy responses to Macpherson's (1999) recommendation that strategies be developed to encourage victims of racist crime to report incidents to the police and that better methods of recording such reports be developed. In addition to recommending improved practice, Macpherson also offered a definition of racist incidents which has become the standard approach to their classification. Macpherson (1999: 328) proposed that racist incidents be defined as '... any incident which is perceived to be racist by the victim or any other person'. As is discussed more fully below, this emphasis on classification based upon the perceptions of victims or other parties was intended to circumvent the tendency for police staff not to recognize – or not to accept – the racist component of victimization even in circumstances where the victim thought that to be an important part of their experience.

The data represented in Figure 5.4 indicates the number of racist incidents recorded by the police services in England and Wales between 2000/01 and 2009/10, and similar data for Scotland is provided for the years 2004/05 to 2008/09. At the beginning of the period, against a context of reforms to reporting and recording that followed the Macpherson Report, the number of incidents fluctuated but followed an upward trend to a peak of 62,071 incidents in 2006/07. Since then the trend has been downward. The number of incidents recorded across different

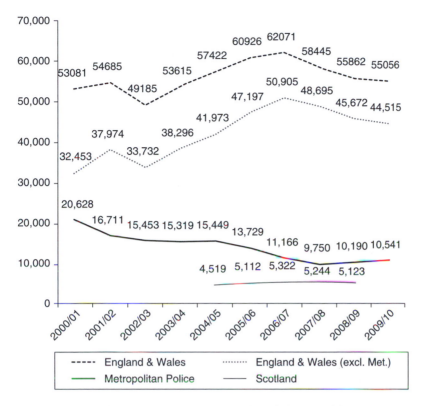

Figure 5.4   Racist incidents recorded by police, 2000/01 to 2009/10

Source: Ministry of Justice (2010) and Scottish Government (2011)

police force areas continues to vary considerably, but across the period as a whole the Metropolitan Police Service (MPS) has accounted for a significant proportion of the total. Often against the trend in the rest of England and Wales, figures for the MPS have consistently declined in the last decade, and while they accounted for more than 19 per cent of the total in 2009/10, they had contributed nearly 39 per cent at the start of the period. However, the apparent decline in incidents recorded by the MPS needs to be understood against a previous increase from 5,480 in 1994/95 to a peak of 23,346 in 1999/00 (Home Office, 2000).

In 1981, the Home Office estimated that there were approximately 7,000 racist attacks in England and Wales. Although changing demographic patterns, definitional changes and a host of other factors make comparisons across time fraught with difficulty, few would argue that the much higher figures recorded in recent years reflect a real increase in absolute levels of racist crime. Instead, the rising trend is understood in terms of improved levels of reporting and recording. McLaughlin (1991) noted that the police service had begun publicity campaigns to encourage victims to report their experiences in the mid-1980s and local authorities and various pressure groups, such as the Newham Monitoring

Project, also seem likely to have contributed to a social climate in which reporting rates are improved. Additionally, post-Macpherson, other initaitives, such as
allowing incidents to be reported to the police via third party organizations, have
also been cited as causes of the increase (Chakraborti and Garland, 2009).

The British Crime Survey estimated that there were 179,000 racially motivated
crimes in 2004/05 and that less than 1 per cent of white adults and around 2 per
cent of Black and Minority Ethnic (BME) adults were at risk of being a victim
(Jansson, 2006). Differences were apparent in terms of the proportion of offences
that were perceived as racially motivated. For all 'household offences', white
respondents reported that less than 1 per cent were racailly motivated but for
BME households the rate was 9 per cent. Vandalism against property was
reported to be racially motivated in 31 per cent of cases by BME respondents and
vandalism against vehicles in 16 per cent of cases; for both offence types the corresponding figures were less than 1 per cent for white households. Violent incidents were perceived to be racially motivated by 27 per cent of BME responents,
compared to 3 per cent of white victims and the rates for 'threats' were 40 per
cent for BME adults compared to 3 per cent for whites. As noted above in relation
to BSC data on victimization in general, these findings do not include the experiences of those younger than 16 years and, being a national study, do not account
for localized patterns of racist victimization (Webster, 2007).

A key challenge in the development of more effective criminal justice
responses to incidents of racist crime has been that they tend to be characterized
as relatively low-level forms of criminal behaviour, often not prioritized in terms
of police investigation, prosecution and sentencing. Figure 5.5 provides recent
statistical evidence confirming Bowling's (1993) argument that the types of racist
offending experienced by victims often take the form of relatively minor incidents that are not severe in themselves but assume greater signficiance because
of the repetitive nature. Bowling noted that 'considering racist incidents as discreet individual events fails to recognize the significance of the cumulative
impact continued victimization has on victims. Sampson and Phillips' (1992)
study of racist victimization in East London found that 67 per cent of families
were repeat victims of offences that, taken individually, were often trivial in
nature. Similarly, Chakraborti and Garland (2009) noted that major racist criminal incidents are relatively rare, but that a more significant problem is the mundane experience of racist offending 'reported to be commonplace by the vast
majority of ... research participants and formed a continuum of incidents that
were a constant feature of day-to-day life'. As Figure 5.5 indicates, a clear majority (67.3 per cent) of racially or religiously aggravated offences recorded by the
police in England and Wales in 2008/09 were incidents of harassment. Cases of
actual or grievous bodily harm formed a much smaller proportion of the total.

Racist incidents are often represented as 'stranger crimes', whereby victims
are randomly selected on the basis of their perceived ethnic origin. Research
evidence suggests, however, as with other forms of hate crime, that there is often
some familiarity between victim and offender. Although BCS data suggested that

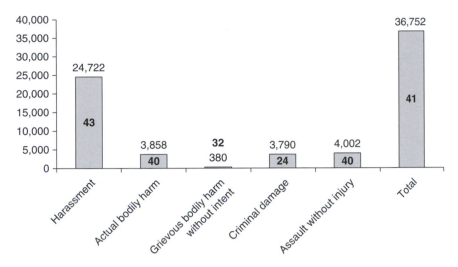

Figure 5.5   Racially or religiously aggravated offences recorded by police by offence type, 2008/09, with clear-up rates (percentages in bold type) for England and Wales

Source: Ministry of Justice (2010)

offenders were strangers to the victim in a majority of cases, in 27 per cent of incidents they were known casually or by sight, and in a further 21 per cent they were known well (Jansson, 2006: 19). Analysis of hate crimes targeted at Jewish people in London between 2001 and 2004 similarly found that perpetrators were either neighbours or business associates of their victims in 61.1 per cent of cases, although this refered only to cases in which a perpetrator could be identi-fied (Iganski et al., 2005). A broad profile of perpetrators can be compiled from BCS data: showing that 70 per cent of offenders were male, 66 per cent were thought to be between 16 and 24 years of age, acted alone in 42 per cent of cases and in groups of four or more in 43 per cent of cases. In 25 per cent of cases the perpetrator was thought to be under the influence of alcohol (Jansson, 2006). While such findings provide some insight into the nature of offenders, they reveal nothing about the motivation of racist crime. Perry (2001) has noted that the lack of research effort devoted to perpetrators of racist offending mirrors the disproportionate concentration on explaining minority ethnic offending. While generally there has been a dearth of research into explaining racist offending, a number of studies have sought to explore the motivations of perpetrators.

McDevitt et al. (2002) developed a typology of hate crime, suggesting that a single set of motivating factors would not adequately explain diverse kinds of offences. They distinguished: 'thrill' hate crimes, in which the offender is moti-vated by a desire for excitement and power; 'defensive' hate crimes provoked by a need to protect resources from perceived external threat; 'retaliatory offences' that are a reaction to a perceived assault or degradation from the target group; and a relatively small minority of 'mission offences', in which the per-petrator is ideologically or politically motivated to eliminate a 'problem' target.

Other analysis of offenders focuses attention on the individual charactersitics of offenders in the context of particular social, economic and cultural contexts, suggesting that factors propelling particular individuals to offend need to be understood in broader terms. Along these lines, for example, Ray et al.'s (2004) study in Greater Manchester found that 'shame' – an emotion stemming from perceived grievances, humiliation, unfairness and powerlessness – led white offenders to commit racist crimes against Asian people who were seen to be relatively, and illegitmately, successful. Offenders, they found, tended to know their victims and targeted them in an effort 'to re-establish control, to escape from shame into a state of pride ... it is an act of bloody revenge ... in this context of revenge against those whose apparent cultural and economic success is an affront to racist assumptions about the "proper" relationship between whites and Asians' (Ray et al., 2004: 356). This study reiterated Sibbitt's (1997) analysis of racist offending by drawing attention to the general propensity of perpetrators to resort to violence to settle disputes of various kinds. Explanations of racist violence need to consider the racist motivation of offenders, but also to establish why some who hold racist beliefs resort to violent offending, while others do not. Sibbitt (1997) identified that perpetrators would engage in wider forms of antisocial and criminal behaviour that was violent, and Ray et al. (2004) noted that racist offenders were 'very rarely specialists in racist violence' and participated in other forms of physical confrontation. In this and other ways, these studies also draw attention to the broader social context in which racist offending occurs, as Iganski et al. (2005: 50) argued:

> Rather than being confined to an extreme and abhorent margin of society, offenders mostly appear to come from the ordinary fabric of society, and incidents occur in the context of the unfolding dynamics of daily life, for many offenders and victims alike. In the case of antisemitic incidents, it is perhaps disconcerting to assert that perpetrators are not confined to an extremist fringe. However, although offenders are expressing a rather more commonplace bigotry in their actions, those who are prepared to act on their bigotry by engaging in criminal activity are without doubt acting in the extreme.

The social and community context against which offences unfold focuses attention on the spatial and geographical dimensions in which racist violence occurs. A central component of racist harassment and violence is the exclusionary intent that underpins such offending and makes the direct impact on individual victims and the broader impact on minorities collectively more serious. Studies of racist violence have noted its association with imagined geographies of white territorialism that serve to define and create boundaries around localities not considered legitimate spaces for minority ethnic people (Hesse et al., 1992; Cohen, 1996). Imagined racialized landscapes serve to organize territory in terms that identify some groups as legitimate and belonging and others as illegitimate interlopers. The spatial context of racist violence can be identified in relation to collective group violence, such as the 1958 riots in Notting Hill where African Caribbean migrants were seen to be 'taking over' the district. More recently, analysis of the 2001 Oldham, Burnley and Bradford disorders has noted how national and international concerns about Islamisist fundamentalism, migration and social policy are interpreted and applied to local geographies such that areas come to be codified by race (Webster, 2003; Kalra and Rhodes, 2009). Ray et al. (2004) and Sibbitt (1997) indicate that individual perpetrators of racist violence also 'read' local space in racialized ways such that their violent actions are an attempt to re-establish lost dominance within the local community. Similarly, Garland and Chakraborti (2006) argue that minorities in the countryside are particularly marginalized by ethnoscapes that imagine rural England as white, and that minority groups properly belong only to urban areas.

The motivations and characteristics of perpetrators, whether as collective action or on a small-group or an individual basis, are clearly complex and multifacted in terms of racism. As has been noted, perpetrators tend not to fit the template of extreme right-wing extremism and their racism often appears to be broadly consistent with that found in society at large. One consequence of this is that criminological analysis needs to focus as much on the violence of perpetrators as it does upon their racism.

Responding to Racist Crime

The failure of the police service, and the criminal justice system more widely, to provide an appropirate response to racist crime has long been noted. Many commentators have contrasted the over-policing of minority ethnic communities as apparent suspects with the under-policing experienced by minority victims of crime (Solomos, 1988; Hall, 2005). Several of the key recent efforts to improve criminal justice responses to racist violence have been noted above, not least the development and adoption of a clear definition of a racist incident and a range of initiatives designed to encourage the public to report, and the police to record, crimes when they have occured. At least tacitly, efforts to more closely record and monitor trends and patterns in racist offences are predicated on an assumption that a lack of reliable data has itself been a barrier to improving agencies' responses. In other related areas, such as recruitment and retention of personnel (as discussed in Chapter Eight), improved ethnic monitoring has been seen as an important first step towards better provision (Fitzgerald and Sibbitt, 1997). The Macpherson Report strongly articulated a link between the poor response to racist violence and wider tensions in police relations with minority communities. As in other areas, the report gave official endorsement to claims widely articulated by campaign groups and academic commentators for several decades when it noted:

> [minority ethnic communities'] collective experience was of senior officers adopting fine policies and using fine words, but of indifference on the ground at junior officer level. The actions or inactions of officers in relation to racist incidents were clearly a most potent factor in damaging public confidence in the Police Service. (Macpherson, 1999: 313)

In addition to adopting an apparently more straightforward definition of what consituted a racist incident, police services have – with considerable support and pressure from government – implemented a range of complementary initiatives to improve the response to racist crime. Alongside extensive training programmes, for example, have been changes to recording practices such that racist incidents are 'flagged' so that patterns and potential 'hot spots' can be identified, and the progress of investigation more easily monitored (Rowe, 2004).

Efforts to improve operational police responses to racist crime have developed alongside legislative changes that created stronger sentencing powers for 'racially aggravated' offences. The 1998 Crime and Disorder Act introduced higher fines and longer sentences in cases where 'ordinary' offences were proven to be 'racially aggravated'. Although a new feature in legal terms, the Act's provisions reflected existing principles included in sentencing guidelines that allowed judges to impose harsher sentences for racist crimes. The 1998 legislation allows for enhanced penalties in cases where it is shown that the offence was motivated by racial hostility. An offender convicted of a regular common assault, for example, is liable to a maximum term of six months' imprisonment or a level-five fine. These tariffs increase to a possible two-year prison sentence or an unlimited fine in a case deemed to be 'racially aggravated'. The comparable concept of 'religiously aggravated offences' was added by the Racial and Religious Hatred Act 2006. The 1998 Act defines 'racial aggravation' in broad and potentially ambigious terms relating to an offence that is:

- motivated by racial hostility, or if
- racial hostility was demonstrated towards the victim either at the time of commiting the offence, or immediately before or after.

As many have noted in relation to debates about hate crime more generally, identifying the precise nature of the motivation of an offender is particularly problematic and is a factor that is often seen as secondary to the distinct matter of the intention of the offender (Morsch, 1991; Jacobs and Potter, 1998). Conceptual difficulties in identifying the motivation, which may only be known by the offender, are overcome, to some extent, by the second clause in the Act, which refers to the more active demonstration of hostility. In this sense, the language used by an offender or their wearing of insignia associated with racist groups would satisfy the criteria of 'racial aggravation' even if their internal motivation was impossible to determine. Even so, commentators have argued that these provisions might prove more effective in relation to offenders who express 'low-level superficial expressions of racism and not deep-seated ideological hatred' (Chakraborti and Garland, 2009: 31). Ministry of Justice (2010) data show that the clear-up rate for all racially or religiously aggravated offences were higher than for non-aggravated offences (at 41 per cent compared to 28 per cent in 2008/09). However, for the largest category of racially or religiously aggravated offences – incidents of harassment – the clear-up rate was lower than that for non-aggravated offences, at 43 per cent compared to 63 per cent. Included in the clear-up rates for racially and regliously aggravated offences were the 11,228 persons cautioned or proceeded against in court in 2008, a slight decrease on the 2007 figure of 11,465 (Ministry of Justice, 2010).

This slight decrease in the number of people cautioned or prosecuted for racially and religiously aggravated offences, and a similar small decrease in the number of incidents recorded by the police between 2007/08 and 2008/09, raises a signficant problem relating to how success and failure are measured in terms of responding to racist crime. A common response to increases in recorded offences of this type is to suggest that this indicates that victims have greater trust and confidence in the police and criminal justice system and so should be welcomed as evidence of improved practice. This may be true, as was noted above, but does this mean that movement in the opposite direction – a reduction in offences recorded – represents a failure? It seems contradictory to argue that a reduction in crime rates represents a setback for the criminal justice system. While efforts over the last few decades to improve reporting and recording practices might have been necessary, this conundrum suggests that a wider approach to preventing and reducing problems of racism and offending in society needs to be developed. This needs to build upon but not be limited to improving the procedures and practices of police and other agencies. If the causes of racist violence are intimately bound up with a contest for scarce resources and the racialization of space and place, coupled with national and international debates about security, terrorism, migration and culture, then efforts to tackle racist violence need to be developed much more broadly than a focus on improvements in ethnic monitoring and enhanced services to victims.

SUMMARY

Victimization studies have reached mixed conclusions in relation to the incidence of crime affecting different ethnic groups. While recent BCS data suggested little difference between ethnic groups, earlier surveys had noted that minorities were at greater risk in terms of household crimes and vehicle theft. Evidence

(Continued)

(Continued)

relating to 'neighbourhood effect' suggests that ethnicity might be among complex social and economic variables related to different crime levels. Minority groups were more likely to perceive increasing crime rates in local areas, higher rates of antisocial behaviour and to be more worried about crime. The quality of ethnic monitoring is problematic in terms of victimization.

Racist hate crime was considered in two dimensions: group violence and interpersonal offences. Historical examples of collective racist violence demonstrate that social problems have been racialized such that minorities have been targeted. These examples indicated that the local context in which collective racist violence occurs is crucial to understanding such processes, a point that was further evidenced in respect of interpersonal racist crime. While the reporting and recording of racist crimes has been the subject of considerable debate and reform, in an effort to develop a more accurate representation of the extent and nature of the problem, concern remains that statistical data fail to properly capture the impact of sustained but low-level incidents that characterize racist offending.

STUDY QUESTIONS

1   Why might the concept of ethnicity provide only a limited account of different levels of criminal victimization?

2   What are the policy and legal implications of understanding racist violence and harassment as continuing and sustained, but low-level, forms of offending?

3   How have studies characterized perpetrators of racist hate crime?

FURTHER READING

Fryer's (1984, Pluto Press) history of black people in Britain provides detailed accounts of racist violence and Garland's (2005) journal article offers a provocative analysis of 'lynching' in the USA. Bowling's (1998, Oxford University Press) *Violent Racism* remains one of the most incisive studies of racist offending and was among the first to focus on the experiences of victims in qualitative terms. More recent work, most notably Garland and Chakraborti's (2006) article, has extended this approach to the context of minorities in rural communities. Useful studies of the perpetrators of racist crime, and hate crime more generally, can be found in the work of Ray et al. (2004) and McDevitt et al. (2002). The report into the racist murder of Stephen Lawrence (Macpherson, 1999, HMSO) provides an exhaustive account of the failures of a police investigation that have been widely noted in cases more generally. Macpherson provided an influential framework for reform of the police and criminal justice that is an important source for understanding developments in these fields more generally over the last decade or more.

6

Race, Conflict and Human Rights

CONTENTS	

OVERVIEW

This chapter will:

- demonstrate that, globally, some of the most serious criminal episodes of the modern era have been closely linked with processes of racial and ethnic conflict. Despite their scope and profile, such events have received little attention in the criminological literature;
- outline key events from world history that indicate the nature and extent of crime relating to racism and the violation of human rights;
- explore ways in which the discipline of criminology might aid understanding of the abuse of human rights;
- examine contemporary criminological interests in environmental harms that breach human rights and have a disproportionate impact on ethnic groups more generally marginalized by globalized forms of neo-colonialism.

KEY TERMS

- Corporate and state crime
- Discipline of criminology
- Genocide
- Rwanda

- Darfur
- Environmental harm
- Holocaust
- Toxic waste

Introduction

It might be assumed that the discipline of criminology would pay greatest attention to those forms of crime that cause the greatest harm to society. Scholarly activity, research funding and institutional organization ought to be concentrated on categories of behaviour that pose the greatest threat to individual victims or to humankind in broad terms. In a liberal democratic society, political and policy responses to crime should focus upon forms of criminal behaviour that cause the most damage to citizens. To a large extent the discussion that follows represents an attempt to understand why criminology has failed to develop a sustained or comprehensive body of work examining the most significant crimes of the last century or so, and to examine ways in which this neglect is coming to be addressed in some contemporary analysis. Efforts to develop a 'criminology of human rights' (Stanley, 2007) might be applied to a range of contemporary concerns, including issues of environmental damage, that will cause considerable harm to significant numbers of people already on the periphery in a globalized world characterized by neo-colonialism and neo-liberalism. The threats that some communities of the 'global south' will face during the twenty-first century are of a different order from those experienced by subject populations of nineteenth and twentieth-century networks of state imperialism, but contemporary harms will similarly impact on the vulnerable and marginalized.

Criminology's failure to examine activities that have had the most deleterious impact is graphically illustrated in relation to the extent of homicide in the form of 'death by government' during the twentieth century (Rummel, 1994, cited in Savelsberg, 2010). Rummel calculated that between 1900 and 1987 more than 169 million individuals lost their lives at the hands of governments, a figure all the more staggering since it excludes those killed in wars. Against this total, Savelsberg (2010: 9) noted, a reliable estimate of the number of victims of homicide at the hands of individuals over the same period amounts to 1.74 million, a total only slightly greater than 1 per cent of those who died as a result of government action. Salvesberg's (2010: 9) observation that 'if criminologists have anything to contribute to our understanding of violent crime, including crime committed by governments, criminological insights should be brought to bear in this enterprise' is difficult to dispute. Of course, not all episodes of death by government are related to racism or to 'ethnic tensions' that might lead to bloody repression of one kind or another: Argentinean death squads of the 1970s and 1980s, for example, 'disappeared' an estimated 10,000 political opponents of the Junta for ideological reasons unrelated to race or ethnicity (Robertson, 2006: 287). Nonetheless, as is demonstrated in relation to selected case studies analyzed below, it is clear that offences against human rights, by no means limited to death by government, cannot be disentangled from broader structural, political and economic patterns closely allied to the marginalization of ethnic groups more generally:

> ... even the most preliminary overview tells us that [human rights] violations regularly occur across state boundaries and with the ideological encouragement, technological assistance or economic support of global parties. Moreover, the imperative of advanced global capitalism, built upon the 'historical' experiences of slavery, colonization and imperialism, cannot be disconnected from the equation; these structural relations of class, intersecting with those of 'race', patriarchy and age, underpin the everyday social injustices faced by those hit hardest by state criminality. (Stanley, 2007: 170)

Human Rights Abuse and the Failure of Criminology

Before considering some specific reasons why criminology has largely overlooked human rights abuses often bound-up with practices of racism and ethnic conflict, it is important to acknowledge that the discipline has not been alone in overlooking crimes of enormous magnitude. As Cohen (2001) has noted, a common response of

participants, witnesses, media, public, professional and political elites has often
been one of a 'state of denial', whereby atrocities are 'forgotten', down-played or
normalized. Cohen argued that just as individual criminals seek to deny their
offending, minimize its impact or develop moral justification for their behaviour,
so too polities deny the import and consequences of atrocities of various kinds.
Cohen distinguished between three related forms of denial. Literal denial, such
that events are said never to have happened; interpretative denial, whereby it is
acknowledged that an event occurred but that it does not constitute an atrocity;
and implicatory denial, such that the outcome or impact of what occurred is either
denied or justified in some way. These processes amount to more than straightforward duplicity, although the conscious presentation of falsehoods in response to
claims of human rights abuses is certainly evident in many cases, since they are
encoded in a range of social and linguistic practices that serve to deny that genocide
and human rights abuses have taken place. Orwellian examples of 'double speak'
and 'double think' are evident in language used to describe state-sponsored human
rights abuse: 'ethnic cleansing' becomes a euphemism for genocide; torture is
re-labelled as 'extraordinary rendition' or 'intensive interrogation'. Cohen (2001:
80) noted how euphemistic language was applied to the killing of Jews by the Nazis:

> ... public Nazi texts were encoded, two-track communications. The extermina-
> tion message was hidden, but barely. It was a pretend concealment – like 'hid-
> ing' objects from children in a game. Concrete terms like 'murder' and 'killing'
> were seldom used. The actions of the *Einsatzgruppen* were referred to as
> 'deportations', 'special actions', 'special treatment', 'executive measures',
> 'cleansing', 'resettlement', 'finishing off', 'liquidation' and 'appropriate treat-
> ment'. The text allows the author to disavow its meaning and the audience to
> claim that they did not understand it.

If the criminal nature of human rights abuses is denied socially, culturally,
politically – even linguistically – then it might be expected that criminological
analysis has been similarly muted. However, other academic disciplines, such
as psychology, political science and law, have developed an understanding of
the circumstances in which atrocities occur and the dynamics that can propel
ordinary individuals to act in extraordinary and heinous ways. Edward-Day
and Vandiver (2000) noted that criminologists have 'paid scant attention to
genocide', yet academic insight from other disciplines has often developed
theoretical insights closely aligned to criminological perspectives on crime and
offending more generally. They argue that this provides hope that a robust
criminology of genocide can be developed, mirroring other efforts to develop
criminological analysis of violations of human rights (Stanley, 2009; Savelsberg,
2010). Ways in which the discipline of criminology might be extended to these
subjects are considered later in this chapter.

Apart from the widespread social and political denial of human rights violations, there are more specific reasons why criminology has not properly addressed
crimes of this kind. The discipline of criminology was nurtured by the state as it

developed in the late nineteenth and early twentieth centuries. In Britain, criminological work was often done by psychiatrists and doctors, for example, whose
scientific research focus was upon prison inmates and 'deviants' (Garland, 1988;
Rock, 1994). Garland (1994: 56) noted that the research work pursued by
Cambridge University's Institute of Criminology in the 1950s consciously sought
to reconcile scientific inquiry with the immediate policy needs of the period, to
the extent that the Institute's programme of work closely resembled that under-
taken by the Home Office Research Unit. Notwithstanding that the institutional
development of criminology eschewed examination of human rights violations,
several leading criminologists had been closely engaged with international
responses to the Holocaust. Leon Radzinowicz, one of the most influential criminologists of the period and founder of the Cambridge Institute, had investigated
Nazi atrocities during the Second World War (Maier-Katkin et al., 2009). In the
1940s, the work of Sheldon Glueck, professor of criminology at Harvard
University, contributed significantly to the establishment of the Nuremberg Trials
(Hagan and Rymond-Richmond, 2009). Interestingly, though, the academic focus
of both men was subsequently diverted to other criminological issues: Radzinowicz
to a history of jurisprudence and Glueck to juvenile delinquency. Hagan and
Rymond-Richmond (2009: 46) suggest that the latter's change of focus can be
attributed to the negative impact that studying the Holocaust would have had on
his scholarly career prospects, in part because of anti-Semitism in the USA.

Funding arrangements and institutional development continue to be heavily
shaped by research council thematic priorities, local and central government
policy agendas, and the priorities of private companies in ways that might inhibit
academic criminologists from examining the crimes of the powerful. The 'fourth
estate' nature of criminology, since its development, contributes to an intellectual
environment in which research agendas are shaped around a need to respond to
crime problems that are socially constructed not according to their innate gravity,
but to the interests of the powerful. As Maier-Katkin et al. (2009: 230–231) argued:

> The safer course to academic respectability and official support for an aspiring
> discipline was to focus on the scientific study of agreed-upon national con-
> cerns such as violent crime, delinquency and drug abuse. ... As a consequence
> of this uneasy marriage between criminology and criminal justice, criminologists
> tended to focus on the concerns of the criminal justice system, such as street
> crime, rather than the study of crimes against humanity in which agents of the
> State are from time to time implicated.

Over the last two decades academic freedom has become increasingly con-
strained by government funding arrangements organized around performance
indicators and the need to demonstrate policy relevance and impact that make
it more difficult to conduct long-term studies into human rights abuses and
state crime (Walters, 2009). Critical criminologists challenge the discipline to
adopt research agendas that expose and confront the crimes of the powerful in
ways that are fundamentally difficult for researchers reliant on funding and

institutional support derived from the state. Even if a radical critique of the established nature of criminology is not endorsed, it is clear that the state-centred basis of the discipline has militated against the study of transnational crimes, especially those committed by states themselves. Hogg (2002) argued that even while it is simplistic to suggest that criminology has been the 'hand-maiden' of the state, there are still grounds to suggest that the 'Hobbesian' nature of the discipline, the strong association between the nation state and criminology, has shaped the parameters and horizon of the discipline. Crime is conceived narrowly in terms of acts that violate state criminal law and justice is understood as the exercise of the authority of a sovereign state (Hogg, 2002). If crime is defined only in terms of acts that break national criminal codes, then acts carried out by states under laws of their own making might not be offences of interest to criminologists. As Maier-Katkin et al. (2009) detailed, some argued that the genocide of the Holocaust was not a crime because it did not violate laws in place in Germany at that period (although the argument proved unsuc-cessful, as the Nuremberg Trials demonstrate). Related to a vacuum created by the absence of law has been the lack of an international criminal justice system. Criminological focus on national courts, prosecutions and penology has lacked an international framework of analysis. Efforts to secure international justice can be traced back to the Middle Ages but, until the 2002 establishment of the International Criminal Court, these have tended to be *ad hoc* interventions in response to particular problems and often have had an uneasy relation with nation-state law (Blattmann and Bowman, 2008). Moreover, criminological research tends to conceptualize offending behaviour in individualistic terms that are incommensurate with human rights violations, for which responsibility is relatively diffuse among large numbers of participants (Stanley, 2007: 169).

For these reasons, the discipline of criminology has been poorly placed to consider activities that are either transnational or carried out by states them-selves, factors that might have been less influential in other academic areas. In discussing the failure of criminology to respond to human rights abuse, how-ever, it becomes apparent that there is a growing body of scholarship that has sought to close this gap. Since the turn of the century, a range of research has begun that has adopted and adapted criminological methods and concepts to human rights atrocities. The following section of this chapter considers the ways in which criminological perspectives have been applied to the Holocaust and to genocides in Rwanda and Darfur.

Towards a Criminology of Genocide

The sheer scale of the murderous activities of the Nazi regime in Germany is difficult to comprehend, let alone respond to. Along with millions of Polish,

Russian, Belorussian and Ukrainian citizens, Russian prisoners of war, Roma, homosexuals and 'mental defectives', the Nazi regime murdered up to 6 million Jews, approximately one-third of the global Jewish population (Shaw, 2003; Valentino, 2004). The crematoria and gas chambers of the 'final solution' represented the most horrific stage in a process of eliminating Jews from Germany that began in the mid-1930s. Valentino (2004) showed how anti-Semitic laws incrementally removed the social and economic rights of Jewish people by banishing them from a series of occupations, restricting their access to public space, and banning marriage between Jewish and non-Jewish people. This was followed by a series of measures designed to remove Jews from Germany to occupied territories in eastern Poland and the development of a plan, never enacted, to deport them *en masse* to Madagascar. These plans were thwarted by Germany's failure to progress against the Allies, especially after the USA joined the war effort. Hitler attributed these setbacks to the pernicious global conspiracy perpetuated by the Jews against Germany, which made more pressing the need to resolve the 'Jewish Question'. It was against this background of anti-Semitism and military defeat that the mass extermination of the Jews, the horrific extension of policies of exclusion and expulsion, was developed. It has been calculated that approximately half of those killed by the Nazis died as a result of shootings or because of the dreadful conditions of life in the ghettos and in labour and concentration camps. The other 50 per cent perished in the death camps – at Auschwitz-Birkenau alone, 1.3 million were killed between late 1941 and the end of 1944 (Browning, 1992; Valentino, 2004).

The extent to which the Nazi Holocaust is a unique episode in human history has been much debated. Cohen (2001) showed how responding to it as an aberrant event only explicable in terms of human capacity for evil was one factor that inhibited analysis of its causes and complexities. Bauman (1989) argued that the Holocaust was the ultimate expression of modernity, entailing as it did murder on an industrial scale organized and delivered bureaucratically against Jews, the ultimate outsider group, a threatening 'other' to the nation state. While this perspective has been questioned, for example by Gilroy (1993), who noted that slavery and colonialism entailed genocide that was similarly organized, there can be little disagreement with Shaw's (2003: 81) claim that the Holocaust is 'the undisputed paradigm of the newly recognized crime of genocide'.

Efforts to explain the involvement of thousands of German citizens in the atrocities of the Holocaust became particularly salient during the Nuremberg Trials of the 1960s. Psychological and cultural perspectives have focused on the extent to which those who implemented the final solution had 'authoritarian personalities' which predisposed them to follow orders that might seem unimaginable to outside observers (Adorno, 1950). Arendt (1963) coined the phrase 'the banality of evil' to explain the ways in which barbarous acts were broken down into a chain of routine processes that were relatively innocuous when considered in isolation, suggesting that ordinary citizens were acting incrementally in ways that effectively disguised the horrific outcome of their collective endeavours. In his 1996 book *Hitler's Willing Executioners*, Goldhagen argued that Germany had a particular national culture of anti-Semitism that encouraged the persecution of Jews. While Goldhagen's analysis of anti-Semitism in German history has been challenged (Browning, 1992, in Savelsberg, 2010), the role of cultural framing in offending behaviour has been a recurring focus of criminological analysis. However, what becomes difficult is explaining how the prevailing general conditions for genocide (in this case 'eliminationist anti-Semitism') become operational in certain times and places. Criminological perspectives on criminalization could help here. For example, Turk (1969) argued that criminalization becomes more likely when powerful authority groups and the subjects of criminalization both have articulated coherent views that conflict with one another. Strong alignment of views between high-level political and legal authorities and frontline officials who enforce the law, coupled with a strong legal framework and institutions, make the active criminalization of outsider groups more likely (Edward-Day and Vandiver, 2000).

Cultural responses and anti-Semitism are clearly important to developing a criminological analysis of the Holocaust and a number of studies have identified similarities between an analysis of this genocide and criminological theory developed in relation to 'ordinary' crime. Kelman (1973, in Edward-Day and Vandiver, 2000: 44–45) has developed a three-fold analysis of the conditions under which ordinary individuals might come to participate in atrocities. He argued that such behaviour requires a loss of constraint and that this relies on processes of authorization, routinization and dehumanization. In terms of authorization, Kelman refers to the means by which activities are ordered or promoted by individuals in positions of legitimate authority. Routinization refers to the breaking down of horrific actions into component parts, such that the individual is sheltered from the outcomes to which they have contributed in only a small degree. Dehuminization relates to the removal of the objects of the activity from the moral community: either they are considered less than human, and so do not warrant the usual ethical consideration, or in some way they might be considered the authors of their own misfortune. As Edward-Day and Vandiver (2000) argued, several features of Kelman's analysis bear close relationship to theories of delinquency developed in the 1950s. In particular, Sykes and Matza (1957) used the concept of 'techniques of neutralisation' to describe ways in which offenders morally justify their behaviour by denying the status of the victim (who is either beneath concern or deserved what they got) and appealing to higher loyalties (the offenders gang, for example). Both components of techniques of neutralization are similar to Kelman's concepts of authorization and dehumanization, and are criminological perspectives that help us to understand the Holocaust. The following section outlines how these and other criminological concepts might address genocide in Rwanda in the 1990s, outlined in Box 6.1.

Box 6.1: Genocide in Rwanda

While the actual numbers of dead will probably never be known, what is known is that over the course of some hundred days in the early summer of 1994, between 500,000 and 800,000 people were put to death through a clear programmatic effort to eliminate Tutsis, along with Hutu 'moderates' believed to be sympathetic to Tutsis. The numbers of those implicated in these killings are even more difficult to estimate, but given the principal methods used – 'inefficient' individual killings by machete – it is assumed that many thousands, perhaps millions, were directly involved. But if the extent of complicity was very probably massive, so was the extent of victimization. Indeed, a UNICEF study posited that five out of six children present in Rwanda during the killings had, at the very least, witnessed bloodshed ...

As many close observers of the Rwandan genocide have repeatedly stressed and as the International Criminal Tribunal for Rwanda has itself confirmed, this was not 'a spontaneous outburst of killing' but the product of a heavily orchestrated campaign that had begun as early as 1990, and dating back to the mid-1993 founding of Radio-Télévision Libre des Milles Collines (RTLM), an ostensibly 'private' radio station founded by leading Hutu extremists from the government, military and business communities. Well before 1994, RTLM began broadcasting vitriolic appeals to private militias and individuals intended to incite killings of Tutsis (along with Hutus regarded as being more sympathetic to Tutsis). As early as 1992, UN officials and non-governmental human rights organizations were warning that radio transmissions within Rwanda were playing a central role in inciting ethnic tensions and ethno-political murders.

Extract from Alvarez (1999: 391–392)

The horrific and extraordinarily intense genocidal slaughter of Tutsi people in Rwanda in the mid-1990s, outlined in Box 6.1, has been subjected to criminological analysis that utilizes many of the concepts referred to in discussion of the Holocaust. As Alvarez (1999) noted, those events were not a sudden or unpredicted outbreak of mindless violence, but neither were they an inevitable result of intractable ethnic conflict. While ethnicity was encoded with social, economic and political significance by Belgian colonialists who afforded a privileged status to Tutsis relative to Hutus, boundaries between the two groups had been relatively fluid to the extent that individuals could switch their ethnic identity from one group to the other. There was considerable intermarriage between Tutsis and Hutus. Clearly, though, racism became the central organizing principle of the violence and should be regarded as a necessary but insufficient condition of the genocide, just as anti-Semitism was in Germany half a century earlier. Indeed, Edward-Day and Vandiver (2000) noted that Tutsi people were 'dehumanized' in much the same way that Jewish people had been in Nazi Germany: they were portrayed as a privileged minority with disproportionate wealth and as being responsible for the problems of the majority.

The role of semi-establishment media in broadcasting racist propaganda about the Tutsi has been widely identified as a central element in their dehumanization. The violence was more widely authorized by elite groups. Smeulers and Hoex (2010: 440) found that 'the planners and instigators were a small and tight group of people who had authority and to whom others listened'. Although the Rwandan genocide was not organized with the industrial power brought to bear in the Holocaust, it was ruthlessly bureaucratic. Edward-Day and Vandiver (2000: 52) describe officials producing lists of people to be killed that were distributed via the civil hierarchy to local villagers:

> The slaughter was so well organized that often the victims themselves knew when their names had been added to the roll call. The army, Hutu militias and peasant groups were mobilized so effectively that even in the absence of technology available to the Nazis (most Tutsis were murdered with machetes and clubs), the death rate over the 100 days of the genocide was three times that of the peak rate achieved by perpetrators of the Holocaust.

A range of criminological concepts help to explain how the bureaucratic, political and cultural organization of the Rwandan genocide at a broad social level were enacted by a significant number of ordinary Hutu people against their fellow citizens, co-workers, kin and neighbours. Haveman (2008, in Smeulers and Hoex, 2010: 436) indicated that 800,000 people are estimated to have been convicted for their involvement in the genocide, a figure amounting to 25–30 per cent of the adult population. Once the violence had been authorized and Tutsis had been dehumanized, group dynamics, differential association and 'hyper-masculinity' – concepts used to explain offending and deviant behaviour more generally – can explain why so many people engaged in such an intense and extensive episode of mass killing.

As well as bringing criminological perspectives to the Rwandan genocide, Smeulers and Hoex (2010) used a methodology that has been applied to analyze other forms of offending: interviews with perpetrators. Based upon an extensive literature review and 29 semi-structured interviews with offenders convicted following their involvement in the genocide, Smeulers and Hoex (2010) distinguished between different types of perpetrator and recognized a range of motivations that led to participation. They categorized participants into three types: planners and instigators, leaders, and joiners. The first comprised senior politicians, government and military officials and media leaders who were motivated by a mixture of hatred for their Tutsi victims, the pursuit of political power and personal careerism. This group included Augustin Bizimungu, who, in May 2011, was sentenced to 30 years imprisonment by the

International Criminal Tribunal for Rwanda (ICTR) for his part in the killing of 800,000 people during his period as head of the army. The second group includes soldiers and police officers who might also have been motivated by political ideology, but also by a commitment to fulfilling their professional duty by implementing directives from senior sources. The third category, the largest, was ordinary citizens motivated by material gain, aggression and sadism, a desire to belong, and fear of reprisals (perhaps to their families) if they did not participate in the genocide.

All of these categories and motivations can be examined and understood through a criminological lens. The concept of differential association, for example, was developed by Sutherland (1949) to explain how individuals come to engage in criminal activity as a result of their interactions with other offenders (Matsueda, 2006). Sutherland first applied the concept to white-collar crime, arguing that offenders learnt both the techniques for committing offences and the attitudes and moral values needed to participate in deviant behaviour. Similar patterns of association were evident in Rwanda. Smeulers and Hoex (2010) examined the micro-dynamics of collective group behaviour in Rwanda and argued that a combination of leadership provided by fanatical perpetrators and criminal gangs, a range of compliance and consensus mechanisms that encouraged wider participation from ordinary citizens and the socio-psychology of collective behaviour explains why events unfolded as they did. They noted that these processes also explain the development of ordinary criminal gangs, although in the context of the Rwandan genocide homicidal behaviour was sanctioned by the authorities who had signalled that such actions would be treated with impunity (Smeulers and Hoex, 2010: 451):

> In many ways, the Rwandan killer groups functioned just like ordinary delinquent groups do: we can distinguish leaders and followers, compliance and consensus mechanisms are operational and group behaviour tends to escalate into extreme behaviour. The crucial difference is that the Rwandan killer groups were formed top-down, the genocidal process was instigated by the political authorities and the groups operated on direct orders of these authorities. ... A final important difference is [that] the Rwandan killer groups differed from the composition of ordinary delinquent groups, as, alongside ordinary criminals and delinquents, many otherwise law-abiding people also participated in the genocide.

That extraordinary crimes can be understood, at least in part, through the application of criminological concepts developed in relation to ordinary offending is also evident from Mullins' (2009) analysis of rape in the Rwandan genocide. Mullins (2009: 731) noted that collective episodes of gang rape during the genocide served to enhance bonding among participants, as it has been found to do in instances of gang rape in other contexts, and to encourage them to 'greater and more atrocious levels of violence'. This perspective echoes Brownmiller's (1975) analysis of the use of rape in war as a means of both degrading and subjugating enemy populations and also as a 'spoil of war', a reward to victorious soldiers that enforces their collective identity. Three categories of rape were identified by Mullins (2009) through an examination of Rwandan court transcripts: opportunistic rape, sexual enslavement and genocidal rape. The first two categories can be identified within broader patterns of sexual violence, and so are susceptible to criminological explanation in terms of masculinity and the exercise of power over women. In the context of war and conflict, however, Mullins noted that forms of 'hyper-masculinity' emerge that allow men to reassert their gender capital through violent assaults on women. Mullin's analysis demonstrated that genocidal rape was practised as a deliberate component of a wider strategy of ethnic violence. The symbolic shaming of rape victims, assaulted and humiliated in public and, in cases where the victim is killed, displayed *post mortem* in gruesome demonstrations of their fate, served to terrorize and destroy the wider Tutsi population. The role of rape in the wider project of genocide in Rwanda is described by Mullins (2009: 732) in the following terms:

> ... to tarnish the reputation and memory of a people before killing them off – ensuring that not only are the final experiences of the population horrible by nature, but the way in which they are remembered by others is also fixed on those end moments (i.e. a nude woman laying along the side of the road with her throat slit and a tree branch inserted into her vagina). Not only is the population itself eliminated, but the final memories of the people's existence are tarnished.

Seawell (2005) similarly argued that rape in the Rwandan genocide, and in the assaults on Bosnian Muslims in the conflict in the former Yugoslavia, was a communicative action, a form of 'social discourse' intended to convey the subordination of victims and their communities. Rape in this context is not an outcome of the social disorganization caused by civil war and conflict, but is an integral part of the conduct of the genocide. Seawell (2005) noted that the international tribunals established in response to the Rwandan genocide, and that in Bosnia, adopted definitions of rape that reflected the wider impact that this form of violence was intended to have in terms of the genocidal intention to destroy or partly destroy national, ethnic, religious or racial groups. In this way, Seawell (2005: 192) argued, the ICTR defined rape in broad terms that 'allows for an understanding of rape as an act of violence with specified intent – an act designed to communicate a particular message of racial or ethnic hatred'. Prosecution of offenders in these terms meant that the prosecuting of offenders in the Rwandan, and Bosnian, context has by-passed some of the legal obstacles associated with bringing charges domestically in the United States. For example, Seawell (2005) demonstrated that many US states rely on a definition of rape that requires that an assault included the use, or threat, of force by the perpetrator on the victim, and that 'force' is constructed in relatively narrow terms. Domestic legal responses to rape that adopted the broader conceptualization applied in the aftermath of genocide, which refer to the intention to 'outrage the personal dignity' of the victim or to cause them 'great suffering or serious injury to the body or health', might prove more effective and better recognize the nature of the trauma experienced by victims. Adopting Seawell's proposed wider legal definition of rape illustrates one way in which a socio-legal analysis of aspects of genocide might enhance domestic criminal justice. This suggests that criminological analysis of genocide might generate new approaches to criminal justice responses to domestic crime in areas, such as sexual violence, where existing responses have been widely criticized.

Box 6.2: Genocide in Darfur

Since early 2003, the government of Sudan has responded to an insurgency by rebel groups in Darfur by unleashing its proxy Janjaweed militias on the rebels' tribal groups. The government supported the resulting ethnic cleansing campaign with well-coordinated air strikes and joint ground operations. The two main rebel groups, the Sudan Liberation Army (SLA) and the Justice and Equality Movement (JEM), are recruited mainly from the largely agrarian Fur and Massalit and the mostly nomadic Zaghawa, the three largest Darfurian groups of African descent. The strategy of the government has been to 'drain the swamp' by driving civilians from their villages, thereby denying the rebels sanctuary in much of Darfur. This campaign has left more than 200,000 dead, most from conflict-related disease and malnutrition. More than two million have been forced from their homes.

Extract from Grono (2006: 624)

The totality of the evidence ... available to us shows that the Jingaweit [Janjaweed] and Sudanese military forces have committed large-scale acts of violence, including murders, rape and physical assaults on non-Arab individuals. Second, the Jingaweit and Sudanese military forces destroyed villages, foodstuffs, and other means of survival. Third, the Sudan Government and its military forces obstructed food, water, medicine, and other humanitarian aid from reaching affected populations, thereby leading to further deaths and suffering. And finally, despite having been put on notice multiple times, Khartoum has failed to stop the violence.

Extract from Colin Powell's evidence to the US Senate Foreign Relations
Committee, September 2004

Much of the international reaction to the events in Darfur, in western Sudan on the border with Chad, have focused on the contentious question of whether the events briefly described above constituted 'genocide', as defined in international law. Legal, scholarly and political debate has focused upon the extent to which the Sudanese government sponsored the violence, whether it was directed at an identifiable group of people or whether it was motivated by economic competition relating to access to land, and whether efforts to categorize the atrocities as 'genocide' would hinder successful prosecution in the International Criminal Court (ICC) (Prunier, 2007). In July 2009, the ICC charged the Sudanese President Omar al-Bashir with three counts of genocide, five crimes against humanity and two counts of murder, making him the first sitting head of state to be indicted by the court. Although charges of genocide were subsequently dropped, and al-Bashir has yet to be brought to trial, the case of Darfur (like that of Rwanda) has been important in terms of international jurisprudence.

As Prunier's (2007) account of the 'ambiguous genocide' in Darfur demonstrates, the roots of the 2003 conflicts run deep in political and historical terms. Unlike in Rwanda, the atrocities briefly outlined in Box 6.2 did not occur as the result of rapid and short-lived escalation, but rather were episodes in a series of violent clashes that had recurred periodically over decades. While the violent assaults primarily targeting Fur, Massalit and Zaghawa tribes of African descent have been committed predominantly by forces such as Janjaweed, closely allied to the Arabic Sudanese government, it is simplistic to suggest that the conflict is an expression of immutable ethnic enmity. Nevertheless, the analysis of the Darfur atrocities conducted by Hagan and Rymond-Richmond (2009) demonstrates that the use of racist epithets was a common feature of the assaults on civilians: shouts of 'Kill the Nuba' [a Sudanese racist term for black Africans] and discussions of black people's status as slaves or monkeys were commonly reported in victims' testimonies. Hagan and Rymond-Richmond (2009: 166–167) noted that these techniques dehumanized victims, in ways illustrated above in relation to the Holocaust and genocide in Rwanda, and that such use of language is also apparent in other forms of criminal offending. In particular, they drew parallels with Katz's (1988) analysis of the ways in which cursing accompanies instances of domestic violence 'to effect degrading transformations' that reinforce the subordination of the victim.

Drawing upon the criminological work of Sutherland and Glueck, Hagan and Rymond-Richmond (2009) developed a criminological analysis of genocide in Darfur based around the concept of 'differential association', which, as has been shown, has similarly been used in the context of other human rights violations. Hagan and Rymond-Richmond explored the balance of group dynamics in favour of crimes occurring compared to those group dynamics that might prevent crimes occurring. In the context of Darfur, the social organization of networks can be identified such that group dynamics that encouraged offending were stronger than those that inhibited offending. As with other forms of criminal activity, relatively closed networks developed among, for example, the Janjaweed militias so that individual interactions were with similar people, ideas and intentions were transparently conveyed, and rigid norms and speech patterns governed behaviour. These closed networks were led by charismatic leaders who mobilized participants. Prunier (2007: 97–98) identified key features of the Janjaweed groups in ways that demonstrate their closely bounded social network and potential for violence:

> Sociologically the Janjaweed seem to have been of six main origins: former bandits and highwaymen who had been 'in the trade since the 1980s; demobilized soldiers from the regular army; young members of Arab tribes having a running land conflict with a neighbouring 'African' group ...; common criminals who were pardoned and released from gaol if they joined the militia; fanatical members of the Tajammu al-Arabi [Union of Arabs]; and young unemployed 'Arab' men, quite similar to those who had joined on the 'African' side.

These dense social networks also provided the material and logistical resources necessary for the violent assaults – weapons were procured, smuggled and supplied, group members were paid and trained, transport and accommodation was provided. As in other forms of group offending, social interaction means that group dynamics develop practical solutions to identified 'problems'. Hagan and Rymond-Richmond (2009) provide detailed analysis of the nature of the criminal organization responsible for the 'joint enterprise' of the violent atrocities perpetrated in Darfur. Links between key individuals within the organization are identified – in particular the role played by Musa Hilal, the son of a prominent Sheikh in North Darfur and a former prisoner with convictions for robbery and murder, in organizing training camps, obtaining weapons, leading attacks and framing the conflict in racialized terms that 'Africans' were the source of the problem. Such a framework of analysis has been used to describe the operation of organized crime groups in other contexts.

The detailed research work, using criminological concepts, conducted by Hagan and Rymond-Richmond (and others) in Darfur demonstrates another route through which criminology can contribute towards the development of a fuller understanding and a more effective response to human rights' violations. Much of the analysis in their study of Darfur is based upon an Atrocities Documentation Survey (ADS) conducted among persons displaced by the conflict into refugee camps in Chad. Developed from crime victimization surveys, discussed in Chapter Five, the implementation of the ADS in the context of Darfur provided a different perspective on the extent of human rights violations than that which had been developed using health-based methodologies more usually employed in the aftermath of humanitarian problems. As Hagan and Rymond-Richmond (2009) noted, World Health Organization (WHO) surveys focused on mortality, morbidity and nutrition in order to estimate risks of disease and starvation within refugee camps. On this basis, the WHO estimated that some 70,000 people had died in the conflict. While this total was subject to revision and debate, official estimates based upon epidemiological surveys in the camps for displaced persons continued not to count death and injury that had been caused prior to persons arriving in the camps. Consideration of the broad picture was not relevant to the need to respond to immediate health crises. In contrast, the US State Department-sponsored ADS was concerned to estimate the extent of violence in wider terms and was conducted in the form of a survey of more than 1,100 people living in camps in Chad, asking them about their own experiences of violence and that of their immediate family members. Unsurprisingly, this method, which included violence before arrival at the camps, led to a much higher estimate of numbers killed or displaced in the conflict: between 300,000 and 400,000 across the whole region of Darfur (Hagan and Rymond-Richmond, 2009: 100).

As Prunier (2007) and Hagan and Rymond-Richmond (2009) amply demonstrate, debates about the numbers killed in the Darfur conflict were highly politically charged. The use of criminological methods not only enables the calculation of estimates that complement those gained through other approaches, but also entails the collection of testimonial material from survivors that develops a stronger understanding of events. While others have used socio-legal methods, such as Mullins' (2009) study of court transcripts to analyze sexual violence in Rwanda, these have not had the advantage of the ADS in uncovering criminal victimization that had gone unreported. Collecting data using a victimization methodology not only bears witness to horrific campaigns of organized violence, it can also be of evidentiary value in terms of bringing offenders to justice. As Savelsberg (2010: 72) noted, Hagan and Rymond-Richmond 'thus achieve what has never been done in empirical scholarship: they mobilize its full potential to provide evidentiary proof of genocide'.

Using case studies of the Holocaust, the genocide in Rwanda and the violent conflict in Darfur, it has been shown that criminological perspectives contribute significantly to understanding human rights violations. While each of these is an extreme episode, the range of concepts that have been developed to understand them is likely to be broadly transferrable to other contexts, as the next section of this chapter seeks to do. Key criminological ideas relating to differential association, techniques of neutralization, hyper-masculinity, power and sexual violence, and the group dynamics of criminal offending have been shown to add important elements to studies of genocide that have tended to draw from other disciplines and focus on broad socio-political patterns of genocide, cultural causes or the psychological processes that might compel ordinary people to commit extraordinary crimes. Traditional perspectives continue to offer much to understanding genocide, but criminological concepts, and techniques, complement these very effectively.

Criminology, Environmental Harm and Neo-colonialism

Criminological analysis of genocide drew upon analysis of corporate and state 'crimes of the powerful' and in turn provides a basis from which emerging problems relating to a range of environmental harms can be better understood.

As with the violations of human rights discussed above, environmental problems have received relatively little criminological attention, although this gap
is being closed, as the discussion below indicates. Many of the most compelling
environmental concerns of the twenty-first century are not illegal and so are
not criminal activities. As has been argued in relation to genocide, a narrow
criminological focus on acts that break the criminal code is particularly problematic when the very states that compose law are implicated in harmful
behaviour. Activities such as the extraction of minerals and timber from the
Amazon might be done legitimately in accordance with Brazilian law (Solinge,
2010) but can be understood as criminal where the terms of the UN Covenant
of Economic, Social and Cultural Rights are breached (Stanley, 2007). Moreover,
the conduct of illegal trade in protected products also often entails attendant
criminal behaviour that further compounds the damage done to local environments and those who depend directly on them. The pressure group Human
Rights Watch found that illegal logging in Indonesia had a huge negative impact
on the livelihoods and environment of indigenous peoples, who are already
marginalized and living in poverty. Moreover, the practice of illegal logging also
entails considerable corruption and the theft of income from the trade:

> the opportunity costs of the lost revenue are huge: funds desperately needed
> for essential services that could help Indonesia meet its human rights obliga-
> tions in areas such as health care go instead into the pockets of timber execu-
> tives and corrupt officials. Corruption and untransparent, unaccountable
> revenue flows in Indonesia are so widespread that a new expression has come
> into common usage in the Indonesian language for such uncontrolled funds,
> 'wild money'. (Human Rights Watch, 2009: 2)

Environmental harm is not motivated by racism or ethnic hostility in any
straightforward manner, but, as with instances of genocide, it is clear that many
of these forms of crime cannot be understood without acknowledging the marginalized status of those most immediately victimized. Although global problems such as climate change threaten all of humanity, it is clear that many
environmental harms disproportionally victimize those already on the margins. As is widely demonstrated in the discussion below of different examples
of environmental damage and attendant human rights violations, the impact of
deforestation, pollution, global warming, the waste industry and mineral
extraction is most keenly felt by populations already on the periphery of global
capitalism. Simon's (2000) analysis of corporate environmental damage draws
upon the notion of 'environmental racism' to describe the differential patterns
in the disposal of toxic waste. He noted that US companies could drastically
reduce the costs incurred in disposing of waste domestically if they shipped it
to developing countries whose poverty made this an attractive source of
national income: 'at times, multinational corporations have provided handsome
financial rewards to the recipient nations. For example, Guinea-Bissau, which

has a gross national product of $150 million, will make $150 million to $600 million over a five-year period in a deal to accept toxic waste from three European nations' (Simon, 2000: 638). Differential victimization from environmental damage, such as pollution, is widely documented in the national domestic context. Social injustice arises since the relatively poor are more likely to live and work in areas adversely affected by environmental harm and lack the economic or political capital to either relocate to other areas or to mobilize against plans to site incinerators or chemical plants in their neighbourhoods. As a lucrative international trade in hazardous waste has developed, these patterns have moved from the local to the global (South, 2010). White (2010) argued that environmental harm at the local, national, regional and global levels is closely interrelated: with a 'butterfly' effect, so that damage committed in one place resonates more widely. This occurs in a very literal sense through what he described as a 'process of transference':

> Harm can move from one place to another. Harm can be externalized from the producers and consumers in ways that make it disappear from their sight and oversight. The global trade in toxic waste (often under the cover of recycling), the illegal dumping of radioactive waste, carbon emission trading, and the shifting of dirty industries to developing countries constitute some of the worst aspects of the 'not in my backyard' syndrome. The result is a massive movement of environmentally harmful products, processes, and wastes to the most vulnerable places and most exploitable peoples of the world. (White, 2010: 11)

Environmental harm has been analyzed criminologically in terms of corporate and white-collar offending and through research that has examined the role of organized crime groups in illegal trade in ivory, waste, 'blood diamonds' and 'conflict timber'. Concepts of differential association and collective criminal enterprise can be applied to aspects of environmental crime, as to 'ordinary' criminal activity, and to genocide. The marginality of the immediate victims within a neo-liberal globalized economy predicated on 'free trade' reflect long-term patterns of colonialism and racism that also provide for the widespread practice of techniques of neutralization. Environmental damage 'disppears from sight', as White put it, partly because those who face the end products of Western consumerism are powerless, unheard and unseen. A United Nations Environment Programme conference in 2006 identified particular problems arising from the lack of capacity of developing nation states to exercise regulatory oversight of waste processing. It noted particular concern relating to the disposal of e-waste, including hazardous substances generated from the dismantling of computers, and chemicals, metals and other by-products released from decommissioning old ships and aeroplanes (White, 2008: 116). Clearly, the impact of Western consumer culture is being felt by the world's poorest peoples, whose invisibility contributes to literal, interpretative and implicatory 'states of denial' through which the global north can neutralize these harms by casting them in terms of the predominant need to maintain lifestyles and sustain economic growth. Such techniques of neutralization are exacerbated further with reference to a 'green consumer' movement that throws an economic lifeline to impoverished people who might benefit from the opportunity to process the waste. Threats to the eco-systems of indigenous communities produced by climate change have often been culturally framed as inevitable collateral damage and neither understood nor responded to as acts of crime.

SUMMARY

The chapter began with the paradox that the discipline of criminology has paid scant attention to serious atrocities that have entailed human death, destruction and misery of a magnitude far greater than that of most other criminal enterprises. The failure of criminology, and other disciplines, to confront human rights abuses of various kinds was explained in terms of the internal history of the discipline as well as the external political, cultural and ideological context. This oversight has begun to be addressed, however, and the chapter reviewed criminological analysis of genocide and other human rights violations. It was argued that theoretically and methodologically, criminology can contribute to efforts to explain and respond to the abuse of human rights. Concepts developed in the study of deviance have been applied to the Holocaust and genocide in Rwanda. Criminological methods have helped to chart the nature and extent of atrocities in Darfur.

Criminological approaches should also be extended to environmental harm. Mineral extraction, timber logging and the dumping of toxic waste has a disproportionate impact on marginalized communities already on the periphery of the global economy, and in some instances threatens the survival of indigenous groups. Critical engagement with race and crime requires attention be paid to emerging forms of environmental crime and degradation.

STUDY QUESTIONS

1 Why has criminology paid so little attention to genocide and the abuse of human rights?
2 How have criminological concepts and methods been applied to events such as the Holocaust, the genocide in Rwanda and the atrocities in Darfur?
3 How might the concept of 'environmental racism' be applied to the illegal trade in minerals and timber?

(Continued)

(Continued)

FURTHER READING

Savelsberg (2010, Sage) provides a clear and concise review of the failure of criminology to engage with state crime and human rights abuse, as well as an indication of how this might be rectified. Another useful approach can be found in Stanley's (2007) chapter and her (2009, Routledge) analysis of human rights violations in Timor-Leste. Smeulers and Hoex's (2010) article in the *British Journal of Criminology* applies criminology to the Rwandan genocide, and Mullins (2009) demonstrates the use of rape as a weapon in the Rwandan conflict in compelling terms. Hagan and Rymond-Richmond's (2009, Cambridge University Press) account of genocide in Darfur is vital reading in respect of all the debates addressed in this chapter. A wealth of evidence relating to these events can be found at the websites of the International Criminal Tribunal for Rwanda (www.unictr.org/) and the International Criminal Court (www.icc-cpi.int/).

7

Disproportionality in the Criminal Justice System

OVERVIEW

This chapter:

- provides detailed evidence of the over-representation of minority groups at various stages of the criminal justice system of England and Wales;
- reviews comparative data relating to other European countries, Australasia and the United States;
- considers debates about the nature of discrimination and over-representation of minorities in criminal justice systems.

KEY TERMS

- Disproportionality
- Institutional racism
- Racism and discrimination

- Ethnic monitoring
- Over-representation

Introduction

It is clear that minority ethnic groups tend to be considerably over-represented in the criminal justice system (CJS) and that patterns of disproportionality have endured across time and between different societies. In Britain, the over-involvement of minorities in the CJS has been well documented for many decades and is apparently authoritatively demonstrated by various government digests of criminal justice statistics. However, not all minority groups are over-represented, and it is also clear that gender, age and other factors influence these patterns. Despite these qualifications, though, it remains the case that Britain's black population remains over-represented in the criminal justice system. A recent parliamentary report starkly outlined the extent of these problems:

> young black people are overrepresented at all stages of the criminal justice system. Black people constitute 2.7% of the population aged 10–17, but represent 8.5% of those of that age group arrested in England and Wales. As a group, they are more likely to be stopped and searched by the police, less likely to be given unconditional bail and more likely to be remanded in custody than white young offenders. Young black people and those of 'mixed' ethnicity are likely to receive more punitive sentences than young white people. (House of Commons Home Affairs Committee, 2007: 5)

A range of other research evidence that elaborates upon this perspective is reviewed later in this chapter and it is also shown that patterns of over-representation also apply to minority and indigenous communities in many other societies. It is apparent that over-representation is linked in complex ways to wider problems of social inclusion and marginalization, and to historical patterns of migration, colonialism and racism. The chapter shows that while demonstrating that minority ethnic groups are over-represented in criminal justice systems is relatively straightforward, identifying the causes and explaining the dynamics of these patterns continues to be among the most controversial challenges facing criminology.

The chapter begins by analyzing the representation of ethnic groups in the criminal justice system of England and Wales in general terms and the ways in which concerns about the apparent disproportionate involvement of minority ethnic groups have emerged over the last few decades. It continues with a detailed consideration of the research evidence relating to the three broad stages of the CJS: police, courts and the penal system. Comparative data across all three stages is then introduced using information from European countries, Australia and New Zealand, and the United States. The chapter concludes by examining the vexed question of how these trends are explained: three broad positions are outlined. First, it may be that the agencies of the CJS play an essentially neutral role and over-representation is a reflection of differences in patterns of offending. Second, it may be that the over-representation is a cumulative process, whereby problems and patterns of discrimination are minor but develop incrementally throughout the system so that decisions at each stage have a significant cumulative impact. Third, it may be that the CJS plays a major role in producing and reproducing patterns of racialization and criminalization that explain the continued marginalization of minority communities in many Western societies.

Minority Ethnic Groups in the Criminal Justice System of England and Wales

Police, Stop and Search

Historically, concerns that minority ethnic groups have been over-represented in the criminal justice system have focused predominantly on relationships between police and minority groups (especially Britain's black population). These debates have existed in various forms for many decades but since the 1950s there has been a sustained critical focus on ways in which police have targeted young black men through stop and search, and subjected them to various forms of harassment and violence. In his study of police relations with 'West Indian' migrants to Britain in the 1950s, Whitfield (2004: 142) noted that police insularity, coupled with their combined role as prosecutors and witnesses for the prosecution, meant that 'many black people were coming to believe that the court system and judiciary legitimized and supported police malpractice'. Hunte's 1965 report *Nigger Hunting in England* provided extensive evidence of police malpractice and abuse of black people. A further report, first compiled in the late 1970s by the Institute of Race Relations (IRR), catalogued a host of examples of police malpractice against black and Asian people organized under headings relating to 'stop, search and strip', 'arbitrary arrest', 'violence on arrest', 'forced entry leading to violence', 'forced confessions', 'fabrication and planting of evidence', and many other sub-genres of abuse of power (IRR, 1987). Such claims were validated by Lord Scarman's (1981: 4.63) official inquiry into the 1981 Brixton disorders that, while denying that senior officers were racist, noted that 'racial prejudice does manifest itself occasionally in the behaviour of a few officers on the streets'. Scarman (1981: 4.67) went on to note that concerns about these problems had grown so that 'the older generation of black people in Brixton has come to share the belief of the younger generation that the police routinely harass and ill-treat black youngsters'.

Although concerns about over-representation of minorities in the CJS are relatively long-standing, what has developed in more recent times – partly as a result of the evidence outlined above – are more robust processes of data collection, ethnic monitoring and reporting. Claims and counter-claims based largely on anecdotal evidence have been supplanted by a growing body of apparently authoritative statistics that provides a definitive picture of the representation of black and Asian people in the British CJS. From the late 1970s onwards, Home Office-sponsored and other research had examined racial disparities in stop and search, arrest, and court decisions (among other things) (Stevens and Willis, 1979; Willis, 1983; Walker, 1989). As is considered at greater length later in this chapter, the consolidation of detailed statistical evidence stretching back to the mid-1990s means that some earlier debates about the 'facts' of over-representation have been resolved: no uncertainty remains, for example, that black people – especially young males – are stopped and searched at rates disproportionate to their presence in the population as a whole. Clearly though, other points of considerable contention persist, and improved monitoring has not resolved fundamental debates and concerns about the position of minorities within the CJS, as is discussed at further length in Chapter Ten.

The tables below indicate, in very broad terms, current patterns relating to ethnicity in the criminal justice system of England and Wales. They are derived from the annual digest *Race and the Criminal Justice System*, a series introduced following the requirements of the 1991 Criminal Justice Act that accelerated the development of ethnic monitoring in police and other agencies of the CJS. The data provide statistical evidence of over-representation that confirms long-standing concerns of the kind outlined above. Table 7.1 compares the position of various ethnic groups at key stages within the criminal justice system and confirms that minorities, black people in particular, are over-represented at each and every stage when compared to their presence in the population as a whole. Initial contact via stop and search by the police disproportionally impacts on the black population, who accounted for 14.8 per cent of these contacts compared to their presence in the population at 2.6 per cent. To a lesser extent, Asian and mixed groups are similarly over-represented in police stop and search. It might be that disproportionality in police contacts then prompts subsequent and cumulative disparities at later stages in the CJS, as will be examined in the discussion below.

Table 7.1   Percentage at different stages of the criminal justice system compared with ethnic breakdown of general population, England and Wales 2008/09

	White	Black	Asian	Mixed	Chinese or other	Not stated/ unknown	Total
Population aged 10 and over 2007[1]	89.4	2.6	5.2	1.3	1.5	0.0	100
Stops and Searches[2]	67.0	14.8	8.8	2.8	1.3	5.4	100
Arrests	80.6	7.6	5.4	2.8	1.4	2.2	100
Cautions[3, 4]	82.6	6.7	4.9		1.5	4.3	100
Court ordered supervision by probation service	82.0	6.0	4.7	2.7	1.2	3.4	100
Prison population (all, including foreign nationals)[5]	72.8	14.4	7.2	3.4	1.7	0.5	100

Source: Ministry of Justice (2010: 8)

Note: Figures may not add up to 100 due to rounding.

[1]Population Estimates by Ethnic Groups supplied by Office of National Statistics.

[2]Stops and Searches recorded by the police under section 1 of the Police and Criminal Evidence Act 1984 and other legislation.

[3]The data in these rows are based on ethnic appearance and, as such, do not include the category Mixed ethnicity (the data in the rest of the table are based on self-identified ethnicity).

[4]These data are for adults only.

[5]Prison population figures are as at 30 June 2009. Please note that these figures include those awaiting deportation.

In 2010 the Equalities and Human Rights Commission (EHRC) reported that disparities in the use of stop and search powers against different ethnic groups were rooted in police policies and practices that could not be justified in terms of offending rates or demographic trends. The Commission (EHRC, 2010) threatened to issue enforcement notices against police forces that continued to exhibit high levels of disproportionality against black and Asian people. The extent to which minorities are over-represented in police stop and searches is shown in Table 7.2. The data show that in 2008/09, 23.9 per 1,000 of the population of England and Wales were stopped and searched by the police: for white people the rate was 17.9 per 1,000, for Asians 40.1 and for the mixed group 51.7. While these minority groups were over-represented, this was not as significant as for the black group, who were stopped at a rate of 135 per 1,000, amounting to 5.65 times the rate for the overall population. The dispro-portionality gap had widened since the previous year.

Debates about police use of stop and search and the disproportionate use of these powers against minority groups have continued for many years, but rela-tively recent studies have suggested that the categorization and conceptualization of stop and search data might be misleading. There are a number of causes of concern. First, the ethnic classifications themselves are problematic. Usually they are based on perceived ethnicity rather than self-classification and the categories themselves are not clear-cut ('white', for example, combines many ethnic groups). The aggregation of ethnic groups into headline categories serves to obfuscate significant differences: while the 'Asian' rate above was 40.1 per 1,000 in 2008/09, for Bangladeshis the rate was 16.4 (lower than whites), but for Pakistanis it was 109.2 – a proportionality ratio of 4.57. Second, there is some evidence to suggest that police officers are more likely to formally record details of minority ethnic people than others, perhaps because they have become sen-sitized to the need to comply with regulations that they might not consider when dealing with the majority population (Fitzgerald and Sibbitt, 1997). Third,

Table 7.2   Police stop and searches per 1,000 population, by ethnic group, England and Wales, 2007/08 and 2008/09

	2007/08		2008/09	
	Rate per 1,000	**Proportionality ratio**	**Rate per 1,000**	**Proportionality ratio**
White	16.5	0.76	17.9	0.75
Black	108.5	5.01	135.0	5.65
Asian	33.5	1.54	40.1	1.68
Mixed	42.5	1.96	51.7	2.16
Chinese/ other	17.7	0.82	20.2	0.84
Total	21.7	1.00	23.9	1.00

Source: Ministry of Justice (2010: supplementary tables)

the comparator group used to contextualize this data may not be the most appropriate (MVA and Miller, 2000; Waddington et al., 2004). Simply put, most of the data compares patterns among police stop and search practices with the ethnic characteristics of the local resident population. Thus, the data are presented such that the proportion of those who are stopped who are Asian is compared to the proportion in the local resident population who are of Asian ethnicity. On this basis, there is considerable evidence to suggest that minorities are over-represented among police stop and search data. This picture is less clear, however, if the comparator group is not the local resident population but, instead, the population of the local area *available* to be stopped and searched. The use of a group of 'available' population stems from research findings that demonstrate that stop and search powers are not implemented in random patterns but rather are concentrated on particular localities and at particular times. Some residents of local areas are less likely to be exposed to the possibility of being stopped and searched because they do not frequent key locations at times when police are most likely to use these powers. When using the available population as the comparator group, studies have produced a picture radically at odds with the predominant narrative based upon Home Office data outlined earlier:

> ... the findings of this research did not suggest any general pattern of bias against those from minority ethnic backgrounds. This was true for minority ethnic groups as a whole, as well as any particular minority ethnic group. Asian people tended to be under-represented in those stopped or searched, compared to their numbers in the available population, with some notable exceptions. The general picture for black people was mixed. For example, in Greenwich, and Chapeltown, they were mostly under-represented among those stopped or searched, yet in Hounslow and Ipswich, they were far more likely to be stopped or searched in vehicles than their available numbers would suggest. Perhaps surprisingly, the most consistent finding across sites was that white people tended to be stopped and searched at a higher rate than their numbers in the available population would predict. (MVA and Miller, 2000: 84)

Waddington et al. (2004) reproduced this methodology in Reading and in Slough. They too found that this measure of police stop and search led to an important change in prevailing explanatory frameworks. As with any methodological approach, however, this approach has limitations, key among them that the factors that make some groups more 'available' to stop and search, such as school exclusion or unemployment, are themselves influenced by racism and disadvantage. The 'availability' thesis does not explain why minority groups in one area experience radically different levels of stop and search compared to similar groups in other police force areas. For example, comparison of force-by-force data shows considerable differences in the overall use of stop and search and large variations in disproportionality. In Dorset, for example, black people were stopped and searched at a rate of 54.5 per 1,000 while the comparable rate in Durham was 7.0, even though the respective rates for the white population were broadly similar across the two constabularies (9.6 in Dorset and 9.7 in Durham). Clearly, developing a reliable basis for the statistical analysis of police stop and search practices is important, and the generation of more detailed information reveals significant insight. Nevertheless, the experience of 20 years or so of data collation and ethnic monitoring has not led to appreciable improvements in policing of minority communities and clearly significant political, legal and operational challenges remain. Bowling and Philips (2007) argued that police use of stop and search ought to be curtailed since they are indicative of racist prejudice that the service has been unable to regulate. While limiting stop and search powers might remove one basis on which minorities are unjustly targeted by police officers, it is far from clear how such a move would address the myriad informal police practices that also disproportionally impact on black and Asian communities.

The over-policing of Asian communities, who have generally experienced lesser disproportionality than other minorities, has been subject to intense scrutiny in the last decade, in the context of debates about security, terrorism, multiculturalism and Islamaphobia. Section 44 of the 2002 Terrorism Act gives police power in defined localities to stop and search vehicles, people in vehicles and pedestrians for articles that could be used for terrorism 'whether or not there are grounds for suspecting that such articles are present'. In this way, the Act moves beyond PACE provisions outlined earlier that require officers to have 'reasonable grounds' relating to individuals who are stopped and searched. Government officials and police have sometimes maintained that Asian people, likely to be identified as synonymous with Muslims, can expect to be stopped and searched more frequently and that security demands prevail over civil rights concerns (as though the two are mutually exclusive). Concerns about the use of these powers stem from a perception that they have little impact in terms of preventing or detecting terrorism, that they are used too broadly to stop and search people where there is no credible relation to terrorist action, and, coupled with these problems, that their disproportionate use against minorities might serve to undermine community relations and so prove counter-productive. The number of arrests arising from these stops and searches has been very small (in the two yearly quarters shown in Table 7.3, 50 and 54 arrests resulted, and many of those were for offences unrelated to terrorism; similarly, less than 10 per cent of PACE stop and searches led to an arrest in 2008/09). Table 7.3 shows that the number of stops and searches conducted under the 2000 Terrorism Act reduced considerably in the last quarter of 2009, compared to the same period in 2008. While the absolute number dropped, the disproportionate impact on the Asian community became greater: in 2008, 15.8 per cent of those stopped under this legislation were Asian, but in 2009 the proportion had risen to 19.7 per cent.

Table 7.3   Stop and searches[1] under section 44 of the 2000 Terrorism Act, 2008 and 2009[2], number and per cent

	2008		2009	
	No.	**Per cent**	**No.**	**Per cent**
White	34,675	60.3	10,630	59.3
Black	6,397	11.1	1,811	10.1
Asian	9,100	15.8	3,526	19.7
Mixed	1,300	2.3	358	2.0
Chinese/ other	2,572	4.5	746	4.2
Not stated	3,422	6.0	855	4.8
Total	57,466	100.0	17,926	100.0

Source: adapted from Home Office (2010b: 17)

[1]Does not include vehicle-only searches

[2]October to December each year

Minorities in the Court System

Similar patterns of over-representation are evident in the outcomes of courts cases, although the difficulty of accounting for ethnic differences is also equally complex and has not been resolved by improved data gathering. Table 7.4 indicates that, especially at magistrates' court, minority ethnic defendants tend to have a lower conviction rate than white people. The table shows that 60.8 per cent of adult defendants are convicted in magistrates' courts in England and Wales, but that this rate is considerably lower for Black, Asian and 'Other' ethnic groups (50.7, 49.1 and 50.8 per cent, respectively). These differences extend to juveniles appearing before magistrates' benches.

That a higher proportion of Black, Asian and other minority ethnic defendants are acquitted in English and Welsh magistrates' courts contrasts with the position in Crown Courts, where differences between ethnic groups are less pronounced for both adults and juveniles. These patterns raise a host of questions relating to the possibility that minorities are 'over-charged', such that they are more likely to be prosecuted on insufficient evidence or charged with offences associated with higher acquittal rates. Perhaps the courts correct disparities or discrimination introduced earlier in the criminal justice system. The data represented in Table 7.4 are also problematic. Although the Ministry of Justice (2010) argues that there has been a considerable improvement in the collection and collation of court data relating to ethnicity in recent years, it continues to be incomplete and problematic on a number of grounds; it is based on perceived rather than self-identified ethnicity, for example. Furthermore, the 'unknown' category is sizeable for both adult and juvenile cases: in 2008, 337,436 adults were proceeded against in magistrates' courts, the ethnicity of 47.9 per cent of them was not recorded; for juveniles in magistrates' courts, ethnicity was not

Table 7.4   Conviction rate[1], at magistrates' courts and the Crown Court, indictable offences only, per cent, 2008

Conviction rate			White	Black	Asian	Other	Unknown	Total
Magistrates' courts	Adult	London	60.5	51.7	53.2	56.3	57.4	57.1
		Rest of E&W[2]	63.6	49.5	47.0	47.2	60.9	61.5
		E&W	63.3	50.7	49.1	50.8	60.3	60.8
	Juvenile	London	75.1	68.3	67.3	65.5	70.0	70.5
		Rest of E&W	76.8	66.3	66.0	71.3	74.2	75.1
		E&W	76.6	67.6	66.5	68.3	73.4	74.3
Crown Court	Adult	London	71.3	73.9	66.9	75.8	71.3	72.0
		Rest of E&W	81.7	83.2	77.7	81.7	81.0	81.4
		E&W	80.4	78.0	74.2	78.9	79.3	79.5
	Juvenile	London	54.9	62.5	58.2	61.5	63.4	60.7
		Rest of E&W	75.0	79.4	80.0	72.3	75.3	75.6
		E&W	73.0	67.8	73.3	67.5	72.6	71.8

Source: Ministry of Justice (2010: 35)

[1]Percentage of those proceeded against who are convicted
[2]England and Wales

recorded in 45.6 per cent of the 58,842 cases proceeded against. In the Crown Courts, incomplete data were less significant although ethnicity was not known in relation to 19.8 per cent of the 81,259 cases brought, and for juveniles the rate was 19.0 per cent of the 3,567 people proceeded against. While improved ethnic monitoring is desirable, it does not necessarily mean that effective policy solutions will be developed, as the experience of police stop and search has shown.

Similar gaps in the data apply to records of sentences passed on those convicted in English and Welsh courts. Table 7.5 shows that white adults and juveniles were more likely to receive a community sentence than black, Asian or 'other' ethnic groups. Conversely, a greater proportion of black adults and juveniles (73.9 and 62.5 per cent respectively) were sentenced to immediate custody than their white, Asian or 'other' peers.

Table 7.5   Percentage of persons sentenced to community or immediate custodial sentences, adults and juveniles, England and Wales, 2008

		White	Black	Asian	Other	Unknown	Total
Community sentences	Adult	25.9	18.8	19.6	14.9	27.2	25.6
	Juvenile	73.8	67.8	69.0	64.7	73.9	73.2
Immediate custodial sentences	Adult	71.3	73.9	66.9	75.8	71.3	72.0
	Juvenile	54.9	62.5	58.2	61.5	63.4	60.7

Source: Ministry of Justice (2010: 37)

Again, though, these patterns might reveal more than straightforward discrimination, even though they may be shaped by broader social processes of racialization and marginalization. The Ministry of Justice report noted that a range of factors contribute towards understanding the data outlined in Table 7.5, including the nature and seriousness of crimes committed. Community sentences are less likely to be passed for offenders who do not have stable family patterns, a fixed job or home – and black and minority ethnic offenders are more likely to be excluded due to these 'legally relevant criteria', a point returned to towards the end of this chapter. Defendants who plead guilty to an offence may receive a deduction in their sentence of up to one-third, and the research evidence suggests that black and minority people are more likely to enter 'not guilty' pleas. The Ministry of Justice (2010) suggests that this might also explain the greater likelihood that those groups be sentenced to custody.

International Comparisons

European Patterns

The over-representation of minority ethnic people in the British criminal justice system mirrors the experiences of other liberal democratic societies, although the particular contexts, history and politics of different countries means that there are important nuances in patterns and explanations in each case, which means that generalized accounts across societies cannot be drawn. In many European societies, systematic data relating to the representation of minorities in the CJS are not recorded; there is, however, a body of evidence from individual countries that raises concern about disproportionality. The position of Turkish 'gast arbiters' in the German CJS, Eastern European and Russian migrants to Sweden, Moroccan communities in Spain, and Muslims across many EU member states has been subject to considerable analysis and debate (Albrecht, 1997; Open Society Justice Initiative [OSJI], 2009).

In Bulgaria, research shows that the Roma community is over-represented at different stages of the CJS in much the same way as has been outlined in the British context. Gounev and Bezlov (2006) demonstrated that the police stop Roma at a greater rate than the Bulgarian population in general, that they are treated differently during pre-trial investigations (a feature of the CJS that has no direct counterpart in the British system), and appear more frequently in court. They argued that the cumulative impact of these patterns in Bulgaria reinforces crime patterns among Roma and further entrenches their social marginalization:

A disproportionate number of Roma end up in prisons, temporary detentions facilities, or with criminal records. The result is a 'revolving cycle' in which an increasing critical mass of the Roma male population becomes involved in the criminal justice process, which in turn becomes a source for fostering a culture of deviant behaviour in many (but not all) Roma communities. In turn, over-policing of the Roma community has become a factor in the increasing criminalization of the Roma community. (Gounev and Bezlov, 2006: 317)

Discrimination by police in Italy against Roma/Gypsies was further reported by the European Commission against Racism and Intolerance (ECRI), which also noted that the over-policing of minorities was coupled with legal discrimination in the courts and prison system (ECRI, 2002). Gounev and Bezlov (2006) noted that Bulgaria is one of the few countries in Eastern Europe to collect and publish data relating to ethnicity in the CJS, and the incompatibility of data gathering, analysis and dissemination make cross-national comparison difficult, as do differences between criminal justice practice and process. According to a review of the policing of minorities in Europe, only Britain collects systematic data relating to contacts between minorities and criminal justice agencies (OSJI, 2009). For historical and cultural reasons, among other factors, statistical data is limited in many other societies. In France, for example, the collection of personal information relating to ethnicity, religion or race is legally prohibited. Data relating to citizenship, though, is collected and shows that non-citizens were more heavily represented as suspects, those convicted and those sentenced to lengthy terms in prison. Pager (2008) used data relating to citizenship to disaggregate these patterns. He found that when variables including crime type, social, demographic and economic characteristics were factored into analysis of the rates at which foreigners were subject to pre-trial detention, judicial control and criminal conviction, there was no relation between status as non-citizen and being detained. In other words, the over-representation of foreigners was related to factors other than their status as non-citizens. However, for the particular sub-group of foreigners of a North African background this was not the case, Pager found. Controlling for the same set of other variables, he concluded that 'no other variable more consistently or powerfully predicts the severity of criminal justice interventions than those measuring nationality and country of origin' (Pager, 2008: 387).

Australasia

In Australia and New Zealand, 'first nations' or aboriginal peoples are clearly over-represented in criminal justice systems. The plight of Indigenous people in the Australian CJS has been subject of political concern for many decades. In 1987 the Royal Commission into Aboriginal Deaths in Custody was established to identify reasons why Indigenous people were dying in large numbers in Australian prisons and in police custody; Blagg (2008) noted that 99 people died between 1980 and 1989. The Commission found that Indigenous prisoners did not die in custody at a rate greater than their non-Indigenous counterparts, but that the high number of fatalities was due to the relatively large number of Indigenous people being imprisoned in the first place. Moreover, the Commission did not attribute the problem to individual failings or oversights, but pointed instead to structural and institutional matters to do with rates of imprisonment, the recruitment and training of staff, and a raft of management issues. In 2009, Indigenous people were imprisoned in Australia at a rate of 1891 per 100,000: a proportion 14 times greater than non-Indigenous. For juveniles, in 2007, the discrepancy was even sharper, with Indigenous people aged 10–17 being 28 times more likely to be detained than non-Indigenous youths (Taylor, 2007: 30). As Figure 7.1 indicates, the extent of this over-representation in Australian prisons has grown in recent years, a trend described by Cunneen and Schwartz (2008: 38) as 'an ever-deepening crisis'.

A 'whole-of-system' perspective on the over-representation of Indigenous people in Australian prisons has led, as elsewhere, to analysis of disproportionalities at early stages of the criminal justice system. The data clearly show that police have disproportionate contact with Indigenous people but that the extent of this varies between states. Figure 7.2 shows the proportion of all police contacts that are with juvenile Indigenous people in Australian states. In New South Wales, for example, 17 per cent of police contacts with male juveniles are with Indigenous young men and 16 per cent of contacts with young women are with Indigenous females. In two of the states, Western Australia and Southern Australia, there are

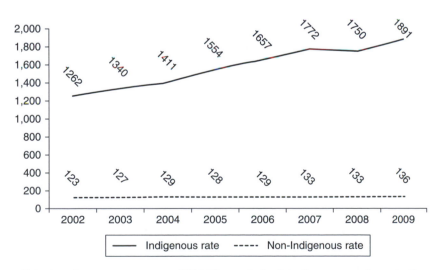

Figure 7.1   Imprisonment rates per 100,000 population*, Indigenous and non-Indigenous Australians, 2002–09

Source: Australian Bureau of Statistics (2009)

* Age-standardized

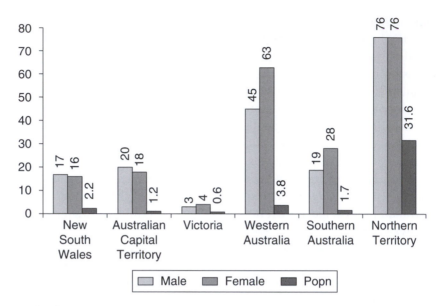

Figure 7.2   Proportion of police contact with Indigenous juveniles, by jurisdiction and sex, and overall proportion of Indigenous people in state population, Australia[1]

Source: Richards (2007: 40)

[1]Data compiled from various reports in the period 2005 to 2007

stark differences between males and females, such that Indigenous females feature more heavily than their male counterparts. Clearly, in all cases Indigenous juveniles feature much more heavily in police contacts than their proportion in the overall population (of all ages) would suggest. Although the Northern Territory, subject of a controversial 2007 federal intervention to tackle problems such as child sex abuse, alcoholism and drug addition (Brown and Brown, 2007), has the highest overall level of contacts between police and Indigenous juveniles, it is also the state with the largest overall Indigenous population so that the extent of over-representation is smaller than in other jurisdictions.

More detailed analysis shows that Indigenous people are more likely to be treated formally in ways that propel them further into the criminal justice system. Conversely, police are more likely to deal with non-Indigenous people in relatively informal ways that curtail their involvement. Figure 7.3 presents outcomes of police contacts in New South Wales, the most populous Australian state, between 2000 and 2004 showed that Indigenous people were more likely to be charged or issued with a Court Attendance Notice (CAN) and less likely to receive a warning or a caution.

In New Zealand, several recent reports have noted that the over-representation of Māori in the criminal justice system is long-standing and continues (Department of Corrections, 2007; Morrison, 2009). As in other countries, disproportionality can be identified at each stage of the justice system so that the overall problem might be best understood as a process of bias amplification,

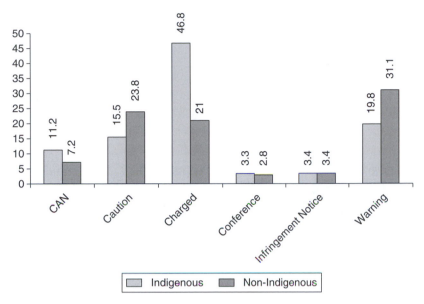

Figure 7.3   Police interventions by Indigenous status, New South Wales, 2000–04, per cent

Source: Cunneen et al. (2006: 63)

whereby discretionary judgments in individual cases aggregate into serious patterns of over-representation (Morrison, 2009). Contacts between police and Māori and Pacific Island peoples indicate that disproportionality is evident from the point of initial contact with the criminal justice system. As Figure 7.4 indicates, in 2008, 221,806 apprehensions were made by New Zealand police – in 41.5 per cent of cases these involved Māori people and in 8.9 per cent Pacific Island people. On this basis, it appears that Māori, in particular, were considerably more likely to be apprehended by police than their presence in the overall residential population suggests: 14.9 per cent of the population (according to 2006 estimates) were Māori and 7.2 per cent were Pacific Islanders.

Once apprehended, Māori are more likely to be prosecuted than New Zealand Europeans (in 2005, 67 per cent compared to 61.6 per cent [Department of Corrections, 2007: 19]). Prosecution rates between Māori and New Zealand Europeans also varied considerably between offence types, however, which suggests that disproportionality is not uniform and needs to be related also to other factors, as the discussion towards the end of this chapter further demonstrates. Figure 7.5 shows that Māori accounted for 47.3 per cent of cases sentenced in 2008, compared to 35.6 per cent involving New Zealand Europeans. These proportions were almost reversed, however, in relation to drug offences, where New Zealand Europeans accounted for 53.3 per cent of cases sentenced and Māori 39.2 per cent. These differences suggest that a challenge for accounting for ethnic differences in criminal justice outcomes of various kinds is to establish

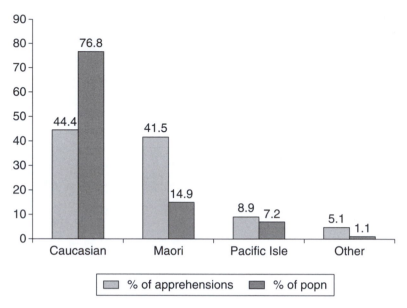

Figure 7.4   Apprehensions by New Zealand police, 2008, by ethnicity

Source: Statistics New Zealand (www.justice.govt.nz/)

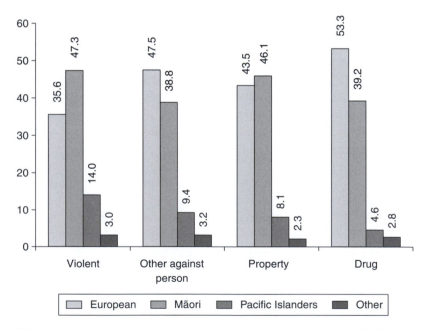

Figure 7.5   Cases sentenced, by crime type and ethnicity, New Zealand 2008, per cent

Source: Statistics New Zealand (www.justice.govt.nz/)

commensurate cases where the only significant point of difference relates to the ethnicity of the individuals involved. In terms of the above data, for example, it might be that the ethnic differences in terms of sentences imposed by the courts relate to patterns and characteristics of offending rather than ethnicity itself.

Moreover, one of the first statistical studies of disproportionality against Māori in the New Zealand criminal justice system suggested that harsher sentences in court might be related, in part, to other factors, including the denial of bail, and that Māori defendants were less likely to have legal representation (O'Malley, 1973). While these contextual factors have been held to account for tougher sentences imposed on minority groups in criminal justice systems in other countries, as was noted earlier, these cannot be held to deny that there is a 'race effect' at work, since they themselves tend to be highly correlated with ethnicity (Spohn, 2000; Morrison, 2009). For complex reasons, it is clear that the courts in New Zealand have tended to impose harsher sentences (i.e. custody) on Māori than on New Zealand European or Pacific Island offenders. As Figure 7.6 illustrates, 15 per cent of Māoris convicted received custodial sentences, compared to 9.4 and 9.3 per cent of New Zealand Europeans and Pacific Islanders respectively. Conversely, only slightly more than one-third (34.5 per cent) of Māori offenders were sentenced to a monetary penalty, whereas almost half of New Zealand European offenders were penalized in this way (49.5 per cent).

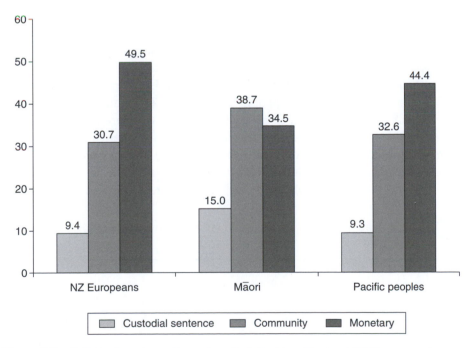

Figure 7.6   Selected sentence type, by ethnicity, New Zealand 2008, per cent

Source: Statistics New Zealand (www.justice.govt.nz/)

United States

By a considerable margin, the United States has the highest imprisonment rate in the world. Globally, more than half of all prisoners are in the USA, which had in 2007 an incarceration rate of 756 per 100,000 compared to a global mean of 158 per 100,000 (Walmsley, 2009). Table 7.6 shows that in 2008, 846,000 black males were in prison, constituting 40.2 per cent of the male prison population (West and Sobel, 2009). The US Census Bureau estimated that in the period 2006–08, the black population of the USA amounted to 12.3 per cent of the total, while the white population was 74.3 per cent. In these crude terms, then, black people are heavily over-represented in US jails.

Other ways of conceptualizing this disproportionality confirm this stark picture, such as Hogg et al.'s (2008) calculation that African American males can expect to spend on average 3.09 years in prison or jail over their lifetime compared to Hispanic and Caucasian males, who can spend on average 1.06 and 0.50 years, respectively. Similarly, other data reveals that a higher proportion of the black and Hispanic populations of the USA have been incarcerated at some point in their life. Table 7.7 indicates that 6.5 and 0.9 per cent respectively of males and females aged 35–44 years have been incarcerated at some time: among black males, however, the figure is more than three times greater at 22 per cent and for Hispanic males it is 10 per cent (Bonczar, 2003). A much higher proportion (8.5 per cent) of black males aged 18–24 had spent time in prison than had white males of any age cohort.

While incarceration rates in the USA might be higher for African American and Hispanic groups, it is less clear that police contacts are greater, although there appear to be some disparities in outcomes arising from those contacts. Table 7.8 shows that more white people than black or Hispanic had contact with the police in 2005: 20.2 per cent of whites had contact, compared to 16.5 and 15.8 per cent respectively for blacks and Hispanics. However, that category includes all contact (including, for example, reporting a crime) and so covers more than police-initiated encounters. Nevertheless, similar rates across all ethnic groups were stopped by the police while driving, which represented more than half of

Table 7.6　Estimated number of inmates held in prison[1], by gender, race, Hispanic origin, 30 June 2008

Male	White	33.9	712,500
	Black	40.2	846,000
	Hispanic	20.3	427,000
Female	White	45.5	94,500
	Black	32.6	67,800
	Hispanic	16.1	33,400

Source: Bureau of Justice Statistics (http://bjs.ojp.usdoj.gov/)

[1]State or federal prisons, or in local jails

Table 7.7   Per cent of adult population ever incarcerated in a state or federal prison by gender, race, Hispanic origin and age, 2001

	18–24	25–34	35–44	45–54	55–64	65 or older
Gender						
Male	2.7	6.0	6.5	5.3	4.0	3.1
Female	0.2	0.7	0.9	0.6	0.3	0.2
Race/Hispanic origin						
White	0.6	1.6	2.0	1.7	1.4	1.1
Male	1.1	2.8	3.5	3.1	2.5	2.0
Female	0.1	0.3	0.5	0.3	0.2	0.2
Black	4.4	10.9	12.1	9.5	6.7	5.9
Male	8.5	20.4	22.0	17.7	13.0	11.6
Female	0.4	2.1	2.8	1.9	1.1	0.9
Hispanic	2.2	5.1	5.8	5.2	3.6	2.2
Male	4.0	9.0	10.0	9.5	6.6	4.1
Female	0.3	0.8	1.1	0.9	0.6	0.3

Source: Bonczar (2003: 6)

Table 7.8   Police contact with US citizens, 2005, by ethnicity

	White	Black/African American	Hispanic/Latino
Per cent who had contact with police	20.2	16.5	15.8
Mean no. of times stopped	1.6	2.0	1.6
Per cent stopped while driving	8.9	8.1	8.9
Per cent of stopped drivers searched by police	3.6	9.5	8.8
Per cent of stopped drivers arrested	2.1	4.5	3.1
Per cent of stopped drivers no enforcement action	13.4	17.6	11.6
Per cent stopped who experienced force	1.2	4.4	2.3

Source: Durose et al. (2007: 2)

all contacts in overall terms. Disparities are apparent, though, in terms of subsequent outcomes: black and Hispanic drivers were much more likely to be searched following a stop than whites, who were also less likely to be arrested. However, black drivers were more likely to have no enforcement action taken as a result of being stopped: this might mean that they were stopped unnecessarily or that officers treated them with discretion. Black people stopped, in any circumstance, were more likely to experience force than were Hispanics, who in turn had a higher rate than did white people who had been stopped.

Explaining the Over-representation of Minorities in Criminal Justice Systems

This review of international data clearly indicates that minorities tend to be over-represented in criminal justice systems in broad terms and that disparities are apparent at each of the various decision-making stages and at each point at which police officers, prosecutors and court officials exercise their discretion. The discussion above has referred to a wide range of contextual factors that preclude any straightforward claim that this evidence demonstrates that the criminal justice system is racist, although it is equally apparent that any analysis of these patterns that excluded factors of racism, prejudice and discrimination would be highly unconvincing. As will be noted at the end of this section, evaluation of the extent to which these patterns are indicative of racism entails normative judgements about how racism is conceptualized and operationalized. Before that, three broad positions are outlined that might explain the trends and data presented above. First, it is possible that they reflect differences in patterns and extent of offending between ethnic groups. Second, it might be that decisions are made in relation to legitimate factors, but in ways that indirectly discriminate against minority communities. Third, the structural and institutional role of criminal justice systems might explain how marginalized groups are disproportionally regulated and controlled in ways that sustain more fundamental social inequalities.

Evidence relating to different levels of offending across ethnic groups was outlined and analyzed in Chapter Four, and will not be reprised here. Analysis of disparities in the criminal justice system might reflect, to some extent, different absolute rates of offending. If minority ethnic communities experience higher levels of social deprivation and marginalization in a range of ways, then this might explain their greater involvement in the criminal justice system. Demographic characteristics vary across ethnic groups, which might mean that a greater proportion of some groups are in the peak ages for offending and contact with the criminal justice system. Karmen's (1996, cited in Bowling, 1999: 536) analysis of gun homicide in New York City in the early 1990s, for example, showed that rates were highest in areas that experienced high levels of multiple deprivation, had low social mobility and a relatively high number of 16–19 year olds. These areas were also districts with large African American and Hispanic communities. Alternatively, patterns and types of offending might vary across ethnic groups. Minorities might not commit crime at a greater rate than white people, but they participate in criminal activities that are more likely to be the subject of police attention and treated more harshly in the court system. Along these lines, critics of the US 'war on drugs' drew attention to the ways in which harsher penalties for crack use impacted disproportionally on poor addicts, while users of cocaine, a more expensive drug, were treated relatively leniently. Mustard (2001: 288–289) noted:

Over 90 percent of those convicted of possessing 5 grams of crack cocaine, a felony offense that carries a 5-year minimum sentence, are black. This contrasts sharply with penalties for powdered cocaine users, who are predominantly white. Conviction for possessing 5 grams of powdered cocaine is a misdemeanor punishable by less than a year in jail.

Similarly, 'crimes of the street' are more likely to be committed by marginalized groups, including some minority ethnic communities, and are relatively strongly policed compared to corporate 'crimes of the suite' that are more likely to be committed by respectable higher-status individuals, who are more likely to belong to ethnic majority communities. Given these different trends and patterns, this perspective holds that the criminal justice system is a neutral broker and ethnic disparities are a reflection of processes and practices that are shaped outside its domain in broader society.

Another broad model recognizes that indirect discrimination might occur within the criminal justice system but suggests that this is a by-product of consideration of legitimate factors. Hood's (1992) study of the over-representation of black and Asian people among those convicted in courts in the West Midlands, for example, suggested that much of the disparity was related to 'legally relevant criteria', such as the employment status and prior record of offenders. Only a small proportion – around 5 per cent – of the over-representation apparent in some courts could be attributed, Hood found, to the 'race of the defendant effect'. Along similar lines, Snowball and Weatherburn (2007) found that the disproportional use of custody in New South Wales was related to the greater likelihood that Indigenous offenders: had received a prior suspended sentence or periodic detention; were more likely to have previously been imprisoned; were more likely to have been convicted of concurrent offences; were more likely to have a large number (8 +) of prior convictions; and were more likely to have been convicted primarily of a serious violent offence. In other words, judicial discrimination or prejudice does not explain longer custodial sentences imposed on Indigenous convicted offenders, but rather that such individuals are more likely to have characteristics that the judiciary ought legitimately to consider in sentencing decisions. This model does not deny that racial stereotyping can lead to discrimination, but only that not all disproportionality can be accounted for in this way.

Commentators have often referred to this model as a 'focal concerns' approach, which directs attention to key criteria that police, prosecutors and judges legitimately consider but against which minorities do worse than other groups. Frieburger et al. (2010: 84), for example, found that African American defendants in Philadelphia were more likely to be kept in pre-trial detention because of 'judges' perceptions of black defendants as being more dangerous, blameworthy, and better able to serve time incarcerated'. The dangerousness of a suspect is a legitimate criterion for consideration, notwithstanding that the stereotyping that can influence judgement undermines claims to a rational scientific basis for risk management (Steen et al., 2005). Other research has also found that minorities are less likely to be given bail or released on home detention because their living conditions are less likely to meet legitimate criteria in terms of security and related concerns. Similarly, studies have found that minorities are less able to provide financial sureties to secure bail, and that their relatively poor employment status also makes it less likely they will be released ahead of trial (Free, 2002, and Cole et al., 1995, cited in Morrison, 2009). For a range of interrelated reasons, Bowling and Phillips (2002: 170) noted that 'a consequence of social inequality is that African/Caribbeans suffer discrimination where homelessness, unemployment and disrupted families ... influence "legally neutral" decisions'. These findings are particularly troubling since minorities detained in custody ahead of trial are less likely subsequently to be given a custodial sentence than their white counterparts (Morrison, 2009). Hood (1992) noted that being remanded in custody makes it difficult for defendants to sustain employment and housing, hard to prepare a defence with a solicitor, and more difficult to present a smart appearance when appearing in court. Just as the over-representation of minorities in stop and search data, discussed earlier in the chapter, is related to the availability of different groups for contact with the police, apparently relevant criteria have disproportionate impacts. Decision-making in the criminal justice system draws upon authoritative knowledge about crime and risk management that are not articulated in terms of race and ethnicity but, when operationalized, have disproportionate impacts upon minority ethnic communities that are already socially, economically and politically marginalized.

The context of the structural marginalization of minority ethnic communities is the focus of analysis for theorists who explain patterns of over-representation in terms of the broader role of the criminal justice system in producing and reproducing social relations. Keith (1993) argued that the criminalization of the black community in Britain in the 1980s was inextricably bound up in the process of racialization related to social, economic and political projects associated with Thatcherism and the New Right (see also Gilroy, 1987). From this perspective, Keith argued that the role of the criminal justice system had moved from one of punishing offenders to a broader project of disciplining whole populations. This focus on criminalization and ethnicity extends to explanations of the status of Asian and Muslim populations in Britain and other Western societies in the context of terrorism and securitization, as is discussed at greater length in Chapter Nine (Spalek and Lambert, 2008).

This focus upon the broad context and dynamics of crime and justice is shared by Christie (2000), Garland (2001), Simon (2007) and Wacquant (2001, 2009), who have argued that the huge growth in the use of imprisonment, disproportionally incarcerating large numbers of black people, needs to be explained in terms of a wider process of social control. Christie (2000) noted that African Americans had once been subject to mechanisms of social control based around slavery, had then become segregated in ghettoes, but were increasingly subjects of the criminal justice system. Since conviction means the denial of the franchise in many US states, disparities in imprisonment rates across ethnic groups have significant consequences in terms of civil participation. Contemporary imprisonment rates means that 30 per cent of black men will lose the right to vote at some point in their lives, and in states where conviction means the permanent denial of the franchise as much as 40 per cent will be excluded from the political process (Christie, 2000: 97). Along similar lines, Garland (2001) maintained that the criminal justice system has expanded in Western societies in recent decades as a mechanism to control 'problem' communities, including many minority ethnic groups that are no longer incorporated into society through mass employment and related welfare systems. In Australia, Blagg (2008) argued that over-representation is particularly pronounced in circumstances where the 'domain' of Aboriginal culture and society comes into close proximity with dominant white Australia. Similarly, Broadhurst (1999) and Hogg (2001) emphasized the role of law and criminal justice agencies in the historical and contemporary process of colonialism and subjugating troublesome subject communities. Wacquant (2001: 95) noted that his conceptualization of criminal justice systems requires thinking beyond the penological functions of the criminal justice system to consider it as 'an instrument for the management of dispossessed and dishonoured groups'. While such perspectives provide a compelling conceptualization of recent expansion of punitive crime control that have had a disproportionate impact upon minority ethnic groups, they have been criticized on a number of grounds, including that they find it difficult, for example, to account for counter-trends such as examples of declining imprisonment rates (Pratt, 2008).

SUMMARY

The over-representation of minority ethnic groups in criminal justice systems is linked in complex ways to wider problems of social inclusion and marginalization, and to historical patterns of migration, colonialism and racism. While demonstrating that minority ethnic groups are over-represented in criminal justice systems is relatively straightforward, identifying the causes and explaining the dynamics of these patterns continues to be among the most controversial challenges facing criminology.

In the UK, the consolidation of detailed statistical evidence since the mid-1990s means that earlier debates about the 'facts' of over-representation have been resolved: no uncertainty remains, for example, that black people – especially young males – are stopped and searched at rates disproportionate to their presence in the population as a whole. Clearly though, other points of considerable

(Continued)

(Continued)

contention persist, and improved monitoring has not resolved fundamental debates and concerns about the position of minorities within the CJS. Using the examples of Australia, New Zealand and the United States, it has been shown that disproportionality persists in various ways across many societies.

A wide range of contextual factors precludes any straightforward claim that the criminal justice system is racist, although it is equally apparent that any analysis that excluded factors of racism, prejudice and discrimination would be highly unconvincing. Three broad positions might explain the over-representation of minorities in the CJS. First, differences in patterns and extent of offending between ethnic groups. Second, it might be that decisions are made in relation to legally relevant criteria, but in ways that indirectly discriminate against minority communities. Third, the structural and institutional role of criminal justice systems might explain how marginalized groups are disproportionally regulated and controlled in ways that sustain more fundamental social inequalities.

STUDY QUESTIONS

1 What are the key differences in measuring stop and search in terms of 'resident' and 'available' populations? What are the strengths and weaknesses of each approach?

2 Compare and contrast patterns of over-representation found in the UK, Australasia and the USA.

3 Why might 'legally relevant criteria' that impact on disproportionality in sentencing practices still indicate a 'race effect'?

FURTHER READING

Extensive statistical information relating to disproportionality within criminal justice can be found at the Ministry of Justice website, www.justice.gov.uk/publications/statistics-and-data/criminal-justice/race.htm. A useful overview and analysis of the position of young black people can be found at www.publications.parliament.uk/pa/cm200607/cmselect/cmhaff/181/18102.htm. Comparative data for the USA can be found at the Bureau of Justice Statistics (http://bjs.ojp.usdoj.gov/), at the Australian Institute of Criminology (www.aic.gov.au/en.aspx), and at the New Zealand Ministry of Justice (www.justice.govt.nz/). Smith's chapter (1994) in the first edition of *The Oxford Handbook of Criminology* provides a clear conceptual framework for understanding disproportionality. Hood (1992, Clarendon Press) is a classic account of disproportionality in the court system, and Bowling and Philips's (2007) article provides a strong analysis of the over-representation of minorities in police stop and search practices.

8

Diversity and Representation in the Criminal Justice System

OVERVIEW

This chapter will:

- outline the 'normative whiteness' of criminal justice systems in many jurisdictions, closely associated with the under-representation of minority ethnic groups in the workforce, which has been widely associated with disproportionality;
- outline and explain trends and patterns relating to the representation of minority ethnic communities as staff in agencies of the criminal justice system;
- explore efforts over recent years to recruit a more representative workforce and to promote diversity in wider terms;
- critically assess the contribution and limitations that these initiatives might deliver in terms of institutional performance.

KEY TERMS

- Career progression
- Diversity
- Legitimacy
- Normative whiteness

- Organizational culture
- Recruitment
- Staff associations

Introduction

The over-representation of some minority ethnic groups in the criminal justice system highlighted in the previous chapter has been widely attributed, in part, to a lack of ethnic diversity among staff across most criminal justice agencies. There are a number of reasons why improving the representations of minority ethnic groups among criminal justice personnel might be advantageous, and these are outlined in the final section of this chapter. Key among these has been a perceived benefit in terms of the exercise of discretion, which forms an important element of criminal justice decision-making at many points of the system. It was noted towards the end of Chapter Seven that one set of reasons for the over-representation of minorities relates to the exercise of bias in discretionary decision-making that has negative consequences for minority ethnic individuals. This bias can either take the form of conscious or unconscious racism and prejudice that might hold some minorities to be a greater criminal threat than other groups. Consistent with this model was the finding of Frieburger et al. (2010) that white judges in the USA were more likely to perceive

African American defendants as dangerous and blameworthy, and that this partly accounted for their greater representation in pre-trial custody. Alternatively, it might be that police officers, magistrates or parole boards fail to understand diverse cultural norms and values and that it is this that leads to illegitimate differences in outcomes. In the context of police stop and search, for example, it has been found that police officers misread the body language and manner of black people in ways that constitute them as disrespectful or suspicious so that they are more likely than other groups to be arrested (Mooney and Young, 2000). This model can be understood in terms of 'normative whiteness' in that the behaviour, motivations and characteristics of diverse communities are not recognized in the criminal justice system.

In an effort to address these problems criminal justice agencies have, as is indicated in more detail below, embarked upon a range of strategies designed to more effectively meet the needs of a diverse society. Much of the focus has been upon recruiting greater numbers of staff from a minority ethnic background so that the profile of agencies comes to more closely represent that of society at large. Other measures have sought to complement greater recruitment through developing diversity within organizations by establishing staff associations and support networks, community engagement projects and a broad range of training programmes intended to enhance understanding of diverse cultures and ethnicities. The discussion that follows reviews many of these developments before considering at greater length the various reasons why diversity and representation in the criminal justice system have become such significant issues. In conclusion, the chapter identifies critical conceptual and practical pitfalls that remain to be addressed.

Recruitment, Retention and Promotion

Data collected by the Ministry of Justice indicate that minority ethnic populations are represented to varied extents across the various agencies of the criminal justice system. Collectively, minority ethnic groups were estimated to form 11 per cent of the total population of England and Wales in 2007. In stark terms, Table 8.1 shows that minority ethnic people were under-represented as police officers, special constables, in the National Offender Management Service (NOMS), and as magistrates. Only among police Community Support Officers (CSOs) and the staff of the Crown Prosecution Service (CPS) were minority ethnic communities represented at rates consistent with their presence in the overall population. The extent to which ethnic monitoring is conducted across the criminal justice system, however, is clearly inconsistent – despite

Table 8.1   Ethnicity of criminal justice staff, 2009

	White	Minority ethnic	Not stated
Police officers	94.3	4.4	1.3
Special constables	88.6	9.6	1.8
Community Support Officers	88.0	11.5	1.1
Crown Prosecution Service staff	65.7	11.6	22.7
National Offender Management Service	85.7	5.7	8.6
Magistrates	92.4	7.6	0.0

Source: Ministry of Justice (2010)

being a statutory responsibility – with almost a quarter of CPS staff and 8.6 per cent of NOMS staff returned as ethnicity 'not stated'.

This general pattern of under-representation becomes more complex when considered in further detail, and the discussion that follows will examine ethnic representation in a more finely grained way in relation to the police service, the CPS, among magistrates and judges, and the National Offender Management Service. Each agency is considered in terms of recruitment trends over time, differences between various ranks and grades (which relate to promotion prospects) and, where available, information relating to rates at which staff from different ethnic groups leave the criminal justice system.

The Police Service

Of all the component agencies of the criminal justice system, the police service has experienced the most sustained pressure to recruit a workforce that is more diverse in terms of ethnicity. This pre-eminence might be due to the relatively high visibility of the police and their pivotal role as gatekeepers to the criminal justice system and that individually and collectively police exercise discretionary powers over fellow citizens that are particularly stark. A litany of enquiries, reports and policy statements has developed over recent decades to recommend that police services must increase the number of minority ethnic officers. The 1999 Macpherson Report, following the public inquiry into the racist murder of Stephen Lawrence in London in 1993, included three recommendations relating to the recruitment and retention of minority ethnic police officers. That report led to the establishment of detailed targets for each police service, based on the proportion of the local population in each service area that is of a minority ethnic background, and so established a specific framework of action not always stipulated by other analysts. However, the need to develop more effective recruitment had been iterated many times. In the mid-1990s two reports, one produced by the Commission for Racial Equality (CRE) (1996) and one by

Her Majesty's Inspectorate of Constabulary (HMIC) (1996), urged that steps be taken to ensure that the ethnic diversity of British society was more closely reflected within the police service. Both of these studies noted that demands to improve equal opportunities had been made in earlier documents produced by powerful police bodies. The CRE report, for example, pointed out that a 1990 policy document issued by the Association of Chief Police Officers (ACPO), *Setting the Standards for Policing: Meeting Community Expectations*, had argued that 'forces should strive to improve equal opportunities within the organisation'. It also referred to a 1992 HMIC report, *Equal Opportunities in the Police Service*, and one from the late 1980s, *Employment in Police Forces: A Survey of Equal Opportunities* (CRE, 1996). Additionally, the CRE report noted that the 1981 Scarman Inquiry had emphasized that 'a police force which fails to reflect the ethnic diversity of our society will never succeed in securing the full support of all its sections' (Scarman, 1981: 5.12).

Turning to the Scarman Report itself, it too noted that the under-representation of black and Asian people within the police had been a fairly long-standing matter of concern and that various attempts to rectify the problem had been made since the mid-1970s. Scarman (1981: 5.6) pointed out that while the service had made efforts to recruit minority officers, there was clearly some reluctance among the black community to seek careers within the police service. The precise findings and recommendations of these various reports will be explored below, but the apparent intractability of the issue is worth noting at this stage. Report upon report (and those mentioned above are but a few of the total) have apparently expressed concern and dismay at the situation, suggested broadly similar solutions, and then joined the litany of documents to be cited in subsequent investigations. It is not being suggested that the police service has done nothing to address the problems so frequently identified, and some details of the measures taken are included below. However, despite decades of recruitment drives and associated activity, the number of minority ethnic police officers remains low, as Table 8.1 indicates. The 2009 figure of 4.4 per cent of officers of a minority ethnic group represents more than twice the proportion of a decade earlier (in 1999, 2 per cent of police officers were of a minority ethnic background), although the police continue to lag behind the other agencies included in the table. Moreover, the minorities are further under-represented amid the higher ranks of the police service. The nature of police careers and the structure of the promotion system clearly mean that how officers progress up the rank hierarchy develops over time, which might mean that relatively recent increases in recruitment have yet to lead to improved representation in middle and senior positions. Table 8.2 indicates the representation of minorities across the rank structure and shows that progress has been made at senior levels: Association of Chief Police Officer ranked officers (including Chief Constables, their Deputies and Assistants, and Commissioners in the Metropolitan Police), for example, were 100 per cent

Table 8.2   Ethnicity by rank in the police service, 1999 and 2009

Rank	White		Asian		Black		Chinese or other		Mixed[1]	Not stated	
	2009	1999	2009	1999	2009	1999	2009	1999	2009	2009	1999
ACPO	93	100	2	0	0	0	0	0	1	4	0
(Chief) Superintendent	96	99.5	1	0.1	1	0.3	0	0.1	1	1	0
(Chief) Inspector	96	99.1	1	0.3	1	0.4	0	0.3	1	1	0
Sergeant	96	98.6	1	0.5	1	0.6	0	0.3	1	1	0
Constable	94	97.8	2	0.7	1	0.9	1	0.5	1	1	0

Source: Home Office (1999) and Ministry of Justice (2010)

[1]The category 'mixed' was not used in presentation of the 1999 data.

white in 1999 and now have 7 per cent of minority or 'mixed' background. Indeed, a clear contrast across the decade is that the most diverse group in 2009 were the ACPO ranks, which had been the least diverse in 1999.

It might be that the future representation of minorities becomes more aligned to that of the general population as a higher proportion of new entrants to the police service are of a minority ethnic background compared to the overall profile of the 43 English and Welsh forces. Seven per cent of 'joiners' to the service in 2008/09 were of a minority ethnic group, a higher rate than across the service as a whole (4.4 per cent) (Ministry of Justice, 2010). Moreover, only 3 per cent of leavers are of a minority background, which might be explained in part by their younger age profile as a cohort that has joined recently relative to other groups.

The Crown Prosecution Service (CPS)

As in the context of policing, the CPS has had an agenda to develop a more diverse workforce for some years, driven partly through a series of employment tribunals and legal challenges as well as pressure from the Commission for Racial Equality (Taylor, 2009). In the wake of these developments, the CPS established an independent inquiry into employment practices – the Denman Inquiry. Denman found that minority ethnic people were under-represented in the CPS, particularly at more senior grades, and that management practices were weak and complacent, and lacked strategic direction (CPS, 2001, cited in Taylor, 2009). In 1999, 8.8 per cent of CPS staff was of a minority ethnic group, a figure much higher than the comparable rate for the police service – even in

Table 8.3   Crown Prosecution Service by ethnicity and grade, per cent, 2008/09

	White	Mixed	Asian	Black	Chinese or other	Not stated	Total (N)
SCS	63.8	0.0	5.0	2.5	5.0	23.8	80
G6/G7	64.9	1.6	4.4	3.3	1.3	24.5	3,197
EO/HEO/SEO	67.4	1.3	4.3	4.7	0.9	21.4	2,994
AA/AO	64.9	1.2	6.3	4.7	0.9	22.0	2,663
Total	65.7	1.4	5.0	4.2	1.1	22.7	8,934

Source: Ministry of Justice (2010)

SCS = Senior Civil Service; G6/G7 = Grade 6/Grade 7; EO = Executive Officer, HEO = Higher Executive Officer, SEO = Senior Executive Officer; AA = Administrative Assistant, AO = Administrative Officer

2009. However, at the most senior grade this proportion was much lower, at only 1.9 per cent for senior administrators and 1.8 per cent for senior lawyers. A decade later these figures had changed significantly, as Table 8.3 indicates.

Unlike some other criminal justice agencies, the CPS has a relatively high proportion of minority ethnic staff at a senior level: 12.5 per cent of the 'senior civil servant' grade was Asian, black, Chinese or 'other' in 2008/09. However, also in contrast to some agencies, such as police services, was the relatively high percentage at all levels for whom ethnicity was not stated. Clearly there is still some problem with the coverage of ethnic monitoring in the CPS. As with the police service, minority ethnic staff formed a greater proportion of staff entering than leaving the CPS in 2009/10 (CPS, 2010b). More than 500 new appointments were made in 2009/10, of which 16.3 per cent were of a Black or Minority Ethnic (BME) background, 80.9 per cent were white and the ethnicity of 2.8 per cent were not known. Some 721 staff left during the period, 12.5 per cent were BME, 70.6 per cent white, and ethnicity was not known for the further 16.9 per cent.

The Magistracy and Judiciary

The under-representation of minority ethnic groups and women has been noted in a series of reports and inquiries dating back to at least the 1980s, and in 1992 the Lord Chief Justice stated that imbalances would be addressed within a few years (Advisory Panel on Judicial Diversity, 2010). As in other areas, a raft of innovations and initiatives sought to develop a judiciary and magistracy that more closely reflects the wider population. However, the structure of the judiciary is in marked contrast to some agencies within the system inasmuch as individuals are appointed to the bench from other careers.

Since the 'pools' of staff working in those fields are not ethnically diverse, then neither will be judicial appointments. Similarly, magistrates have been selected from sections of society that have not been as ethnically diverse as the population as a whole. Malleson (2009) has pointed out that a 'trickle up' orthodoxy prevailed for many decades such that it was (complacently, she argued) assumed that as diversity improved within the legal profession the majority white and male character of the judiciary would change over time. Barmes and Malleson (2011: 246) characterized the 'gate-keeping' role of the legal profession in the following terms:

> the legal profession, in practice, polices accessibility to the different sections of the judiciary, including its highest echelons. The effect is that the judiciary, and especially the senior judiciary, reflects the systematic disadvantage and marginalisation in the legal profession of certain identity groups; notably but not exclusively, women and members of ethnic minorities.

Focusing on the 'feeder' legal professions as a means of enhancing the diversity of the judiciary and among magistrates is clearly important, although it is clear that the apparent increasing diversity among solicitors and barristers has not yet translated into greater diversity on the bench (Barmes and Malleson, 2011). Table 8.4 indicates that 4.5 per cent of judges were of a minority ethnic background and, as with the police but not the CPS, this proportion is much lower among higher positions. In overall terms the proportion had increased three-fold since 1999. Recorders constitute the highest group in numerical terms (ethnic data was available for 947 of the 1,235 people in that post), of which, as the table indicates, 6 per cent were of a minority ethnic background in 2009. Furthermore, 8 per cent of magistrates were of a minority ethnic background in 2009, compared to 4.5 per cent a decade earlier (Home Office, 1999; Ministry of Justice, 2010).

Table 8.4   Percentage of judiciary of minority ethnic background, 1999 and 2009

	Minority ethnic in post, 2009, per cent	Minority ethnic in post, 1999, per cent
Lord of Appeal in Ordinary/Heads of Division/Lord Justice of Appeal	0.0	0.0
High Court Judge	3.5	0.0
Circuit Judge	2.5	0.1
Recorder	6.0	2.0
Judge Advocates	0.0	n/a
Deputy Judge Advocates	11.1	n/a
District Judge/Deputy District Judge	4.7	1.4
Totals	4.5	1.5

Source: Home Office (1999) and Ministry of Justice (2010)

The National Offender Management Service and the Probation Service

In contrast to other agencies within the criminal justice system, problems of racism within prisons remained largely under-researched until the racist murder of Zahid Mubarek at Feltham Young Offenders Institution in 2000 (Bhui, 2009). Concern that prison staff had failed to protect Mubarek from his cellmate, who committed the murder and had expressed violent racist intentions and had a history of mental illness, prompted a series of inquiries into racism within the prison service. Although Morgan (2006) noted that diversity within the probation service had developed slowly through the 1980s and 1990s, the number of minority ethnic staff had increased more rapidly in the first years of the twenty-first century. Lewis (2009) argued that these improvements could be attributed to strong leadership, accountability and improved monitoring, but that momentum relating to diversity waned in the wake of institutional reorganization.

The National Offender Management Service comprises the prison and probation services. Table 8.5 indicates that the percentage of minorities at senior ranks in the prison service is lower than among officers, administrative and 'other' grades. Overall, 5.7 per cent of NOMS staff was of a minority ethnic background. Data relating to the probation service indicate that, in 2008, 13.4 per cent was of a minority ethnic background. In respect to NOMS and the probation service, the 2008 and 2009 data show increases since 1999 when 8.7 per cent of the National Probation Service was of a minority ethnic background, as were 2.6 per cent of prison officers and 0.8 per cent of prison governors (Home Office, 1999).

In 2009/10, 9 per cent of staff joining NOMS was of a minority ethnic background, a figure rising to 20 per cent of those joining at management grade

Table 8.5   Percentage of National Offender Management Service (NOMS) staff of minority ethnic background, 2009

| | Self-declared ethnicity | | | | | | |
	White	Mixed	Asian	Black	Chinese or other	Not stated	Total
Senior civil servant	67.5	1.3	0.0	1.3	0.0	29.9	77
Senior managers	71.7	1.2	0.9	1.1	0.9	24.3	929
Managers	83.6	1.2	2.0	2.3	0.9	10.0	3,721
Officers	88.2	1.0	1.0	2.1	0.7	6.8	26,266
Administrative	81.2	0.8	2.7	2.9	0.5	11.9	7,134
Other grades	84.7	0.9	1.8	3.2	0.8	8.6	14,829
Total	85.7	1.0	1.5	2.5	0.7	8.6	52,956

Source: Ministry of Justice (2010)

positions. Gender differences were apparent in relation to new entrants as female minority ethnic staff were almost twice as likely as their male counterparts to join at management positions; the largest proportion (28 per cent) of male minority ethnic entrants was prison officers (NOMS, 2011). Minority ethnic staff left the NOMS at a slightly higher rate than their white colleagues (6.3 per cent and 5.2 per cent respectively), a gap that has apparently narrowed in recent years (NOMS, 2011).

Enhancing Diversity within the Criminal Justice System

As discussed, collectively and individually the agencies of the criminal justice system have been under pressure to develop a more diverse workforce for many years. Not all of the diversity agenda has related to ethnicity, and in the last decade or so recognition has increased that other groups are also marginalized. Some of the strategies developed to recruit more minority ethnic staff have been applied to other under-represented groups in an effort to enhance diversity in generic terms. Developments in terms of the ethnic representation of staff, then, cannot be considered separately from the broader diversity agenda and some of the strategies outlined below have been devised in terms of a wider remit that includes recognition of gender, age, sexuality, disability and other factors. Moreover, developments within criminal justice have been located in the context of concurrent concerns across much of the public sector, much of which can be traced back to New Labour's post-Macpherson agenda to promote 'race equality' through a raft of policy and legislative initiatives (Back et al., 2002). While some of these initiatives originated in response to problems identified within the police service, not all of the developments outlined below can be applied to all agencies of the criminal justice system. There are specific organizational factors that make discussion of measures to enhance diversity in the criminal justice system in general terms difficult. The police service, for example, recruits all officers into the junior rank of constable while judges and magistrates tend to be appointed on the basis of prior experience in the legal professions. Notwithstanding the particularities of each agency, though, certain general features emerge across criminal justice efforts to recruit and maintain a more ethnically diverse staff.

A range of barriers to the recruitment of minority ethnic staff have been identified. Some relate to the career choices and paths preferred by minority ethnic individuals. Stone and Tuffin (2000) found that minorities were dissuaded from pursuing careers in the police service because they perceived that they would encounter racism from colleagues, isolation from their families and communities, and would face poor promotion prospects. These (real and perceived) problems are compounded in relation to the police service since, by tradition, recruitment often has been through personal and familial contacts with others already in the service. If minorities do not have friends and relations employed as police officers, then it would be less likely that they would opt for such a career themselves. One perceived advantage of introducing the Community Support Officer (CSO) role from 2001 was that this might provide a vehicle for non-traditional entrants to gain exposure and experience of policing without a full commitment to a lengthy training programme (Johnston, 2006). As was shown in Table 8.1, there are almost three times the percentage of minority ethnic staff employed as CSOs compared to police officers.

Similar pre-application concerns have been identified in relation to the judiciary in terms of the tendency for those in the legal profession to be recruited through an informal 'tap-on-the-shoulder' process, whereby existing staff approached others thought likely to make good candidates (Advisory Panel on Judicial Diversity, 2010). A strong criticism of these informal selection processes is that they tend to reproduce existing staffing patterns and fail to attract the strongest candidates from overlooked non-traditional backgrounds. Efforts to tackle such barriers have focused upon a range of 'outreach' strategies by criminal justice agencies seeking to increase their exposure among minority ethnic groups who might be encouraged to apply for employment. Targeted recruitment drives and advertising campaigns in minority ethnic media, for example, have been developed by many agencies. Pre-application mentoring has been introduced for minority ethnic police applicants in some countries. Such processes are intended to give applicants from under-represented groups advice and support to develop strong applications and can be seen as efforts towards positive action rather than the positive discrimination that might be associated with quota systems (Mossman et al., 2008).

Problematic criteria have been identified in formal regulations and rules concerning employment opportunities, for example language and physical requirements that may indirectly discriminate against minority ethnic communities and may have little relevance in terms of competencies necessary for the performance of particular roles. Procedures and processes of application and selection may also discriminate against minority ethnic candidates. Alfred (1992, cited in Bowling and Phillips, 2002) found that minority ethnic staff interviewed for posts in the prison service were asked questions relating to responses to racism from colleagues and that responses considered inappropriate were among criteria for rejecting applications. Similar questions were not asked of white applicants. In response to identified problems, some police services have revised uniform requirements so that Sikh officers can wear turbans and female Muslims can wear hijabs as part of their formal uniform (Holdaway and O'Neill, 2007). Additionally, police training schools have become more accommodating in terms of dietary and religious requirements of minority ethnic (and other) recruits (Rowe, 2004).

Beyond the process of initial recruitment, criminal justice agencies have developed strategies intended to promote the value of diversity, address institutional racism, and enhance the promotion and retention of minority ethnic staff. Staff associations have developed in police, probation and prison services to support minority ethnic staff and to represent their interests. An early example of these is the Black Police Association (BPA) that emerged in the mid-1990s, initially in the Metropolitan Police Service, from informal social networks of minority ethnic officers who had met to discuss their individual and collective experiences. In a period when concern was growing about the high rate at which minority ethnic officers left the police service, and a number of prominent legal cases alleging racial discrimination had been brought against various forces, the BPA became increasingly prominent throughout the 1990s (Holdaway, 1996; Holdaway and O'Neill, 2007). The BPA was given additional impetus, and enhanced status, by the Macpherson Report into the racist murder of Stephen Lawrence, which recommended that all police services ought to establish branches of the association. Coupled with New Labour's managerialist approach to the police service, the Macpherson Report also prompted the establishment of the National Black Police Association with Home Office sponsorship and incorporation into the police reform and policy-making agenda.

Similar staff associations developed in other agencies of the criminal justice system. In the 1980s, the Association of Black Probation Officers and the National Association of Asian Probation Staff were formed, both with the intention of promoting the interests of minority ethnic staff and forging better relations with wider communities. Similarly, in 2001, the RESPECT association was formed to promote the interests of minority ethnic staff in the Prison Service (Bhui, 2009). Vanstone (2006) argued that the probation associations, and the National Association of Probation Officers, were effective in promoting issues relating to diversity in terms of policy and management initiatives. However, it has also been found that official commitments have not always been translated into practice on the ground and that minority ethnic staff have reported a lack of support from managers in terms of participating in network activities (Morgan, 2006). Perhaps more problematic is the recent transformation of the probation service away from a humanistic approach to rehabilitation towards a role focused on the supervision and management of offenders, a shift that might endanger the services' ingrained commitment to liberal values of anti-racism. Bhui (2006: 179) argued that staff association efforts to promote diversity could not withstand the reshaping of the core purpose of the probation service: 'the focus on race equality diminished as attention was focused more on cost-efficient services, and a discourse dominated by risk, while developing complacency about race issues in probation was left unchecked'. While managerialist reform might have promoted the activities on minority ethnic staff associations in the police service, they have eroded the 'diversity agenda' within probation. This serves as a reminder that the internal development of diversity and representation in criminal justice agencies occurs against particular political contexts and cannot be assumed to follow a progressive path, or to move in the same direction across agencies. Moreover, as Heer and Atherton's (2008) study of Asian staff in the probation service found, attitudes towards diversity in the workplace are also shaped by broader developments, such as an Islamaphobic discourse that casts Asian people as terrorist sympathizers.

In addition to reconfiguring personnel profiles by recruiting, retaining and promoting minority ethnic staff, criminal justice agencies have developed extensive diversity and 'race relations' training programmes for new and continuing staff. The focus of these programmes has varied considerably over time and between agencies, but has ranged from the promotion of equal opportunities, the nature and impact of institutional racism, community engagement and 'cultural competency', whereby staff are introduced to historical, social, religious and other cultural aspects of minority ethnic communities. Tamkin et al. (2003) highlighted the importance of clarity in terms of the aims and objectives of training programmes and, in particular, whether they are intended to challenge or change the attitudes or the behaviour of participants. Rowe (2004) noted, in the context of police training, that different approaches in this respect reflect different assumptions about the nature and impact of racism among staff. One training strategy has been to persuade staff of the importance of recognizing and valuing cultural diversity, and the concomitant need to confront racism. This can be characterized as a 'hearts and minds' strategy. An alternative approach, sometimes favoured in the police service, has been that which seeks to change the behaviour of staff in terms of the language that they use, the manner in which they interact with different groups, the processes and procedures that they follow, and to encourage them to report inappropriate or unethical behaviour among colleagues. This can be characterized as a professional practice strategy.

There has been considerable impetus to develop and deliver diversity training in criminal justice, engendered by recommendations from the Macpherson Report (Macpherson, 1999) and the inquiry into the murder of Zahid Mubarek (Keith, 2006). As a result of these pressures, agencies of the criminal justice system have expended significant resources on diversity training. The Metropolitan Police, for example, trained 35,000 people between 1999 and 2002 at a total cost of more than £14 million (Rowe and Garland, 2007: 45). The impact of these programmes is difficult to assess, in part because systematic evaluation has not always been conducted (Rowe and Garland, 2007; Heer and Atherton, 2008). Concerns have been identified in relation to the extent to which the impact of training has been short-lived and that programmes have faced budgetary problems affecting training more generally, and a misplaced sense that training detracts from frontline service delivery (Bhui, 2009). It is also contradictory that diversity training programmes introduced as a response to identified problems of institutional racism in the criminal justice system have often been focused upon affecting the attitudes and behaviour of individual staff (Rowe, 2004).

Promoting the Diversity Agenda

As the previous discussion illustrates, it is very apparent that the principle of developing greater ethnic diversity has been widely endorsed and has led to considerable policy effort to improve the recruitment, retention and promotion of minorities. Amidst all of these developments, the reasons for encouraging greater diversity and the outcomes that might be accrued in terms of organizational performance have often not been articulated. The advantages of enhancing diversity have often remained implicit, but coalesce into three main areas: a moral case related to the legitimacy of the criminal justice system, a business case with internal and external impact, and a regulatory case in response to legal and governance pressures. These may be complementary reasons to promote diversity and there may be overlap between them. Articulating the potential benefits of the various and extensive schemes outlined above, which represent only a fraction of what has been done in practice, is important since it is not possible to assess the overall impact that they may have without a sense of the fundamental purposes and prospects of diversity.

The Moral Case

In a framework of social democracy it is widely held that public institutions need to be broadly reflective of the population. That the police service has been a bastion of white male employment for most of its modern history has belied the canonical principle of policing discourse in Britain, and many other countries, that the police service ought to reflect the policed. If the 'people are the police' and the 'police are the people', then it becomes a matter of legitimacy to strive towards ensuring that the profile of staff more closely represents society. This principle underpins Lord Scarman's argument, cited earlier, that the police service cannot secure the support of the public unless it is seen to represent them. In an era in which the politics of identity and debates about multiculturalism have become increasingly salient, diversity matters in terms of securing legitimacy. This perspective was articulated in a 1994 report published by the Council of Europe, which referred to the police in particular and other agencies more widely:

> Europe is now becoming multiracial and multicultural ... the composition of police forces (like that of every public administration) should normally be representative of the community it serves. This diversification of recruitment will establish a more trusting climate between the police and the different population groups. (Council of Europe, 1994: 16)

While morality and institutional legitimacy are important considerations across the public sector – and beyond – they are particularly important in relation to criminal justice agencies that have particular powers to curtail the rights of citizens through the use of force. Prenzler (2009: 22) argued that while criminal justice agencies are subject to ethical frameworks that apply more broadly across the public and private sectors:

> it could be argued that public service ethics are most imperative in [the criminal justice] component of government. Most government departments require people to act in certain ways, but often the processes are persuasive or coercive. In criminal justice there is much greater reliance on direct force. Criminal laws and related legislation authorise government agents to deprive people of their liberty to subject them to trial and punishment, and forcibly punish or coercively treat them. ... Some systems even authorise the execution of offenders.

Given the stark powers of the criminal justice system, legitimacy through ethical practice is particularly important. Just as other forms of ethical misconduct, such as corruption and deviance, are often regarded as more grievous when committed by police officers or judges, so too racist and discriminatory practice in terms of personnel management are understood as moral priorities. Along these lines, the Crown Prosecution Service links the promotion of inequality to maintaining public legitimacy and ensuring better organizational performance, the 'business case' outlined in the following section:

> Crime affects all communities, as does our work. We must have the public's trust and be seen by all communities as their prosecution service. We must act fairly at all times in the interests of justice. To be trusted to make fair prosecution decisions, we realise that our workforce needs to reflect the population we serve and we must treat all employees with respect. For us, treating people fairly in the workplace is firmly linked to providing a fair prosecution service. (CPS, 2010a: 4)

The Business Case

Perhaps in an effort to couch the promotion of diversity in terms that do not invite scepticism relating to 'political correctness', some policy statements emphasize that the development of workforce diversity will allow criminal justice agencies to perform more strongly in terms of their core functions. The business case for diversity addresses internal and external capabilities of agencies. The internal aspect relates to the need that organizations have to recruit and retain the most able staff in terms of key competencies and the need to ensure that advertising and recruitment drives attract the strongest people from sectors of society that have traditionally been overlooked. The Deputy Commissioner of the Metropolitan Police argued that, in an era when officer recruitment was increasing, ensuring that prospective staff were attracted from across the whole population was vital:

> ... for the most basic of business reasons. The future survival of this organisation ... which needs to recruit two-thirds of its police staff over the next ten years, depends on its ability to attract and retain the most talented employees from all our communities. (Police Review, 2001: 14)

In addition to workforce development, much of the business case for diversity has been couched in terms of delivering quality service in a more heterogeneous society. Again in respect to the police service, it has long been seen as operationally beneficial to deploy staff who are 'matched' to the ethnic profile of the community. Although the diversity agenda has been associated with liberal programmes in the relatively recent past, the business case was evident in older colonial policing models. In New Zealand, police leaders adopted a degree of ethnic matching even during the era of colonial quasi-military policing, relying on Māori officers to provide effective policing of Māori communities (Hill, 1986). In other colonial policing systems, too, the recruitment and deployment of minorities was seen as expedient and efficient. Regarding the Indian Police Service, a Royal Commission in 1912 recommended greater efforts to recruit Indians, appoint them to senior posts, and equalize salaries (Griffiths, 1971: 189). During the era of Jim Crow racial segregation in the United States, black officers were employed to police African American communities (Roberg et al., 2005). Black officers were also employed to police racial segregation in apartheid South Africa (Cawthra, 1993).

More recently there has been an emphasis on deploying staff with the appropriate cultural and linguistic skills necessary to work effectively in a multicultural context. The organizational need to better understand the complex social context in which offending occurs has underpinned the need to recruit more minority ethnic staff in policing, probation and NOMS, and the court service (Rowe, 2004; Bhui, 2006; Advisory Panel on Judicial Diversity, 2010). Similarly, Ward et al. (2009: 759) noted that the drive towards recruiting more diverse personnel to the US courts system has been pursued for 'business case' reasons:

> ... calls for equal representation among legal decision makers commonly suggest that this should substantively and symbolically enhance the quality of justice administration, by incorporating prerogatives, sensibilities and skill sets of a more representative cross-section of society and increasing the apparent democratic legitimacy of government institutions.

The Regulatory Case

Whatever the ethical or organizational benefits that may, or may not, accrue, criminal justice agencies have been required to introduce strategies and monitor performance in terms of workforce diversity by a raft of legislative and policy interventions. While the 1976 Race Relations Act prohibited discrimination in the provision of goods, facilities and services, the extent to which this, the primary piece of legislation in terms of tackling racial discrimination, applied to the criminal justice system was limited. The 1976 Act did not apply to operational aspects of policing, such as the use and abuse of stop and search powers that are discussed elsewhere in this book. They did, however, apply to some aspects of policing that might be construed as service provision, for example, the manner in which crime prevention advice is given to the public. In terms of the impact of the 1976 Act on issues relating to the employment of civilian staff, it is clear that the legislation against racial discrimination contained in section 4 applies equally to the criminal justice system as to any other organization.

However, it is also apparent that, as with the public services more generally, the 2000 Race Relations (Amendment) Act significantly changes the legal context against which the recruitment, retention and promotion of minority ethnic staff in criminal justice takes place. In keeping with Macpherson's demand that 'the full force of the race relations legislation should apply to all police officers, and that Chief Officers of Police should be made vicariously liable for the acts and omissions of their officers' (Macpherson, 1999: 328), the 2000 Act fully includes the police service. Under the terms of the Act, the police service now has a proactive legal duty to tackle racial discrimination and promote 'race equality'.

While the 2000 Act made the recruitment and retention of minority staff the focus of particular legislation applicable across the criminal justice system, health services, schools and universities, and the public sector as a whole, other managerial and regulatory factors have also been developed. Consistent with techniques associated with New Public Management more generally, criminal justice agencies have been required to establish priorities and achieve targets relating to diversity. In respect of diversity in the workplace, as in most other aspects of organizational performance, agencies of the criminal justice system have been subject to management by target setting, the development of performance indicators, auditing and the compilation of league tables (McLaughlin, 2007). The results of these processes are evident in the annual reports, strategy documents and performance reviews on which analysis of progress in relation to workforce diversity was based earlier in this chapter. The coalition government formed in 2010 pledged to develop democratic accountability to replace the audit culture of the last few decades – and some of the employment targets established for the police service in the late 1990s had been abandoned in any case – but statutory duties to promote diversity continue.

Workforce Diversity: Necessary but Insufficient Conditions for Reform

For a combination of moral, operational and legislative reasons the development of a more ethnically diverse staff in the criminal justice system will continue to be a priority. However, the measures outlined earlier in this chapter have limited effect in addressing disproportionality within agencies, the poor response to problems of racist violence, and enhancing the legitimacy of the criminal justice system. While there are clear reasons to welcome the continued development of ethnic diversity within the criminal justice system, there are associated limitations and dangers relating to ethnic essentialism. Holdaway and O'Neill (2007) have argued that the Black Police Association (and the argument can be extended to other minority staff associations within the criminal justice system) reproduces an ethnic essentialism reflective of dominant racialized discourse. While BPAs have developed an anti-racist agenda that challenges established stereotypes and racist attitudes towards minority staff, they have done so in terms that continue to foreground ethnic identity. Politically, this might have been opportunistic in the context of post-Macpherson policing but, like many of the other programmes and policies outlined in this chapter, it risks creating an ethnic identity that is fixed and uncontested. This concern extends more widely to ethnic monitoring practices within criminal justice that are analyzed further in Chapter Ten. No doubt the collective experience of racism and discrimination means that minority ethnic staff within the criminal justice system might have some shared identity, just as do female staff, those who are gay or lesbian, or those with a disability. Any group that might be outside the normative white, male, heterosexual and able-bodied working environment that has characterized the criminal justice system has some shared identity on the basis of their relative marginalization but cannot be understood in one-dimensional terms on that basis.

Problems emanating from a lack of diversity cannot be resolved on the basis of a deficit model such that rectifying a lack of (in this context) minority ethnic representation will be a sufficient response. There are a number of reasons why such a strategy is limited. The ethnic identity of staff does not simply equate to improved legitimacy. Cheliotis and Liebling (2006) found, for example, that the perceived quality of race relations in prisons was 'most significantly associated with views on respect, humanity, fairness, [and] relationships with staff' – factors related to legitimacy – but that minority ethnic prisoners' perceptions were not related to the ethnicity of prison staff. The killing by police of Sean Bell in New York City in 2006 led to considerable debate about racial profiling and aggressive policing in black neighbourhoods – factors also related to legitimacy, ethics and morality. In response to these concerns, the Police Commissioner Kelly noted that these allegations had continued even during a period in which minority ethnic staff had been recruited in greater numbers and allegations of racism in this case arose even though three of the five officers involved in the shooting were black (Cardwell, 2007). Clearly, in these contexts the ethnicity of personnel is of secondary importance to operational behaviour and institutional dynamics. In other respects an approach of 'ethnic matching' of staff to clients or the wider public is likely to be flawed if it fails to recognize other dimensions of identity, relating to class, gender, age, employment and education, among many things. Ethnicity is but one part of profoundly unequal and antagonistic relations between staff, prisoners, suspects, victims and public. Without critical engagement with the concept of ethnicity – such that its complexity and multiplicity and social constructed nature are recognized – strategies to improve operational performance through enhancing diversity will remain fundamentally flawed.

As was outlined in Chapter Seven, disproportional practices and outcomes within the criminal justice system must be understood in terms of the lack of diversity of staff. Patterns of prejudice and discrimination cannot be explained without reference to the normative whiteness of agencies that have failed to reflect the ethnic diversity of wider society. Recruiting more minority ethnic staff might begin to address these cultural and institutional problems, although the extent to which recruits are able to transform established cultural forms might be questioned. This is a particular challenge when there might be compelling reasons to subscribe to existing norms and values as a means of self-preservation in what might be a hostile environment. Minority ethnic women might internalize and sustain existing gendered norms in the face of racism and sexism (Stone and Tuffin, 2000; Westmarland, 2002). Not all issues relating to disproportionality, though, can be addressed through changing the profile of criminal justice employees. Institutional and operational practices that underpin much of the disproportionate treatment of some minority ethnic groups cannot be transformed solely through more effective recruitment, retention and promotion of minorities, which are necessary but insufficient conditions for reform.

SUMMARY

The under-representation of minority ethnic people among the staff of criminal justice agencies has long been recognized and is often associated with problems of disproportionate treatment of victims and offenders and the 'normative whiteness' of the system. Across police, the CPS, the courts, NOMS and the probation service, minorities tend to be under-represented compared to their presence in the overall population. Furthermore, minority ethnic staff tend to be under-represented to a greater extent among more senior ranks. Ethnic monitoring has been one element of a wide-ranging programme of innovations that has

(Continued)

(Continued)

sought to recruit, retain and promote minority staff. Other approaches have included pre-recruitment programmes, advertising and recruitment campaigns, and changes to employment regulations that have been indirectly discriminatory.

There are three complementary reasons why the development of a more ethnically diverse workforce has become a priority for the criminal justice system. There is a moral case, relating to public legitimacy and ethics, a business case, relating to recruiting a more effective workforce, and a regulatory case, relating to the need to comply with statutory and policy responsibilities. While there are strong reasons why workforce diversity ought to be pursued, it will not resolve institutional and structural social problems that underpin criminal justice inequalities and the disproportionate treatment of minority ethnic communities.

STUDY QUESTIONS

1 What organizational differences between criminal justice agencies might make differences in terms of the recruitment of a more ethnically diverse workforce?

2 What have been identified as the key barriers to the recruitment of a more diverse workforce?

3 In what ways might improved workforce diversity enhance the legitimacy of criminal justice agencies? For what reasons might this have a limited effect?

FURTHER READING

In the wake of the Stephen Lawrence Report (Macpherson, 1999, HMSO) the Home Office conducted a series of studies relating to ethnicity and police careers. Key among these is Stone and Tuffin's (2000, Home Office) study, which provides a good overview of the issues outlined in this chapter. Johnston's (2006) article analyzes ways in which the recruitment of Police CSOs has been used to broaden ethnic diversity within services. A broader overview of recruitment, and other issues, of minorities across the CJS more generally can be found in Bhui's (2009, Sage) collection. Information about the Black Police Association can be found at www.nbpa.co.uk/home/index.php/en/, and details of the Association of Black Probation Officers at http://abponoms.com/ and the National Association of Asian Probation Staff website is www.naaps-noms.co.uk/.

9

Islam, Terrorism and Security

OVERVIEW

This chapter:

- critically examines the ways in which racial, ethnic and religious differences have provided a powerful framework for understanding and responding to contemporary terrorism;
- outlines the context of recent Islamist terrorism and policy and legislative responses;
- critically examines the notion that these responses have accelerated Islamaphobia and established Muslims as a 'suspect community';
- explores ways in which 'security' has become embedded as the primary objective of governance, embroiling networks of global, state, civil and private agencies.

KEY TERMS

- Civil liberties
- Radicalization
- Surveillance [and suspicion]

- Financing terrorism
- Security
- Terrorism

Introduction: Terrorism and Security into the Twenty-first Century

The impact of fundamentalist Islamist terrorism on contemporary society has been deep and wide. Deep in terms of the cost in human lives, the resources that have been dedicated to responding and preventing terrorist actions, and in relation to the impact that the threat of terrorism has had on the political, legal, psychological and cultural fabric of many societies. The symbolic and spectacular nature of incidents such as the 9/11 attacks, the Bali, London and Madrid bombings, to mention only a few of the most high-profile examples, has meant that the impact of terrorist activity has extended far beyond the individuals directly caught up in atrocities. The effect of these incidents has also been wide inasmuch as it has extended into areas of social life not previously associated with security and crime problems. The status and role of religious leaders, issues relating to asylum and migration, relationships between students and teachers, between neighbours, work colleagues and fellow citizens have become subject to concerns about threat and security in ways that profoundly unsettle civic and social relations and redraw boundaries of communities and polities. Notions of risk and insecurity have changed mentalities of crime such that crime control has become an integral part of processes of governance and the responsibility of a host of public and private institutions and private citizens. As Loader and Walker (2007: 9) argued 'security has become *the* political vernacular of our time'.

Charting a history of terrorism is difficult since the concept itself is highly contested. Simply put, what constitutes a terrorist campaign is unclear and there have been myriad examples of individuals once associated with 'terrorism' assuming legitimate political roles, from Menachem Begin, who was active in paramilitary resistance to British rule in Palestine in the 1930s and 1940s and went on to become Prime Minister of Israel, to Nelson Mandela, who was identified as a terrorist by many Western governments before becoming President of South Africa, to Martin McGuiness, who was accused of being a leader of the Irish Republican Army and subsequently became Deputy First Minister of the Northern Ireland Assembly. Defining terrorism in any of its forms, including state terrorism, is beyond the scope of this chapter. Even so, given that a recurring theme of this book is to critically engage with core concepts relating to 'race' and 'crime' it is important to recognize that 'terrorism' is also socially constructed and can only be understood in particular contexts. Indeed, ways in which concerns relating to terrorism have extended to other spheres of religious, cultural, political and civic society is considered later in this chapter. While terrorism remains conceptually problematic, it has been a vivid and visible feature in many societies in recent times. The dates '9/11' and '7/7' have become powerful symbolic reference points in contemporary popular culture, with discursive resonance that condenses concern about extremism, terror and insecurity in late-modern society. The terrorist attacks in the United States in September 2001 and the London bombings in July 2005, along with the Madrid train bombings in March 2004 and the Mumbai shootings in November 2008, have been the most spectacular and widely witnessed crimes in history. In 2007, Prime Minister Tony Blair, in a speech given on *HMS Albion*, argued that 'put simply, September 11 2001 changed everything', and that:

> Terrorism is an attack on our values. Its ideology is anti-democratic, anti-freedom, anti-everything that makes modern life so rich in possibility. When the Taliban murder a teacher in front of his class, as they did recently, for daring to teach girls; that is an act not just of cruelty but of ideology. Using force against them to prevent such an act is not 'defence' in the traditional sense of that word, but 'security' in the broadest sense, an assertion of our values against theirs. (Blair, 2007, cited in Mullard and Cole, 2007: 6)

This brief analysis of the threat of Islamist terrorism encapsulates the cornerstones of the 'War on Terror' propagated by President Bush in the aftermath of the 11 September 2001 attacks, co-joined by Blair, and continued in practice, if not in political rhetoric, by their respective successors. US government lawyers and officials maintained that the killing of Osama Bin Laden in May 2011 was not an illegal or 'extra judicial' act but was legally justified on the basis that the

USA was at war with Al-Qaeda (Bowcott, 2011). Blair's speech clearly cast the struggle against Islamist terrorism as an ideological conflict that extended beyond other terrorist campaigns relating to disputed territory or sovereignty. That the conflict related to 'values' has been a crucial component of arguments that Muslim communities in Western societies have been collectively implicated in the fundamental 'clash of civilizations' that Huntingdon (1997) suggested would shape post-Cold War politics. This thesis casts Islam as inherently incompatible with Western liberal democratic values in ways that, despite being profoundly simplistic (as is discussed at greater length below), have been influential in political discourse surrounding security, terrorism and the future of multicultural society. Before considering the impact that the conceptual framework surrounding contemporary terrorism has had on Muslim individuals and communities in Britain and elsewhere, aspects of the legislative and security agenda that has developed in the last decade or so are reviewed.

Legislative Responses: Britannia Waives the Rules?

As Mythen et al. (2009) noted, even though Britain had a lengthy history of developing terrorism legislation, relative to other countries, a raft of legal measures were introduced in response to Islamist terrorism. Elements of these provisions involved derogation from human rights provisions and established elements of due process. Key among these have been the 2000 Terrorism Act, the 2001 Anti-Terrorism, Crime and Security Act (ATCSA), the 2005 Prevention of Terrorism Act (PTA), the 2006 Terrorism Act, and the 2008 Counter-Terrorism Act. Additionally, New Labour introduced supplementary legislation such as the 1998 Criminal Justice (Terrorism and Conspiracy) Act and the 2000 Regulation of Investigatory Powers Act. Other legislation, such as the 2002 Proceeds of Crime Act, which gives police and other agencies legal powers to confiscate criminal assets, has also been applied to terrorist activity. Clearly, such an extensive legislative programme includes a broad range of measures, analysis of which is beyond the scope of the current discussion. Three key themes have emerged that have been widely held to have had a disproportionate impact on Muslim and Asian communities in Britain and in other countries, and it its these legal provisions that are outlined below.

Unlike other states that had experienced terrorist activity, the British government derogated from the European Convention on Human Rights in order to allow for the indefinite detention of foreign nationals suspected of terror-related offences. In the United States, President Bush issued a Military Order in November 2001 that allowed for similar indefinite detention of foreign nationals at Guantanamo Bay in Cuba. In the UK and the USA a parallel system of justice was established such that foreign terrorist suspects were held and processed in regimes that denied to them the usual rights and due process of the criminal justice system. In the UK, the 2001 ATCSA gave the Secretary of State the right to certify foreign nationals 'reasonably suspected' of being a terrorist or 'with links' to international terrorist organizations and to detain them indefinitely. The Act also linked terrorism with asylum by denying the right of suspected terrorists from applying for asylum (Bosworth and Guild, 2008). In 2004 the Law Lords ruled that the provisions for indefinite detention were contrary to the European Convention on Human Rights (ECHR) since they only applied to foreign nationals and so were discriminatory. While the Law Lords recognized that exceptional security threats might justify the suspension of usual rules of due process, they found that provisions for indefinite detention could not be justified as a long-term measure. They also argued that it was inconsistent to apply such measures only to foreign nationals when there was no evidence that they posed a greater threat than resident citizens (Donohue, 2008: 58–59). In response to that ruling, the 2005 PTA introduced control orders that restricted the rights of those 'associated' with terrorist activity such that they were confined to a designated address for 18 hours a day and denied internet and mobile phones access as well as being restricted in terms of their association with other people. In order to comply with the ECHR, the control orders could be applied to citizens as well as foreign nationals; in March 2011, 10 control orders were in place and all of those subject to them were British citizens.

In the light of considerable controversy about the impact of these measures in terms of human rights and civil liberties, the Conservative-led coalition government announced in 2011 that control orders would be replaced by new provisions: Terrorism Prevention and Investigation Measures (TPIM). Until legislation is passed to enable TPIM, existing arrangements for control orders will continue to apply. TPIM, the government proposed, will differ from control orders in the following ways (Hansard, 2011):

- restrictions that impact on an individual's ability to follow a normal pattern of daily life will be kept to a minimum;
- the legislation will make clearer what restrictions can and cannot be imposed;
- the new measures will have a two year maximum time limit and will only be imposed by the Home Secretary with prior permission from the High Court, except in urgent cases;
- the Home Secretary will need reasonable grounds to believe that an individual is or has been involved in terrorism-related activity – a higher test than under the current regime – and be satisfied that it is necessary to apply measures from the regime to protect the public from a risk of terrorism; and
- a more flexible overnight residence requirement will replace the current curfew arrangements and forcible relocation will be scrapped and replaced with the power to order more tightly-defined exclusions from particular areas and to prevent foreign travel.

Although these proposals suggest a less intrusive regime requiring a higher threshold, the proposed TPIM will continue to mean that those suspected of terrorist-related activity will be subject to executive powers that fall outside the scope of mainstream criminal justice (Mantouvalou, 2006, cited in McGhee, 2008). As has been noted, these arrangements mirror similar measures introduced in the United States, and continued under the Obama administration that had previously pledged to close the camp at Guantanamo and to try suspects in criminal courts, and in other countries, such as Canada and Australia (Oriola, 2009). The removal of legal rights from terrorist suspects in these ways has been criticized by many analysts who argue that defining the 'right to have rights' in ways that create 'internal others' outwith mainstream society has been especially pernicious since those subject to such provisions have usually been Muslim. McGhee (2008) argued that the sacrifice of the rights of the few (Muslim foreign nationals) cannot be justified, even if it were to secure the protection of the many. Such legislative provisions, he argued, amount to an 'inequality of esteem, the denial of shared humanity and dehumanization' (McGhee, 2008: 27).

As was discussed in Chapter Seven, the over-representation of minority groups in police stop and search data has been subjected to continuing and intense debate for several decades. During much of this period, Asian people have tended to be under-represented relative to other ethnic cohorts and arguments about processes of criminalization and racialization have been focused on other groups. Concerns about 'Asian criminality' have developed along a number of lines since the 1990s, relating to, for example, drug-dealing and following the 2001 'Milltown' riots in Oldham, Bradford, Burnley and elsewhere that were often explained in terms of the cultural dysfunctionality of Asian communities (Webster, 2003; Bolognani, 2009). Against this background, Asian people are over-represented in police stop and search data relative to their presence in the general population, as Table 7.1 in Chapter Seven indicated. However, this over-representation is more pronounced in relation to stop and search powers introduced under section 44 of the 2000 Terrorism Act. The Act included provisions that enable police officers to stop and search persons or vehicles in designated areas to find articles 'of a kind which could be used in connection with terrorism'. Unlike the provisions of the 1984 Police and Criminal Evidence Act, there is no requirement that the officer has 'reasonable suspicion' relating to the person stopped and anyone in the given location can be stopped. In 2008/09, more than 200,000 stop and searches were carried out under section 44 powers: 61.1 per cent of those involved were white and 15.4 per cent were Asians. While Asian people are over-represented in terms of 'general' (PACE) stop and search practices, there is still greater disproportionality in relation to the powers intended to be used to prevent terrorism.

In addition to extending police stop and search powers, the 2000 Terrorism Act also granted the Home Secretary power to proscribe organizations involved in terrorist activity. Civil liberty campaigners have argued that the Act defines terrorism in broad terms so that many groups involved in protest movements might fall under the remit of the Home Secretary's power. These concerns were exacerbated by the 2006 Terrorism Act which extended the grounds on which organizations could be proscribed to include activities that 'glorify' terrorism. Membership, professed membership, expression of support and the wearing of clothing or articles associated with proscribed organizations are all criminal offences. In 2011, 46 organizations were proscribed, two of which were listed for glorifying terrorism. While not all of these groups were associated, by the Home Office, with Islamist terrorism (the list includes the Basque separatist group ETA, for example) a majority are and it has been argued that outlawing organizations in this way has been at one end of a spectrum that has cast suspicion on a wide range of Islamic charitable, business, educational and religious groups. This point is returned to further below in discussion of the argument that Muslims constitute a 'suspect community' in contemporary Western societies.

Policy Responses: Suspicion and Radicalization

In addition to these legal developments, the British government has developed a broader strategic response to terrorism. In 2003 the 'Contest' strategy was launched to counter terrorism. The strategy has been updated several times and is the subject of an ongoing review that encompasses all aspects of terrorism policy. Across its various iterations, Contest has comprised four key elements that collectively seek to address the environment in which terrorism develops, to stop terrorist attacks from happening and to improve the management of incidents when they do occur. The four dimensions of Contest are:

- Pursue – to stop terrorist attacks;
- Prepare – where we cannot stop an attack, to mitigate its impact;
- Protect – to strengthen our overall protection against terrorist attacks;
- Prevent– to stop people becoming terrorists or supporting violent extremists.

Many of the legal powers granted to the police and other agencies have been developed as components of these four themes, and some of the impact that these might have had on Muslim communities in Britain have been outlined in the discussion above. In this section, attention focuses on the fourth strand of the Contest strategy – Prevent. This strand has entailed developing policy and operational practice that have sought to engage Muslim communities in efforts to address the recruitment of terrorists and the spread of ideologies that support such activity. As a number of commentators have suggested, Prevent intends to 'drain the swamp' in which terrorism breeds (Appleby, 2010). This has entailed the extension of partnership approaches to crime and disorder to efforts to tackle terrorism and might be considered as an exercise in 'soft power' through the engagement of community groups and a plethora of local partners in efforts to identify individuals or groups that might be vulnerable to radicalization (Spalek and McDonald, 2009).

As in other crime and community safety contexts (Hughes and Edwards, 2002), a key challenge has related to the conceptualization of communities themselves and the identification of appropriate partners to engage in the Prevent

agenda. Two key concerns emerge. First, the selection of partners, and the identification of priorities, has been developed in terms established by central government itself. The extent to which government foreign policy, for example,
might contribute towards the growth of terrorism is not recognized in official
reports and statements relating to the Prevent strategy. Inviting Muslim groups
to engage in partnership with an agenda already established by central government has meant that they are only able to participate in a 'highly circumscribed
debate' about the nature and causes of violent extremism (McGhee, 2008: 57–58).

Second, engagement has extended only to Muslim groups identified, or self-
selected, as 'moderate'. These groups might not be the most effective in terms
of engaging with those who might be most 'vulnerable' to processes of 'radicalization'. Spalek and McDonald's (2009) study of police engagement found
that Salafi and Islamist groups, whose radicalism meant that they were pejo-
ratively regarded as suspicious, were often the very organizations that could
most effectively build bridges and develop trust with individuals who might
already hold violent extremist positions. Spalek and McDonald noted that local
engagement with radical groups has developed, and has been effective, but
this has been done beyond the scope of the Contest/Prevent framework, which
has maintained a values-based approach seeking only to engage with Muslim
groups that are seen as legitimate in terms defined by central government.

Much of the difficulty of identifying and engaging with community partners
reflects broader problems with multi-agency working in crime and antisocial
behaviour more widely. As was noted in Chapter Four, community groups that
might engage in projects face difficult strategic and funding dilemmas.
Accepting a role within local networks might offer opportunities to shape the
direction of community interventions and a share of related resources.
However, risks might arise from being co-opted by dominant agendas and
programmes. In circumstances where admission to partner status is defined in
terms of adherence to a broad and ill-defined community of values, Muslim
organizations have found themselves inhibited from addressing concerns
about Western military interventions and other grievances. Arguably, their
ability to participate in democratic debate has been curtailed by a dominant
agenda that requires Muslim organizations to demonstrate loyalty. McGhee
(2008: 76) expressed the government's approach in the following terms:

> Rather than broaden its counter-terrorism strategy to include a national debate
> on the possible relationship between British foreign policy and the radicalization
> of young British Muslims, [the government] has chosen to narrow the parame-
> ters of permitted debate. Rather than attempting to foster 'open and honest'
> debate on 'difficult issues' with the members of Muslim communities in Britain,
> the government is clearly attempting to close down debates, especially in rela-
> tion to foreign policy.

A central aim of the Prevent agenda has been to develop strategies to stop the radicalization of people vulnerable to recruitment to terrorist ideology and activities.

This has entailed 'hard power' activities to detain and deport 'preachers of hate' such as Abu Hamza and Omar Bakri Mohammed. Other approaches to tackling radicalization have involved local partnerships and communities identifying individuals who might be becoming engaged in extremist behaviour. Key among these initiatives has been the 'Channel' programme, described in the following terms in a report by the House of Commons Communities and Local Government Committee (CLGC) (2010: 14):

> *Channel* is an intervention which for some witnesses has met with success and, for others, courted much controversy. The *Channel* process identifies an individual's risk of vulnerability to becoming violently extreme and their influence on others. These individuals may not have committed any criminal offence but information is received, sometimes from community members, about their activities. This might include accessing terrorist websites, frequently talking about taking violent action or other negative behaviours. If the risk assessment suggests that interventions are required, then a partnership of police, statutory partners, councillors and appropriate local community leaders will consider what community interventions are available and appropriate in each case. Unlike *Prevent, Channel* focuses on all types of extremism, not just that inspired by al-Qaeda.

Nevertheless, as is outlined below, it has been argued that Prevent activity has tended to focus simplistically on the Muslim community in generic and one-dimensional terms. This has reinforced, it is argued, dominant media and political discourse that has problematized the Muslim community and sustained Islamaphobia (Hoskins and O'Loughlin, 2009; Meer and Modood, 2011). The CLGC (2010: 8–9) report noted that the Prevent programme was widely criticized for subsuming debates relating to community cohesion under the rubric of security and counter-terrorism. The community cohesion agenda – developed in the wake of the 'Milltown disorders' of the early 2000s – has itself been criticized on the grounds that it explained social and community tensions in terms of an apparent self-isolation of Muslim communities that was propagated by a failed model of multiculturalism (Modood, 2007). Just as the community cohesion agenda tended to locate the 'problem' within the Muslim community itself, so too the Prevent agenda has been criticized for suggesting that the potential for extremism and radicalization is inherent within Muslim culture. This perception was widely documented in the CLGC (2010: 9) report, as illustrated in the evidence given to the Committee by the Islamic Society of Britain:

> The term 'Prevent' lends itself to the idea that there lies a dormant terrorist within Muslims; that somewhere, entwined in their instincts and licensed by their religious beliefs, there is the possibility that some, albeit very rarely, will turn to terrorism against the state. And so we must do everything to 'prevent' that from happening.

Hoskins and O'Loughlin (2009) argued that media representation of radicalization have adopted narrative formats portraying a linear journey taking 'ordinary' youths on a path towards violent extremism in a manner that suggests a continuum between normative mainstream social relations and risky terrorist threat. This suggests that the cultural, religious and other aspects of communities associated with terrorism are themselves problematic since they contain the potential for radicalism. This continuum underlies Prevent initiatives focused broadly upon Muslim communities that problematize cultural and religious practices as 'breeding grounds' for radicalization. One of the difficulties of the Contest approach to counter-terrorism, Richards (2011) has argued, is that the fundamental concept of radicalization is poorly understood. Key tensions and questions relating to radicalization are not addressed in government strategy that defines the phrase in straightforward terms as 'the process by which people come to support violent extremism and, in some cases, join terrorist groups' (Home Office, 2009, cited in Richards, 2011: 145). Linking radicalism with violence is problematic and serves to widen the category of risky suspects in ways that are unhelpful not only in terms of responding to security threats, but also as they serve to stigmatize and marginalize groups that might otherwise be important allies in counter-terrorism. As Lambert (2008) and Richards (2011) have noted, when used in other contexts the term 'radical' is usually not considered in a negative sense. Political parties themselves, for example, might proclaim the radical nature of their policy proposals. Moreover, the notion of radicalism has not previously been applied to other forms of terrorism; it was not used, for example, in relation to the recruitment of individuals from nationalist or Catholic communities in Northern Ireland who might have been vulnerable to recruitment to Irish republican terrorism. Equating radicalization with violence, as the Home Office definition does, is unhelpful since it fails to distinguish between Islamist groups, such as Salafi Muslims, who advance a radical creed but reject terrorism and violence. Conjoining radicalism and violence not only serves to stigmatize communities, it also denies opportunities to challenge terrorist ideology (Abbas, 2007). This is a fundamental category error, which, as Spalek et al. (2009: 180) have noted, can be counter-productive if radical but non-violent groups are considered part of the problem rather than as potential components of a solution:

> ... the fact that al-Qaida spokesmen often invoke and subvert Salafi and Islamist approaches to Islam in an attempt to legitimize their violence helps illustrate why it is that Salafi and Islamist community groups often have the best tools with which to undermine al-Qaida propaganda within their own youth communities.

The role and status of Muslim civil society and community groups has also been problematized by the aspects of the 'War on Terror' focused upon the financing of terrorism. In late September 2001, President Bush signed Executive Order 13224 entitling him to freeze the financial assets of individuals and entities suspected of being linked to terrorism. Sanctions can be imposed by the US government on financial organizations (even those foreign to the USA) that deal with those subject to these executive orders. The framework developed by Bush was extended through United Nations Resolution 1373, which requires that all member states freeze the assets of listed groups and individuals, a process that McCulloch and Pickering

(2005: 476) argued 'gives states enormous latitude to unilaterally attach the label of terrorism to individuals or organisations and financially cripple them'. In the UK, the 2001 ATCSA empowered the government to confiscate money thought to relate to terrorist activity, whether or not there were court proceedings relating to such offences. The Act also requires that those who have assets frozen disclose information, or face up to two years' imprisonment, expands the range of agencies that can seize assets, and places a statutory duty upon the 'regulated' sector (such as solicitors or financial institutions) to inform law enforcement authorities if they had reasonable grounds to suspect others of involvement in terrorist-related activity.

While the disruption of financial activity might be regarded as a relatively benign aspect of counter-terrorism when considered in contrast to high-profile controversies relating to control orders, the use of torture and the removal of legal rights for suspects, such measures have had disproportionate negative impacts on Muslim communities in many countries. In the period up until April 2005, for example, Executive Order 13224 was applied to 743 people and 947 organizations: almost all of which (98 per cent of the people and 97 per cent of the organizations) were Muslim or Arab (Donohue, 2008: 168). It might have been, of course, that the orders were properly targeted at individuals and groups associated with terrorist activity but the impact of the US legal framework has meant that the impact of efforts to tackle terrorist finance has been felt across wide swathes of business and charitable work. Donohue (2008) noted that Islamic charities and religious groups have received reduced donations, publications have had a decline in advertising revenues, and prominent banks have adopted policies that require employees not to deal with Islamic or Arab enterprises. Globally, the institution of changes to financial and banking systems has been targeted at informal systems that are seen as vulnerable to exploitation by terrorist groups and difficult to regulate. Such informal banking systems are more common in developing countries. A prominent form is the Hawala system that was developed in India and relied upon familial financial networks. Targeting such systems is identified by McCulloch and Pickering as a form of corporate neo-colonialism whereby dominant Western practices become the norm that must be applied. This is based on 'the notion that non-Western, particularly Muslim, users of financial systems, like Islamic charities and NGOs, which operate outside the corporate mainstream, are inherently suspect' (McCulloch and Pickering, 2005: 480). Donohue (2008: 180) cited the example of the al-Barakat remittance company, through which some $500 million was distributed into Somalia each year by private citizens and agencies including the United Nations, an amount greater than the foreign aid given to that country. Donohue (2008: 181) noted that curtailing such financial systems not only has significant humanitarian consequences, but is counter-productive in security terms as the policy 'does not marginalize fundamentalists; it makes them more powerful'.

Charities providing international aid to Muslim people have also been negatively affected by counter-terrorism financial regulations. Partly perhaps, in the

UK, this has been due to legal provisions that criminalize donors to organizations that might be engaged in terrorism (which is, as noted above, defined in very broad and loose terms). In 2003, President Bush listed a UK-based charity, Interpal, in connection with terrorist-related activity. As a result, the UK Charity Commission froze its bank accounts, which had been used to work with Palestinians in need in the West Bank, the Gaza strip, Jordan and Lebanon. After an investigation, however, the Commission found that there was no evidence to support the claims made against Interpal and its assets were released (Donohue, 2008: 176).

In addition to an impact on charitable activity, concerns relating to security and counter-terrorism have reshaped the framework for state disbursement of overseas development aid. Although the 2000 international Millennium Summit led to a commitment to poverty reduction, the 'war on terror' has established a different agenda for development aid based upon twin pillars of the extent to which recipient states are strategic allies and their vulnerability in terms of developing terrorist threat. While the amount of overseas development aid has risen in absolute terms, it has been increasingly allocated in terms relating to terrorism rather than the amelioration of poverty. Aning (2010: 20) has argued that 'the crosscutting influence of security has had a major influence on aid policy as a whole. The main direct effect has been the securitisation and skewed disbursement of aid'. Additionally, the securitization of development aid has altered relations between recipient country governments and civil society organizations. Muslim groups have been subjected to extensive scrutiny in ways that have deterred campaigning on human rights issues that might be construed as challenging established state practices (Howell and Lind, 2009). In countries including China, Uzbekistan and Zimbabwe, governments have sought to suppress civil society groups campaigning for regional autonomy, democratic reform and human rights on the grounds that they are engaged in Islamist terrorism; evidence that Howell (2006: 126) argued demonstrates a broader conflation negatively affecting development issues:

> Given the complex interweaving of meanings and language around terrorism, Islam, refugees and asylum-seeking, any kind of claim-making actions, social movements and organisations advocating around issues of justice, religious freedom, immediately become suspect.

Muslims as 'Suspect Communities'

The above discussion provides many examples of the various ways in which Muslim individuals, organizations and communities have been subjected to heightened degrees of suspicion in response to the threat of Islamist terrorism during the last decade or so. Much of the critical debate surrounding legal and organizational dimensions of counter-terrorism has focused broadly on the increased powers that states have assumed over citizens, the morality, legality and efficacy of using torture in the interrogation of suspects, and the extent to which efforts to prevent terrorism have involved the denial of the very rights that define democratic polities threatened by violent extremism (Mullard and Cole, 2007; Walker, 2007). In relation to Muslim communities in Britain and elsewhere, these concerns have coalesced in the form of arguments that this group have been subject to processes of racialization and criminalization such that they form a contemporary 'suspect community', marked as different from and dangerous to mainstream society. Having broadly outlined the thesis that Muslims have been identified as a 'suspect community', the discussion moves on to identify central underlying processes that have led to this formation. In the final part of the chapter, it is argued that the 'suspect community' thesis provides a convincing perspective on the development of anti-terrorism measures and their relation to Islamaphobia, but that important questions remain and that the concept needs to be further refined.

The concept of a 'suspect community' was developed by Hillyard (1993), who argued that measures introduced by British governments in the 1970s in response to republican terrorism in Northern Ireland had been implemented in practice such that all Irish people were conceptualized as potential offenders. Irish people – or those perceived to be Irish – were subject to various controls, for example when travelling from the north of Ireland to the mainland of Britain, that were not applied elsewhere. Hillyard argued that these measures were ineffective in terms of preventing or investigating terrorism. Moreover, as others have also maintained, they served to alienate Irish people subject to coercion and surveillance and so were counter-productive in that they reinforced nationalist claims of state oppression. Pantazis and Pemberton (2009) have extended Hillyard's analysis to contemporary policing and security measures intended to prevent and detect fundamentalist Islamist terrorism. The Muslim community in Britain, and many other European countries, it is argued, form a twenty-first-century 'suspect community'. Mythen et al. (2009: 738) argued that while it is legitimate that nation states seek to protect the security of citizens, contemporary security measures have gone further:

> It is, of course, only to be expected that the state should seek to reduce threats to public security through the range of powers at its disposal, including proposing appropriate criminal justice legislation, conducting intelligence operations and engaging in legitimate policing. This point accepted, we would argue that in each of these areas, the British state has sanctioned and implemented disproportionate forms of regulation that have had grim ramifications for Muslim minority groups. In particular, the inequitable application of these modes of regulation have contributed to the wider process through which British Muslims are labelled as dangerous, risky 'others' that threaten the security of the nation.

Pantazis and Pemberton (2009) suggest that legal, policing and operational activities have combined with Islamaphobic political and media discourse that have sought to identify Muslims as suspect communities in Western countries. Thus, the banning of organizations associated with minority ethnic, refugee and Muslim community groups, powers to stop and search individuals without reasonable suspicion, and the establishment of control orders and similar measures that have disproportionally impacted upon Muslim communities – all of which have been detailed in this chapter – have a symbiotic relationship with established political and media discourse that has created the Muslim community as threatening. As Burnett and Whyte (2005) and Appleby (2010) have noted, 'Muslim' has become a contested and discursively constructed category in relation to contemporary terrorism. A singular Muslim identity, that denies the plurality of religious perspectives and ethnic identities, emerges such that 'Muslim' becomes a politicized category beyond a matter of personal faith. Chakraborti (2007) argued that the discursive construction of identity has 'created a culture of suspicion against Muslims throughout Europe whose presence is widely perceived to be a threat as the "enemy within" on the war on terror and whose adherence to Islam is seen as a direct challenge'. The presence of Muslims has been constructed as problematic in various European countries. In 2009, voters in Switzerland supported a referendum calling for a ban on the construction of minarets. The Swiss referendum was developed by a small right-wing party similar to that of the Dutch politician Geert Wilders, who has warned about the potential 'Islamification' of Europe and labelled the Koran a 'fascist book'. Similar warnings have been made by the Danish People's Party. This context of populist Islamaphobia creates the conditions that identify Muslims as a suspect community, a development described in relation to Italian society in the following terms (Maneri, 2011: 87):

> Investigative, intelligence and police operations thus become news and are translated into a language of common sense that constructs a pre-interpreted problem. This portrays religious differences as problematic only in the case of a threatening, fundamentalist Islam, which infiltrates when it does not invade and whose nature is by and large criminal. This kind of connotation also characterizes a range of other connected themes, from integration (Muslims as bearers of customs that violate accepted norms) to the freedom of worship (mosques as hideouts for fundamentalists).

Connotations of suspicion, risk and threat have also surrounded debates in various European countries about the right of Muslim women to wear the burqa. Legal prohibitions on the wearing of the burqa in French schools have been in place since 2004 and were extended, in 2011, to a wholesale ban in public places. Alongside debate about the status of the burqa in terms of secularism in French society and in relation to the oppression of Muslim women, proponents of a ban on the wearing of veils in public spaces have articulated concerns about the security implications of concealed identity. The notion that efforts to evade the reach of surveillance technologies are themselves grounds for suspicion apply in relation to other forms of behaviour that also conceal identity, but have been advanced in relation to Muslim women in a number of European countries in the context of counter-terrorism. Just as the discursive construction of Muslims as risky communities has underpinned much of the legislation, policy and operational practice examined in this chapter, the specific issue of the burqa can be seen to underpin a range of surveillance techniques applied to Muslim communities. The surveillance of the suspect Muslim community has adopted a number of forms and is conducted at various levels in a range of ways. Routine technological techniques such as CCTV have been targeted at Muslim neighbourhoods, as illustrated by a project developed, although subsequently cancelled, in Birmingham (as outlined in a newspaper report shown in Box 9.1).

Box 9.1

Birmingham stops Muslim CCTV surveillance scheme

A project to place two Muslim areas in Birmingham under surveillance has been dramatically halted after an investigation by the Guardian revealed it was a counterterrorism initiative.

Bags are being placed over hundreds of cameras which were recently installed in the neighbourhoods of Washwood Heath and Sparkbrook, to reassure the community that their movements are not being monitored until a public consultation takes place.

Announcing that the cameras would not be turned on, West Midlands police and Birmingham city council apologised for not being 'more explicit' about the funding arrangements of the project, which stipulated they should be used to combat terrorism.

But officials insisted the £3m project could still go ahead if the consultation showed support for the cameras. The programme could also be shelved altogether, which would require police and the council to take down the cameras.

Under the initiative, Project Champion, the suburbs were to be monitored by a network of 169 automatic number plate recognition (ANPR) cameras – three times more than in the entire city centre. The cameras, which include covert cameras secretly installed in the street, form 'rings of steel' meaning residents cannot enter or leave the areas without their cars being tracked. Data was to be stored for two years.

(Continued)

(Continued)

There were angry public meetings in the city last week, after the Guardian disclosed the cameras were paid for by the Terrorism and Allied Matters (TAM) fund, administered by the Association of Chief Police Officers. Its grants are for projects that 'deter or prevent terrorism or help to prosecute those responsible'. Police sources said the initiative was the first of its kind in the UK that sought to monitor a population seen as 'at risk' of extremism.

Extract from *The Guardian*, 17 June 2010

The collective identification of communities and neighbourhoods targeted for surveillance mirrors concerns about the racial profiling of individual suspects targeted in police stop and searches conducted under section 44 of the 2000 Terrorism Act or of Muslim prisoners, as examined earlier. Only a very small proportion of these stops and searches result in a conviction relating to terrorism – in the year to September 2009 there were more than 200,000 stop and searches under section 44, but only 201 arrests and in just 72 cases did these result in terrorism-related charges (Home Office, 2010b). Proponents of the 'suspect community' thesis argue that such data demonstrates that police stop and search powers – in this context directed disproportionally at Asian people – is evidence of racial profiling that subjects thousands of people to unwarranted police attention and is a central feature of counter-terrorism policy and practice that ensures that 'Muslim communities continue to endure the spectre of state suspicion' (Pantazis and Pemberton, 2009: 662). The connection between stop and search practices and surveillance was illustrated by claims that security services have exerted pressure on individuals who have been stopped to covertly spy on Muslim communities (Dodd, 2011). Racial profiling in the context of 'ordinary' crime has been widely criticized on the grounds that it is an ineffective, as well as ethically problematic, means of predicting offending behaviour and the targeting of terrorist suspects on the basis of their ethnic and religious identity is similarly flawed. Simon (2007: 273) noted that the 9/11 attackers did not exhibit the risk factors that form the basis of profiling techniques: 'they were not born addicted to crack; they did not grow up in single-parent, female-dominated homes; nor did they blow off school, do drugs, or fall into repeated low-level conflicts with the police'. For similar reasons, Sivanandan (2006: 4) argued that the 7/7 bombers did not fit the model of vulnerability to radicalization that underpinned counter-terrorist policy:

None of the suicide bombers could be said not to have been integrated into British society. Abdullah Jamal (formerly Jermaine Lindsay) was married to a white, English woman, Mohammad Sidique Khan was a graduate teacher who helped children of all religions with learning difficulties, Shehzad Tanweer was also a graduate and often helped out in his father's fish-and-chip shop and

Hasib Hussain was sent to Pakistan because he had fallen into the English culture of drinking and swearing. You can't get more integrated than that, not within a couple of generations. And yet, they were prepared to take their lives and the lives of their fellow citizens in the name of Islam.

Much of the critical analysis of the ways in which Muslims have become 'suspect communities' traces the ways in which practices developed in the context of Irish terrorism, in the 1970s and 1980s, have extended to contemporary communities of risk. As the above discussion indicates, there is extensive evidence suggesting that police, customs and security services in many countries have developed policies and practices that have come to define Muslims as risky and problematic. Less widely noted in the research literature is that these processes of state surveillance have extended and become embedded in the practices of complex networks of government agencies, public sector organizations, private companies and individual citizens. Policing and security are increasingly understood in terms of plural networks of governance that engage state and government agencies at a range of transnational, national, subnational agencies, as well as civil society and private organizations (Loader, 2000; Wood and Shearing, 2007). The impact of plural policing has been widely noted in studies of contemporary approaches to crime control in general terms and also characterizes the processes that have made Muslim communities suspect. Mazerolle and Ransley (2005) identified a range of legal and regulatory interventions that have contributed to 'third party policing', whereby private, public and civil society organizations have been incorporated into crime control and prevention. In England and Wales, to cite a prime example, local authorities have been given responsibility for a range of crime control and community safety activities (Hughes, 2007). Similarly, private companies and public bodies have become embroiled in monitoring the behaviour of citizens who might be suspicious or risky in the context of security and terrorism. The banking and finance sector are required to submit Suspicious Activity Reports detailing transactions that might be related to terrorism or to organized crime. Donohue (2008) has noted that such requirements have been part of a wider process that has disproportionally impacted upon Muslim businesses and charities. The surveillance of Muslim and Arab communities has been widely noted in the context of profiling and security practices of private companies operating in airports (Ramirez et al., 2003). Public sector organizations have also become nodes in networks of policing and security. Universities have been identified as potential sites of radicalization and academic staff are urged to report the suspicious activity of Islamic societies and individuals who might be encouraging violent extremism. Similarly, community and religious groups are encouraged to report potentially problematic individuals or activities. While there is nothing inherently misplaced in widening processes of surveillance, concern does arise given the wider context of Islamaphobia and racism perpetuated in the media and public discourse more widely. The

stereotyping of Irish people, in terms of terrorism and 'the troubles', under-
scored wider practices of socio-economic and political discrimination and
perpetuated the marginalization and disadvantage of those communities.
Similar practices in the context of contemporary Muslim communities
become more entrenched, however, in the context of pluralized policing and
security that integrated wider swathes of organizations and individuals. In a
'maximum surveillance society', in which wider nets have narrower meshes,
processes of control have greater reach and a more significant impact.

Perhaps the extent to which discourse of security and practices of surveillance have impregnated social relations is most evident in the context of individual interactions directed towards those perceived to be Muslim. Although
the extent of incidents motivated by Islamaphobia has been less widely analyzed than other forms of hate crime, there is considerable anecdotal evidence
that Muslims, and those perceived to be Muslim, have been surveilled and
targeted on such a basis. Moreover, Spalek (2002) found that the fear of being
targeted by those who associated Islam with terrorist atrocities had an impact
on the routine behaviour and lifestyle of some Muslim women. At the other
end of the spectrum are more passive forms of surveillance such as those
encouraged by publicity campaigns that encourage private citizens to observe and
report suspicious behaviour. Finn (2011) noted that the study of surveillance has
paid relatively little attention to the experiences of those under observation
and has also failed to adequately consider 'citizen-to-citizen' surveillance
encounters. South Asian women in the United States, Finn's study found, had
extensive experience of surveillance from fellow members of the public in
routine encounters on transport systems, in the supermarket, the workplace
and leisure contexts. Although these might appear relatively innocuous when
considered as individual experiences, Finn argued (2011: 423–424) that 'surveillant staring' is an important part of 'othering' racialized minorities. That
they are routine and 'trivial' incidents occurring in everyday settings makes
them more, not less, invidious, Finn (2011: 424–425) maintained:

> Whilst technological surveillance, such as CCTV, airport screening, and compu-
> terized databases, does disproportionately affect South Asians and other non-
> white persons, often these forms of surveillance are occasional encounters, or
> they are invisible to the person concerned. ... However, person-to-person sur-
> veillance is a more democratic practice that is experienced more often and is
> more visible to the person being surveilled ... it is the surveillance 'encounter'
> that is significant in bringing about the racialized effects of this surveillance.

There is clear evidence that Muslim communities have become 'suspect communities' in ways previously applied to Irish communities and that this has
been exacerbated by the increasingly embedded nature of surveillance in the
practices of a range of agencies and among citizens. Nevertheless, a number of
caveats can be applied to the 'suspect community thesis'. First, as Greer (2010)

argued, for all that government ministers and policy documents have at times misidentified Muslim communities as risky and vulnerable to violent extremism and radicalization, there have also been a recurring instance that the majority of Muslims are law-abiding and opposed to terrorist activity. In some respects the 'suspect community thesis' is an argument for which supporting examples can easily be identified but for which there remains relatively little research evidence. That policy and practice have been developed in some local circumstances that run counter to the prevailing thesis is significant. As Lambert's (2008) study demonstrates, police have run programmes in conjunction with radical Muslim groups that the 'suspect community' thesis would suggest have been irredeemably problematized. While the suspect community thesis is convincing at the macro-level, it belies the fact that local actors, agencies and networks might operate in ways that sometimes run counter to prevailing policy discourse and ideology. Moreover, during the same period in which legislation has extended state powers to stop and search, detain suspects and conduct surveillance, there have been other developments that have extended the legal protection of ethnic and religious minorities. As detailed in Chapter Five, the Racial and Religious Hatred Act of 2006 introduced stronger tariffs for such forms of hate crime. The Race Relations (Amendment) Act 2000 imposed a statutory duty on all public agencies to promote equality and extended previous legal provisions against racism to the police service, which had been partially exempted from the 1976 Race Relations Act. Much of the public and criminal justice field has been subject to considerable reform engendered by the 1999 Lawrence Report's analysis of institutional racism. Clearly, the identification of Muslims as a 'suspect community' has not developed in a straightforward or uncontested manner. It must also be noted that other communities and groups have also been subject to public discourse and 'cultures of control' that identify them as problematic subjects for suspicion (Garland, 2001). Other ethnic groups, such as Gypsy Traveller communities, have been extensively criminalized in the popular media, the focus of disproportionate police attention, and subjected to surveillance by plural networks of police and members of the general public (James, 2007). Furthermore, other 'risky' communities – youth, for example, are often subject to similar processes and patterns that cast them in generic terms as threatening. Muncie (2004) has argued that the demonization and criminalization of young people has proceeded in ways that mirror the 'othering' of Muslim communities. Walker (2009) goes further still to argue that the development of 'neighbour terrorism' – threats from familiar internal elements of society – has led to the development of 'all-risks' policing that subjects everyone to the attention of surveillance. In an era in which security, risk and control have become the pre-eminent focus of governance, engaging a broad range of networks and agencies, Muslim communities might come under specific forms of suspicion that are distinct from those applied to other groups, but that are not confined only to the Muslim community.

SUMMARY

Contemporary concerns about terrorism have resulted in legislative and policy initiatives that have constructed Muslim individuals and groups in terms of risk and threats to security. The development and deployment of control orders, the proscription of organizations and efforts to block the funding of terrorist activity have led to considerable debate about the balance between human rights and civil liberties and security that have implications for all citizens. In practice, however, these have had particular impact upon Muslims such that many have argued that, coupled with Islamaphobia in political and media discourse, they have become 'suspect communities' in the twenty-first century. Many forms of surveillance – conducted by the state, private companies and individual citizens – have concentrated upon Muslim communities and culture. While the 'suspect community' thesis has much evidence to support it, it must be acknowledged that there has been a series of developments that have sought to extend legal protection to Muslim people and that other groups, such as young people and Gypsy Travellers, have also been subjected to similar processes of criminalization and suspicion.

STUDY QUESTIONS

1 Are the restriction of legal rights and limitations on civil liberties inevitable consequences of the threat of contemporary terrorism?

2 Why might the concept of 'radicalism' be unhelpful in terms of preventing terrorism?

3 What are the strengths and weaknesses of the 'suspect community' thesis as applied to Muslims in Britain?

FURTHER READING

Chapters by Chakraborti (2007) and Spalek, Lambert and Baker (2009) outline developments in policing and criminal justice treatment of Muslims in Britain during the 'post 9/11' period. Legal and criminal justice responses to terrorism in the United States and in Britain are thoroughly documented and reviewed in Donohue's (2008, Cambridge University Press) *The Cost of Counterterrorism*. The strengths and weakness of the 'suspect community' debate, as it applies in relation to Muslims in Britain, are reviewed, from different perspectives, in Pantazis and Pemberton's (2009) and Greer's (2010) articles in the *British Journal of Criminology*.

10

Race and Crime: a Critical Engagement

OVERVIEW

This chapter:

- summarizes key debates and reiterates that race and crime have been closely intertwined since criminology emerged in the mid-nineteenth century;

- identifies limitations with forms of ethnic monitoring that have become an important component of criminal justice responses to problems of disproportionality and argues that these risk sustaining the fundamentally flawed engagement between race and crime;

- argues that criminology needs to develop a more critical approach that: recognizes the problematic status of the concept of race; should focus on the racialization of crime; and needs to continue to develop recent engagement with forms of crime and harm that have significant impacts on groups marginalized by broader processes of racism and disadvantage. These include abuses of human rights, genocide, and environmental harms.

KEY TERMS

- Class, gender, age and other variables
- Criminal justice system
- Critical engagement with race and crime
- Media and cultural representation of race and crime

- Criminalization
- Criminological theory
- Ethnic monitoring
- Racialization

Introduction

This book has demonstrated that an enduring, problematic and pernicious engagement between 'race' and 'crime' has dominated much criminological debate, within and beyond the academy, throughout much of the period since criminology developed from the middle of the nineteenth century. Conversely, it has been shown that there has been an under-appreciation of types of crime, such as human rights abuses, and other forms of social, political and environmental harms that have had grave consequences for some ethnic groups. Furthermore, there has been an under-engagement in terms of a failure to theorize, analyze and respond to the impact of 'race' and racist discourse, which have been significant in the oppression of minority ethnic groups and marginalized groups within global political and economic networks.

The Over-engagement of Race and Crime

Too much critical engagement between race and crime has been evident in the continuing development of theoretical approaches to criminal behaviour. While the crude biological racism evident in the work of early theorists was keenly contested even as it emerged in the nineteenth century, associations between race and crime have persisted in various forms throughout subsequent decades. Biological and genetic perspectives were overtaken by environmental and socio-logical approaches derived from urban sociology in the first decades of the twentieth century. However, the concept of race continued to be a largely unquestioned variable of criminological analysis. Race might have come to be understood as a sociological, rather than a biological, variable, but positivist approaches continued to rely on it as an independent factor to be included in analysis of social patterns and problems. Just as criminological analysis has dis-proportionally concentrated on apparent criminal propensities of the working class, so too racialized minority ethnic groups have tended to be regarded as problematic. Critical challenges to the concept of race emerged in sociology, cultural studies and elsewhere, but criminology has paid insufficient attention to the problematic status of race. Approaches to race and crime that emphasized political and ideological processes of racialization developed in the 1970s and 1980s in response to the 'mugging' phenomenon and to urban unrest, but much of this work was rooted in cultural studies, sociology and geography, rather than criminology (Hall et al., 1978; Gilroy, 1987; Solomos, 1988; Keith, 1993).

More recently, the resurgence of scientific interest in genetics has been applied to the study of crime as it has to a broad spectrum of human behav-iour, including sexuality, intelligence and pathology. Biosocial explanations of criminality that have developed since the 1980s have often sought to eschew racist perspectives evident in earlier periods. However, some studies have claimed to identify racial differences rooted in biology that explain different levels of offending. As was demonstrated in Chapter Two, such analysis is conceptually flawed, based on highly problematic data, and ignores the impact that differential institutional practices might have on different groups' levels of engagement with the criminal justice system. Although biosocial approaches acknowledge that human behaviour needs to be understood in terms broader than biology or genetics, there remains a problematic failure to recognize that the concepts of race and crime are socially constructed and cannot be analyzed as objective independent variables.

Although biosocial perspectives on crime have tended not to pay attention to such practices, it is evident that criminal justice agencies have applied a critical engagement between race and crime through the sustained and extensive dispro-portionalities experienced by some minority ethnic groups. In Britain during the post-war period, the established position of senior police officers and politicians tended to be that newly arrived migrants were relatively under-involved in criminal behaviour compared to the wider population. Before that period is identified as a 'golden age', however, it should be noted that street-level practices of police officers, journalists, local politicians and members of the public often racialized and criminalized the behaviour of male migrant workers from the Caribbean and elsewhere (Rowe, 1998; Whitfield, 2004). Then, as now, the class and status of migrant workers, as well as their ethnicity, raised concerns about their impact on society. The development of ethnic monitoring within criminal justice since the mid-1980s, discussed more fully below, has meant that partial, limited and anecdotal claims that minorities have been subjected to discrimination at various stages of the criminal justice system have been complemented by statistical evidence of the kind analyzed in Chapter Seven. The interpretation of this statistical evidence is problematic and has become contested. Nevertheless, it is apparent that black and Asian people in Britain, and other groups elsewhere, experience disproportionality in terms of police stop and search, prosecution and imprisonment. Although these patterns of racialization and criminalization are mediated by class, gender, age and location, the criminal justice system critically engages race and crime through overt and covert practices and policies that both reflect, and in turn reinforce, theoretical and political discourses of risk and offending.

Race and crime have been mutually reinforcing concepts in much media and political representation. As analyzed in Chapter Three, the news media has both misrepresented and exaggerated offending committed by minority ethnic communities and broadly failed to cover those groups in terms of problems of racist victimization and the wider news agenda. While academic analysis has uncovered dynamics of media organizations and the news agenda that explain why crime coverage features so predominantly in the press and on TV, there has been relatively little focus on related representation in other media forms. Cinema, literature and fictional TV programmes have drawn upon racist and ethnic stereotypes that not only suggest minorities are over-involved in some forms of crime, but also that such practices are intimately bound up in the culture and ethnicity of offenders. The critical engagement between race and crime is also evident in emerging digital media formats that might not rely upon crude racist stereotypes but still reconfigure familiar images of urban decline, crime and lawlessness that have been widely racialized in news media, infotainment formats and traditional fictional genres.

Ethnic Monitoring in Criminal Justice

In Britain, ethnic monitoring in criminal justice has developed since the 1980s. The ethnicity of individuals in contact with every stage of the criminal justice system is recorded, from myriad police interactions with the public, through prosecution and courts, and into prisons and offender management. The ethnicity of victims, witnesses, suspects, defendants in court, people convicted, as well as the broad range of staff employed in the criminal justice system is recorded, collated, aggregated and published. Much of the data analyzed in Chapters Four, Five, Seven and Eight are an outcome of these monitoring processes. Fitzgerald and Sibbitt (1997) noted that an early step in the development of ethnic monitoring was the publication of a 1983 Home Office Statistical Bulletin, which outlined crime statistics in the Metropolitan Police District (MPD) by ethnic group. A longitudinal perspective followed in 1984 with the publication of similar data relating to the period 1977–1983, and in 1989 the Home Office published statistics showing ethnic patterns relating to victims, suspects and those arrested in the MPD during 1987. Since 1996, the Home Office, and now the Ministry of Justice, has published 'Race in the Criminal Justice System' annual reports under section 95 of the Criminal Justice Act 1991. During a 20-year period, analysis of 'racial differences' in offending and the criminal justice system has been transformed. Previous debate was based upon relatively narrow studies of the practices of particular agencies in specific localities (such as Hood's 1992 study of the practices in two courts, or Norris et al.'s 1992 study of police stop and search) or on qualitative evidence (for example, the Institute of Race Relations' 1987 report *Policing Against Black People*). Particularly since the section 95 reports have been published, the evidential basis of debates has been transformed by the accrual of a mass of statistical data that provide apparently authoritative evidence that some minority ethnic groups are over-represented at many stages of the criminal justice system. Much of the discussion of offending, victimization and criminal justice practice in earlier chapters of this book has drawn upon this body of statistical evidence. It has been shown that this detailed data on ethnicity, race and crime has not resolved debates about the causes of disproportionality, or, perhaps more importantly, provided for effective responses to identified problems. Nevertheless, it has formed an authoritative picture informing policy analysis, institutional and legal practices, and political and public debate relating to criminal justice in a diverse society.

However, critical problems with ethnic monitoring remain largely unaddressed. Ethnic monitoring within criminal justice in Britain risks reifying, rather than problematizing, race and ethnicity as variables with explanatory reach. Just as the establishment of groups such as the Black Police Association, and other staff organizations, tends to solidify and entrench ethnicity as a key component of internal cultural and human resource development, so too a focus on ethnic monitoring is problematic. During a period of 20–25 years the collation and publication of statistics relating to race, crime and justice have moved from being a taboo activity to something that is highly routine. Perhaps initial opposition to the collation of such data (from those of the Left who saw it as potentially authoritarian during a period in which national identity, immigration and law and order were high on the agenda of the New Right) has been super-seded by a contemporary failure to focus critical attention on the status of ethnic monitoring. It is demonstrated below that the collection of data relating to ethnicity within the criminal justice system is problematic for a number of reasons, including that the categories on which collation and analysis is based are unsatisfactory. Centrally important though that is, a more significant concern is the continuing failure to identify the fundamental purposes of ethnic monitoring. Statistical data relating to criminal justice practices may be unsatisfactory but, when considered in conjunction with other research findings, it is clear that some minority groups experience disproportionate treatment within the criminal justice system. If ethnic monitoring were introduced in order to develop authoritative evidence, then it has done so. The evidence relating to the over-representation of some minorities in police stop and searches, to cite a prime example, is extensive, although explanations of this remain keenly contested. Equally apparent is the under-representation of minorities among the staff of agencies within the criminal justice system, which varies in degree but persists to some extent across police, courts, prisons and probation. In respect to these examples of over-representation and under-representation, however, there remains a failure to effectively tackle the problems that ethnic monitoring apparently identifies. Ethnic monitoring, it is argued below, needs to remain a feature of criminal justice, albeit one that needs to be refined and to be more related to other dimensions of social diversity. These reforms will not prove effective, however, unless fundamental issues relating to accountability and management within the criminal justice system are also addressed, alongside broader social processes of racialization and criminalization that operate at structural levels, rather than the micro-level analysis of criminal justice interactions with the public that are the subject of current ethnic monitoring processes.

Although ethnic monitoring within the criminal justice system has become established in Britain, Australasia and the United States – but not in other Western liberal democracies such as Canada or much of Western Europe – it has been subject to relatively little critical analysis. Two broad categories of problem are explored in the discussion that follows. The first category refers to the processes and practices of ethnic monitoring and considers whether they are effective and appropriate in their own terms. The second is a broader category that raises fundamental questions about the extent to which ethnic monitoring can provide a basis for significant reform.

As has been noted, ethnic monitoring is not practised in many countries, and this is sometimes explained in terms of the particular historical and cultural context of different societies. In France, to give a prime example, republican ideals of universal citizenship explain political resistance to ethnic classification in public policy and criminal justice. Equally, historical, social and political dynamics inform processes of ethnic monitoring in countries that have adopted such practices. This is particularly evident in terms of the different categories developed across different societies. In the United States, individuals are categorized into either one of two 'racial' groups (white or black) or in terms of a wider set of 'ethnic' categories that include 'Asian' and 'Hispanic'. Clearly, this set of typologies has developed in the particular context of US society, just as the classification used in Britain reflects the politics of post-war migration. In the UK, ethnic monitoring in criminal justice has been organized around 16 different categories (plus the additional 'not stated' option), as shown in Table 10.1.

This typology is problematic for a number of reasons. First, the categories fail to encapsulate the breadth and diversity of ethnicity in contemporary British society. 'White' is a highly nebulous ethnic category. Recent migrants from Eastern European countries, for example, do not easily fit this template, which might mean that specific experiences of racist violence, for instance, are obscured amid myriad categories. Gypsy and Traveller groups are similarly difficult to place within this framework, as are people from the Middle East. Second, the typology is sometimes based on national identities but at other times on skin colour. This means that the categories are incommensurate with one another: comparing people of Bangladeshi descent with those who are of 'any other black background' appears rather meaningless and confuses familial lineage with skin pigmentation. While fine distinctions are drawn between some groups of different national background, there is nothing in the classifications to recognize religious identity: Muslim and Jewish people, who have particular histories of victimization, for example, are not captured in the ethnic classifications. The category 'B9 – any other black background' implies that B1 and B2 similarly apply to people who are black, and so fails to acknowledge the ethnic diversity of both the Caribbean and Africa. The Asian categories of Indian, Pakistani and Bangladeshi reflect migration to Britain since the 1960s but clearly do not adequately acknowledge the breadth and diversity of the continent that represents around half the population on the planet. More puzzling still, 'Chinese' is listed

Table 10.1 UK ethnic classifications

W1 – white British	A9 – any other Asian background	M3 – white and Asian
W2 – white Irish	B1 – Caribbean	M9 – any other mixed background
W9 – any other white background	B2 – African	O1 – Chinese
A1 – Indian	B9 – any other black background	O9 – any other ethnic group
A2 – Pakistani	M1 – white and black Caribbean	
A3 – Bangladeshi	M2 – white and black African	NS – not stated

as a separate group altogether. The vagaries and contradictions of these categories, on which much analysis of race and crime is based, led Young (2011: 118) to note with exasperation that:

> The measures of ethnicity are a scandal. To judge ethnicity, as in the United States, by a mixture of melanin level in the skin (black/white), continent (Asian), and, oddest of all, 'hispanic' veers on the edge of the preposterous. The use of 'black' in terms of one 'drop' of African ancestry would have delighted a white supremacist from the apartheid days in South Africa. As the saying goes, a white woman can have a black baby, but a black woman can't have a white one (unless, of course, as is frequently the case, she is looking after it!). Thus American descendants of slaves, people from a large number of cultures in the Caribbean, African businessmen from anywhere south of the Sahara, etc. are all bundled together in the most chaotic categories imaginable. So many cultures reduced to one posited gene base. 'Asian' – from the world's largest continent becomes Chinese in the United States and Indian in the UK. 'Hispanic' includes a middle-class Argentinean, a poor indigenous Peruvian and a Catalan from Barcelona. And if any of these categories had even a modicum of approximation of reality in the past, they are demolished by the hyperpluralism of today. What significance do they really have other than satisfying the prejudices of the right or creating fictitious power blocks for the left? Yet they are the very stuff of opinion polls, policy demographics and political analysis. The recent US 2010 Census does not even seem to have taken on board that 'race' is a biological nonsense; it is the false object of racism not the subject of ethnicity. Yet in a fashion that would make a national socialist bureaucrat rub hands in disbelief, the census deems to list Hmong, Laotian, Thai, Pakistani, Cambodian, Fijian and Tongan together with the usual 'black', Hawaiian, Korean as separate 'races'. It adds with caution 'for this census Hispanic origins are not races' (US Census 2010). And where is everyone else: white Brazilian, Israeli, Russian, Australian, French, German, British, etc? They are, of course, in the most ragbag category of all: 'white'.

For all that the 16 + 1 typology used in the UK is confused and confusing, it is at least based upon self-classification, such that each individual can locate themselves – even with some difficulty – into the category of their choosing. In terms of specific criminal justice data, however, this is not always possible. In cases where an individual is not apprehended and so cannot be asked to express their ethnic identity, police use the Phoenix Codes that catalogue ethnicity in highly problematic terms. The Police Phoenix Codes categorize people as north European; south European; Black; Asian; Chinese, Japanese, South East Asian or Middle Eastern; or 'unknown'; a series of labels so crude and flawed that the fact they are collated on the basis of the subjective judgement of an individual police officer, or reporting victim or witness, makes them not much more problematic than they would otherwise be.

This catalogue of problems, contradictions and limitations relating to ethnic categories used as a basis for policy development in criminal justice might suggest that such practices be abandoned altogether. That would be a retrograde step that would detract from the pursuit of social justice. As has been noted tackling injustice and discrimination within state organizations is important for reasons of legitimacy; in the context of criminal justice – through which the state can exercise the legitimate use of force against citizens and can deny them liberty – legitimacy and procedural justice are particularly significant (Smith, 1994). What the limitations and problems identified do suggest, though, is that ethnic monitoring needs to be reconfigured in ways that more closely reflect contemporary social diversity. Introducing new ethnic categories is not without disadvantage if it means that longitudinal analysis becomes impossible due to a break in the format of data organization. That, however, is an argument for never re-categorizing, which poses the greater risk that ethnic monitoring practices will become increasingly difficult to reconcile to the ethnic diversity of late modern societies. Whatever categories are developed, criminological and policy analysis needs to remain focused on their limited explanatory power and that ethnicity is a fluid concept; identity is not fixed in the ways that such categorization implies. Criminological analysis cannot continue either to ignore the problematic status of ethnic categories or only acknowledge them in a relatively cursory manner before continuing an analysis based upon data that is fundamentally flawed.

Banton (2005) has argued that developing racial typologies – however relevant or reflexive they might be – is a particularly Western practice that makes little sense in terms of cultural or group identity in many parts of the world. A consequence of the continued use of such terminology is to sustain the 'racial coding' of social problems that are categorized on an unsatisfactory basis. The second category of problems relating to ethnic monitoring in criminal justice develops from this concern and is related not – as with the problems identified above – to classification and data collation processes, but to outcomes that arise as a result. One difficulty is that ethnic monitoring is conducted in relative isolation. Even if the concerns about ethnic categorization identified above were resolved, or could be resolved, other factors likely to influence the extent and nature of contact with the criminal justice system are not monitored, collated or analyzed to anything like the same extent as race and ethnicity. In Britain, and elsewhere, the influence of age and gender, can be discerned from official sources broadly comparable to the data sets on which discussion of race and criminal justice is based. Although these variables can be subject to similar critical analysis that has been applied to ethnic categorization, there is at least scope to examine trends and patterns relating to age and gender, as well as flawed ethnic categories. However, other factors, such as religion, sexuality, and – perhaps most significantly – class, are not monitored as part of the routine practices of the criminal justice system. Many of these variables are themselves difficult to define in objective terms: devising categories to capture class or sexuality, to take two examples, is problematic. A consequence of existing approaches is that patterns of disproportionality tend to be analyzed in terms of available data relating to race and ethnicity, which precludes adequate consideration of other factors that might provide more compelling explanations incorporating other variables. The adage that such practices make what can be counted important, rather than counting what is important, is particularly apposite in relation to ethnic monitoring within the criminal justice system.

Debates about police stop and search practices, outlined in Chapter Seven, illustrate something of the extent to which the focus on ethnic monitoring reinforces engagement between race and crime through the omission of data relating to other variables. As has been shown, the data tends to demonstrate that black minority ethnic groups are substantially over-represented in police stop and search, but this judgement is based upon data that fails adequately to address other factors that seem likely to underpin differences in this form of police/public engagement. Several studies have addressed issues relating to spatial and temporal differences in police stops and searches and concluded that the broad patterns of ethnic disproportionality are less clear-cut and vary between different localities (MVA and Miller, 2000; Waddington et al., 2004). The paucity of national performance data relating to such variables means, however, that explanations drawing upon a wider set of variables remain relatively under-explored and that the primary debate continues to be framed in terms of ethnicity. Similarly, a recent study of police custody practices examined ethnic differences in the experiences of prisoners (Skinns, 2010). Other variables – relating to the influence of different types of offence and the characteristics of different custody suites were also considered, but other factors, such as the class background, were omitted from the analysis because related data were not collated by the police and so remained unknown. Unless ethnic monitoring is coupled with greater attention to other determinants, particularly factors relating to class (about which official data tend to be silent), there remains the danger that it serves to sustain rather than challenge the critical engagement between race and crime.

It has been shown that the development of ethnic monitoring, particularly in respect of the different categories that are employed, is related to specific histories of migration and the politics of particular societies. One reason why the ethnic categories applied in criminal justice in Britain are increasingly problematic is because they developed following post-war migration from former colonies and so fail to capture the hyper-pluralism that Young (2011) argued is characteristic of the twenty-first century. The development of ethnic monitoring also needs to be understood in terms of wider practices of managerialism within criminal justice and across the public sector more generally. In this context, ethnic monitoring is a performance indicator against which agencies are inspected and held accountable. This casts equality between ethnic groups in relatively narrow terms of equal opportunity and treatment that serve to marginalize or deny the impact of broader structural socio-economic inequalities between groups (Webster, 2012). Reiner (1993) identified the 'chimera' of pure discrimination in criminal justice and argued that statistical data analysis could never hope to identify in absolute terms that proportion of unequal treatment attributable to racism, prejudice or stereotyping. Almost two decades of sustained ethnic monitoring in Britain has strengthened this argument, especially as the processes and practices applied have been divorced from analysis that incorporates critical engagement with wider factors and offers little in terms of broader policies that might reverse them. As Webster (2012: xx) has argued:

> ... the persistence of this statistical picture may lend itself to reinforcing nega-
> tive stereotypes ... and cuts off alternative perceptions of the crime problem.
> Rather, bureaucratically defined ethnic categories offer a confused, fixed and
> narrow picture, repeatedly presented, of unchanging ethnic groups that con-
> fuse visible 'race' with cultural ethnicity, conflate the variation of ethnic identity,
> and take little account of the new complexity of Britain's ethnic landscape.

The perpetuation of negative stereotypes parallels arguments that fictional represen-tations of crime that seek to subvert established associations between ethnicity, race and offending, of the kind discussed in relation to *The Wire* in Chapter Three, ulti-mately sustain dominant narratives. This unintended consequence of ethnic monitor-ing is also apparent in relation to the role of staff associations within the criminal justice system, and beyond, that have promoted an anti-racist agenda but serve to entrench ethnicity and have contributed to 'cultural wars' within the workforce (McLaughlin, 2007). Holdaway (1996) noted that the Black Police Association provided a strong response to problems of racism, but also that it contributed to the further racialization of policing. In sustaining frameworks of analysis that rely upon racial and ethnic iden-tity, there is a risk that critical engagement becomes muted. This highlights a central challenge to understanding and responding to debates about race and crime examined throughout this book. As has been demonstrated, racist victimization is an extensive and pervasive problem that continues to cause significant harm both to individuals and communities. For all that ethnic monitoring data are flawed, there remains a broader body of quantitative and qualitative evidence, reviewed throughout this book, that minority ethnic people receive worse treatment, both as suspects and victims, from the criminal justice system. For these reasons it is clear that criminology should not aban-don research and analysis into race and crime. However, the problematic nature of the concept of race needs to be at the centre of criminological perspectives.

Race and Crime: Towards a Critical Engagement

On this basis, criminological approaches to race and crime need to entail greater critical engagement conceptually and in terms of the range of offending and social harm subject to analysis. There has been too much critical engagement in terms of theoretical perspectives that seek to identify race, in either biological or cultural terms, as a cause of offending behaviour. While interpersonal violence, street robbery, drug- and gang-related offending pose serious harms and warrant continued criminological attention, the relationship that such problems have to race and ethnicity needs to be re-cast in terms that recognize and critically consider processes of racialization. The interrelationships between class, localities, age, gender, religion and other factors also needs to be subject to sustained analysis.

The relative failure of criminology to critically engage crimes of great magnitude in terms of human misery, and that often take racialized forms, needs to be rectified. As has been shown across several chapters in this book, genocide, human rights abuses, state crimes, and environmental harm have only recently been subject to criminological analysis. Such practices are not necessarily driven by racism, but they often disproportionally impact upon marginalized peoples subject to racism more broadly. It is in response to these challenges that criminology needs to more critically engage with race and crime, while, at the same time, develop a stronger analysis of the deeply problematic associations between the two concepts that have tended to dominate the discipline in the nineteenth and twentieth centuries.

There are a number of ways in which criminology can become more critically engaged with existing and developing types of crime and broader harms that are racialized or have racist consequences. Conceptually, the problematic and unsatisfactory nature of race needs to be foregrounded in discussion of types of crime that have come to be associated in media, political and criminal justice practice with minority ethnic communities. Studies of racist violence have begun to pay more attention to the notion of 'whiteness', reflecting a broader trend within sociology and cultural studies to address ethnicity in more comprehensive terms (Ray et al., 2004). While it may primarily serve to illustrate the limited explanatory power that ethnicity has in relation to offending, there is a need for criminology to consider ethnicity in critical terms as a factor in a broad range of offending. Addressing ethnicity in crimes that have not been racialized, such as, for example insurance fraud, might indicate some of the limitations of understanding any type of offending through the lens of ethnic identity.

Other ways in which criminology can contribute to understanding contemporary forms of social, political and environmental harms that impact upon those at the margins of global neo-liberal networks have been identified at various points in this book. Approaches to genocide have been greatly enhanced through the application of criminological concepts derived from the analysis of corporate crime. Differential association, to take a primary example, contributes to an understanding of forms of white-collar crime, but also to genocidal massacres. Criminological work developed by Hagan and Richmond-Ryder (2009) in the context of genocide in Darfur can be extended to other human rights abuses, not only those with ethnic and racist dimensions. Similarly, these conceptual frameworks can also be applied to other forms of crime and social harm. Environmental racism associated with the global trade in toxic waste, climate change and the illegal extraction of natural resources can be understood, and challenged, using criminological concepts such as 'techniques of neutralization' (White, 2011). Just as those involved in deviance or offending seek to conceptually recalibrate their behaviour so as to rectify any moral dilemmas that might otherwise prove unsettling to them, so too states, corporations and consumers responsible for environmental damage recast their culpability. The depletion of natural resources is not considered a cause for concern in terms of sustainability but rather an opportunity for impoverished people to participate in global markets that offer the promise of enrichment. The destruction caused by climate change, which will impact soonest on politically and economically marginalized groups on the peripheries of global networks, is understood predominantly either as an inevitable price of affluent consumer societies or as a 'natural disaster' for which no one is responsible. Criminology can help to explain and so to challenge the social construction of these forms of crime and harm and to illustrate their connections with wider global relations and patterns of racism.

SUMMARY

Criminology and criminal justice have sustained a critical engagement between race and crime. Theoretically, the discipline of criminology has sought to identify biological and genetic, as well as sociological, causes of offending that treat the concept of race in terms that fail to appreciate its circumscribed explanatory power. Such problems have been reflected in criminal justice processes and practices that have served to criminalize and racialize some minority communities. Popular cultural and political discourse has also often constructed crime problems in racialized terms.

The challenge of responding to the established critical engagement between race and crime is to take problems of discrimination, over-representation and other disproportionalities, and the impact of racism, seriously without further reinforcing the conceptual status of race. It has been shown that the development of ethnic monitoring in criminal justice in Britain has tended not to meet this challenge. Partly, this might be attributed to the poor quality of categorization and management of ethnic monitoring processes. Additionally, the limited impact of ethnic monitoring can be associated with an implicit framework that conceptualizes racism and discrimination in micro-level individualistic terms that do not incorporate structural, socio-economic, cultural or wider processes.

The final part of the chapter argued that it is to these broader dimensions of debates about racialization and criminalization that criminology needs to develop stronger critical engagement. While established concerns with forms of crime and patterns of victimization will properly be continued, criminology needs to pay more attention to corporate crimes, state crime, human rights abuses and environmental degradation that will become increasingly salient in the twenty-first century and pose serious risks to minority ethnic groups within local and transnational societies.

(Continued)

(Continued)

STUDY QUESTIONS

1 What have been the key features of the problematic critical engagement between race and crime evident in criminological theory, criminal justice practice, and cultural and political discourse?

2 What are the central strengths and weaknesses of the practices of ethnic monitoring in criminal justice?

3 Along what lines should contemporary criminology develop a more effective critical engagement with debates about race and crime?

FURTHER READING

Further reading relating to the engagement of race and crime within criminology and criminal justice practices has been identified at the end of the previous chapters. The principles of ethnic monitoring developed in policing, and subsequently across the criminal justice system, are outlined in Fitzgerald and Sibbitt's (1997) Home Office research study. Much information relating to ethnic categorization and the collection and management of related statistical information is available at the Ministry of Justice website, www.justice.gov.uk/publications/statistics-and-data/criminal-justice/race.htm. Included at this site are the results of ethnic monitoring as well as consultation documents and information about underlying process and practice.

Some critical analysis of ethnic monitoring can be found in Back et al.'s (2002) review of race policies developed by New Labour from the late 1990s, and in Webster's (2012) chapter, which argues that such practices need to be more closely aligned to concepts of justice.

Glossary

Academic discipline of criminology: developed from the mid-nineteenth century in Europe and the United States, often dominated by legalistic, psychological and medical perspectives on offenders. The discipline developed sociological and social-legal perspectives from the early part of the twentieth century.

Biosocial theories of crime: seek to explain offending behaviour in terms of the biological and physiological characteristics of offenders but, unlike earlier forms of biological positivism, adopt a framework that recognizes that such characteristics are influenced by the social context in which offenders live.

Classical criminology: developed in the eighteenth century in opposition to the use of extreme and arbitrary punishments. Classical criminology advocated a rational approach that punishment ought to be imposed only to the extent necessary to ensure a deterrent.

Corporate and state crime: critical criminology draws attention to the relatively hidden criminal practices of powerful and established groups. Criminal justice systems and legal frameworks developed by nation states are poorly placed to respond to the crimes of the powerful, even if there were ideological or political motivations to do so.

Crime: in narrow legal terms, crime can be understood as any action or behaviour that violates the criminal law. This 'black letter law' approach to crime is usually regarded as inadequate on a number of grounds. Perhaps most importantly, it fails to account for differences in defining crime between societies at different times and in different places. That an action or behaviour might be criminal in one period but not another, or in one society but not in another, focuses attention on the particular social, political and cultural context in which crime is defined. For these reasons some prefer to focus attention on processes of criminalization, whereby society defines some harmful forms of behaviour as unacceptable, but not others.

Criminalization: given that **crime** is a socially constructed concept, it is important to examine the social, economic, political and cultural circumstances that shape processes that define some forms of behaviour as criminal but do not sanction other activities that might also be considered harmful. The concept of criminalization also focuses attention on the impact that criminal justice agencies can have in terms of focusing attention on groups and forms of behaviour in ways that can further entrench their criminal status.

Criminological positivism: an approach focused on discovering, through the operations of scientific method, causes of offending behaviour, whether rooted in biological, social, psychological or environmental factors.

Digital media: a term applied to diverse forms of new media technology, including computer gaming, online virtual environments and new social media.

Disproportionality: in terms of criminal justice this concept relates to the differences in levels of interaction or in experiences between different sectors of the population. Some differences might be legitimate if, for example, they can be explained by variations in patterns or types of offending. Usually, however, the concept of disproportionality is applied to differences that cannot be explained in terms of justifiable criteria.

Diversity: within criminal justice agencies in Britain and elsewhere, there has been a sustained policy focus on aspects of diversity. In terms of personnel, this has meant a range of initiatives intended to increase the recruitment, retention and promotion of a body of staff that is diverse in terms of ethnicity, gender, age, sexuality and disability. In addition to legal and political imperatives to address diversity, potential benefits have been identified in terms of operational performance and public legitimacy.

Ethnic monitoring: a range of practices developed in criminal justice in Britain in response to evidence of **disproportionality**. By recording and analyzing interactions and outcomes in criminal justice in relation to ethnicity, it is intended that a clearer picture of trends and problems can be identified. The collection of ethnic data was made a legal requirement for criminal justice agencies by section 95 of the 1991 Criminal Justice Act.

Eugenics: a set of beliefs and practices predicated on the notion that the physical and intellectual capacity of future generations can be enhanced through strengthening the genetic and biological 'stock' of the population through selective breeding programmes. The Eugenics Movement was at its strongest in the late nineteenth and early twentieth centuries, and such beliefs were advocated by those from a range of political backgrounds.

Genocide: a term developed in the mid-twentieth century that refers to the wholesale murder of groups of people based upon their race, ethnicity or nationality. A declaration of the United Nations General Assembly in 1946 identified genocide as a crime under international law.

Hate crime: developed in the USA in the 1970s to refer to forms of offending that are in some way motivated by prejudice towards or hatred of the broader social group to which the target is perceived to belong. Hate crimes are considered to have a significant impact beyond the particular properties of the specific offence because they are signal crimes intended to instil fear and insecurity in a community beyond the individual victim. A controversial aspect of legislation addressing hate crime is the notion of 'motivation', which can be difficult to apply in practical evidential terms when prosecuting offenders. Britain does not have generic hate crime legislation although provisions such as those for **racially and religiously aggravated offences** are broadly similar in approach to hate crime legislation enacted in other jurisdictions.

Holocaust: the **genocide** of 6 million Jews by the Nazis between 1933 and 1945 is the central component of the Holocaust (or Shoah in Hebrew). The term is sometimes used to encompass the systematic murder of other ethnic groups targeted by Hitler's regime, such as the estimated 250,000 Roma who also perished.

Infotainment: a media genre that combines the production values of entertainment with a quasi-factual documentary agenda. This form has been particularly common in recent decades, and crime and policing form an important topic of such shows.

Institutional racism: a term that developed in the civil rights era in 1960s, USA. It was used to explain unequal treatment of minorities that was the accumulated outcome of policies and practices that were not themselves inherently racist but were discriminatory in effect. The concept of institutional racism has been particularly influential in Britain in the wake of the Macpherson Report into the racist murder of Stephen Lawrence, which defined it as the 'collective failure of an organisation to provide an appropriate and professional service to people because of their colour, culture or ethnic origin. It can be seen or detected in processes, attitudes and behaviour which amount to discrimination through unwitting prejudice, ignorance, thoughtlessness and racist stereotyping which disadvantages minority ethnic people' (Macpherson, 1999: 6.34).

Labelling theory: first associated with the work of Howard Becker in the United States in the 1950s and 1960s, this perspective emphasizes that crime and deviance are exacerbated by social responses that identify, label and stigmatize individuals such that their problematic behaviour becomes more embedded.

Moral panic: developed by Stan Cohen in the 1960s, the concept refers to the manner in which media, cultural and political responses to social problems can distort and exaggerate their significance in ways that subsequently exacerbate and amplify their seriousness.

'Mugging' and street crime: from the 1970s onwards some minority groups in Britain have been disproportionately associated in media, policing and political debates with forms of street robbery, drug dealing, gang crime and similar offences. The term 'mugging' was first applied to such offences by the media in the early 1970s, even though it has no real meaning in terms of legal or criminal codes, and from the outset was used to connote a 'racial' or ethnic dimension to criminal behaviour of this kind.

Neo-colonialism: a term used to describe global patterns of economic dominance and dependence that persist between societies that were previously part of colonial systems. The pattern of these relationships has persisted despite the formal demise of political governmental dominance.

Normative whiteness: the tendency for organizations, politics, policy and cultural practices to assume that all clients, citizens and the public at large is of the same white ethnic background.

Offending, Crime and Justice Survey (OCJS): along with **victim surveys**, self-report studies provide a useful complementary measure of offending behaviour that supplements data officially recorded by the police. A primary recent example in Britain has been the OCJS, which has included booster samples of minority ethnic groups.

Organizational culture: in the context of criminal justice the concept is used to explain practices and outcomes produced by institutions as a result of the professional discretion exercised by personnel. Organizational culture can explain operational practices that might not be directly evident in policy or legal frameworks. The nature of the work conducted by criminal justice agencies, the relation of personnel to wider society, and the characteristics of those employed in the criminal justice system have been cited in various combinations to explain the persistence of informal working practices. The notion of organizational culture has been used to explain forms of prejudice and discrimination that have persisted despite policy interventions designed to promote equality of opportunity.

Race: the concept of race developed as a means of ordering human beings into distinct populations and suggested that differences in physical or mental capacities could be attributed to biological or genetic lineage. The scientific basis of race has been discredited on the grounds that the biological and genetic variation between human populations are minor and have little explanatory power in terms of differences between them. Although many have argued that the concept should be abandoned in favour of **sociological approaches to 'race'** or that the notion of **racialization** is more useful, 'race' continues to be important since it remains a powerful, albeit flawed, concept through which social life is understood. That it is an essentially contested concept that ought to be treated critically is an important theme of this book.

Racial profiling: the process whereby the association of certain types of offending with particular ethnic or 'racial' minorities becomes predominant such that all people perceived to belong to those groups come under suspicion, regardless of their individual behaviour. Conversely, those who might be engaged in offending behaviour but who are not perceived to belong to the profiled group are not subject to the attention of law enforcement or other authorities. The practice of racial profiling has been especially controversial in the United States, where it is legally prohibited but still widely perceived to inform police activities.

Racialization: focuses attention on the complex ways in which the idea of **race** is socially constructed by exploring the social, economic, political and cultural contexts that sustain the concept as a viable, even though fundamentally flawed, way of narrating and understanding social life.

Racially and religiously aggravated offences: British law provides for stronger penalties for offences that are 'aggravated' by racial or religious factors. This is defined either in terms relating to the motivation of the offender, which may be difficult to determine in legal terms, or by the behaviour or language that the offender displays or uses before, during or after the offence. Unlike in some other jurisdictions, Britain has no generic legislation against **hate crime**, but racially and religiously aggravated offences are approximate to such provisions.

Radicalization: in the wake of the apparent threat of Islamist terrorism, the notion of radicalization underpinned policies that sought to prevent people identified as vulnerable being recruited by violent extremists.

Reporting rates: a key problem with officially recorded crime statistics is that they only reflect the proportion of offending that becomes known to the police and is defined as a violation of the criminal law. Any incident must be reported to the police and then be recorded as a criminal offence; incidents that do not pass this two-stage threshold are not represented in official crime statistics and remain part of what is sometimes known as the 'dark figure' of crime. In the case of racist offending, as well as in other contexts, a considerable emphasis has been placed upon encouraging the reporting of offences so that a more accurate picture of the extent and patterns of victimization can be developed.

Scientific racism: developing in the nineteenth century, scientific racism was based on a bogus positivist empiricism and held that humanity could be classified into distinct categories that could be ranked hierarchically.

Sociological approaches to 'race': dominant since the second half of the twentieth century a broad range of perspectives have developed from a sociological perspective that seek not to understand the concept of 'race' in terms of inherent objective components, but to recognize that the term is socially constructed. Such approaches can be understood as a response to the much-cited observation that while 'race' is not real in itself it is real in its consequences, and is therefore an important topic for research and analysis. Critics argue that such approaches effectively legitimize the concept of race and that the focus ought instead to be on processes of **racialization**, which involve structural relations of power and ideology.

Staff associations: in addition to formal and long-standing staff associations such as the Police Federation and the Prison Officers' Association, there has developed a range of different sectional groups representing particular interests within the criminal justice system. Many of these groups represent female staff or those from a particular ethnic or religious background who share interests that have tended to be under-recognized by the various agencies of the criminal justice system.

Surveillance: as a form of social control, surveillance has been practised by states for centuries. The capacity and reach of surveillance methods have been greatly accelerated by technological innovations. In relation to issues of race and racism, concerns have been expressed in various contexts that minority ethnic communities experience **disproportionality** as they are subject to invasive technology to a greater extent than other groups. Surveillance technology is often linked to claims of **racial profiling**.

Victim surveys: as a result of recognition that officially recorded crime statistics fail to capture a significant proportion of offending that does not, for a range of reasons, come to the attention of police, victim surveys were developed in the United States in the early 1970s to provide a more complete measure of crime trends and patterns. Aided by methodological developments in social survey research methods, victim surveys began to indicate that many types of offence remained under-reported to the police. Similar research methods are applied in the British Crime Survey, which was first conducted in 1982 and has been run as a continuous process since the early years of the twenty-first century. See also the **Offender, Crime and Justice Survey**.

Victimization: criminological research that developed in the early 1970s, partly based on victim surveys, demonstrated that criminal victimization was not a random misfortune but was disproportionally experienced by some social groups and categories more than others. Often the likelihood of criminal victimization has been found to be related to a host of other forms of social disadvantage and marginalization. Such evidence has led to a host of victims' rights pressure groups and to a series of political responses that have sought to place an increased emphasis on the rights of victims within the criminal justice system.

References

Abbas, T. (2007) 'Muslim Minorities in Britain: Integration, Multiculturalism and Radicalism in the Post-7/7 Period', *Journal of Intercultural Studies*, 28: 287–300.

Adamson, S., Cole, B. and Craig, G. (2009) *Hidden from Public View? Racism against the UK's Chinese Population*, London: The Monitoring Group.

Adorno, T. (1950) *The Authoritarian Personality*, London: Harper & Row.

Advisory Panel on Judicial Diversity (2010) *The Report of the Advisory Panel on Judicial Diversity 2010*, London: Ministry of Justice.

Agozino, B. (2003) *Counter-Colonial Criminology: A Critique of Imperialist Reason*, London: Pluto Press.

Albrecht, H.-J. (1997) 'Ethnic Minorities, Crime and Criminal Justice in Germany', *Crime and Justice: A Review of Research*, 21: 31–99.

Aldridge, J. and Medina, J. (2008) *Youth Gangs in an English City: Social Exclusion, Drugs and Violence: Full Research Report*, ESRC End of Award Report, RES-000-23-0615. Swindon: ESRC.

Alexander, C. (2004) 'Imagining the Asian Gang: Ethnicity, Masculinity and Youth after "the Riots"', *Critical Social Policy*, 24: 526–549.

Alfred, R. (1992) *Black Workers in the Prison Service*, London: Prison Reform Trust.

Alvarez, J.E. (1999) 'Crimes of State/Crimes of Hate: Lessons from Rwanda', *Yale Journal of International Law*, 24: 365–483.

Anderson, C. (2004) *Legible Bodies: Race, Criminality and Colonialism in South Asia*, Oxford: Berg.

Aning, K. (2010) 'Security, the War on Terror, and Official Development Assistance', *Critical Studies on Terrorism*, 3: 7–26.

Appleby, N. (2010) 'Labelling the Innocent: How Government Counter-Terrorism Advice Creates Labels that Contribute to the Problem', *Critical Studies on Terrorism*, 3: 421–436.

Arendt, H. (1963) *Eichmann in Jerusalem: A Report on the Banality of Evil*, New York: Viking.

Armelagos, G.K. and Goodman, A.H. (1998) 'Race, Racism, and Anthropology', in Goodman, A.H. and Leatherman, T. (eds), *Building a New Biocultural Synthesis: Political-Economic Perspectives on Human Biology*, Ann Arbor, MI: University of Michigan Press, pp. 359–377.

Australian Bureau of Statistics (2009) *Prisoners in Australia, 2009*, Canberra: Australian Bureau of Statistics.

Back, L., Keith, M., Khan, A., Shukra, K. and Solomos, J. (2002) 'The Return of Assimilationism: Race, Multiculturalism and New Labour', *Sociological Research Online*, 7(2), www.socresonline.org.uk/7/2/back.html.

Back, L. and Solomos, J. (eds) (2000) *Theories of Race and Racism*, London: Routledge.

Banton, M. (1959) *White and Coloured: The Behaviour of British People Towards Coloured Immigrants*, London: Cape.

Banton, M. (1967) *Race Relations*, London: Tavistock.

Banton, M. (1987) *Racial Theories*, Cambridge: Cambridge University Press.

Banton, M. (2005) 'Historical and Contemporary Modes of Racialization', in Murji, K. and Solomos, J. (eds), *Racialization: Studies in Theory and Practice*, Oxford: Oxford University Press, pp. 51–68.

Barclay, G. and Tavares, C. (1999) *Information on the Criminal Justice System of England and Wales, Digest 4*, London: Home Office.

Barker, M. (1981) *The New Racism*, London: Junction Books.

Barmes, L. and Malleson, K. (2011) 'The Legal Profession as Gatekeeper to the Judiciary: Design Faults in Measures to Enhance Diversity', *Modern Law Review*, 74: 245–271.

Battaglini, G.Q. (1914/15) 'Eugenics and the Criminal Law', *Journal of the American Institute of Criminal Law & Criminology*, pp. 12–15.

Bauman, Z. (1989) *Modernity and the Holocaust*, Cambridge: Polity Press.

Becker, H. (1963) *Outsiders: Studies in the Sociology of Deviance*, New York: Free Press.

Benedikt, M. (1881) *Anatomical Studies upon Brains of Criminals*, New York: de Capo Press.

Bhui, H.S. (2006) 'Anti-Racist Practice in NOMS: Reconciling Managerialist and Professional Realities', *The Howard Journal*, 45: 171–190.

Bhui, H.S. (2009) 'Prisons and Race Equality', in Bhui, H.S. (ed.), *Race and Criminal Justice*, London: Sage, pp. 83–101.

Blagg, H. (2008) *Crime, Aboriginality and the Decolonisation of Justice*, Sydney: Hawkins Press.

Blair, T. (2007) 'Our Nation's Future: Defence', 12 January, London: 10 Downing Street.

Blattmann, R. and Bowman, K. (2008) 'Achievements and Problems of the International Criminal Court: A View from Within', *Journal of International Criminal Justice*, 6: 711–730.

Bolognani, M. (2009) *Crime and Muslim Britain: Culture and the Politics of Criminology among British Pakistanis*, London: I.B. Tauris.

Bonczar, T. (2003) *Prevalence of Imprisonment in the U.S. Population, 1974–2001*, Washington, DC: Bureau of Justice Statistics.

Bosworth, M. and Guild, M. (2008) 'Governing through Migration Control: Security and Citizenship in Britain', *British Journal of Criminology*, 48: 703–719.

Bowcott, O. (2011) 'Osama bin Laden: US Responds to Questions about Killing's Legality', *The Guardian*, 3 May, www.guardian.co.uk/world/2011/may/03/osama-bin-laden-killing-legality

Bowling, B. (1993) 'Racial Harassment and the Process of Victimization: Conceptual and Methodological Implications for the Local Crime Survey', *British Journal of Criminology*, 33: 231–250.

Bowling, B. (1998) *Violent Racism: Victimisation, Policing and Social Context*, Oxford: Oxford University Press.

Bowling, B. (1999) 'The Rise and Fall of New York Murder: Zero Tolerance or Crack's Decline?', *British Journal of Criminology*, 39(4): 531–555.

Bowling, B. and Philips, C. (2002) *Racism, Crime and Justice*, Harlow: Longman.

Bowling, B. and Philips, C. (2007) 'Disproportionate and Discriminatory: Reviewing the Evidence on Police Stop and Search', *Modern Law Review*, 70: 936–961.

Broadhurst, R. (1999) 'Crime and Indigenous People', in Graycar, A. and Grabosky, P. (eds), *Handbook of Australian Criminology*, Melbourne: Cambridge University Press, pp. 256–280.

Brogden, M. (1987) 'The Emergence of the Police: The Colonial Dimension', *British Journal of Criminology*, 27(1): 4–14.

Brown, A. and Brown, N. (2007) 'The Northern Territory Intervention: Voices from the Centre of the Fringe', *Medical Journal of Australia*, 187: 621–623.

Browning, C. (1992) *Ordinary Men: Reserve Police Battalion 101 and the Final Solution in Poland*, New York: Harper Collins.

Brownmiller, S. (1975) *Against Our Will: Men, Women and Rape*, New York: Simon & Schuster.

Burnett, J. and Whyte, D. (2005) 'Embedded Expertise and the New Terrorism', *Journal for Crime, Conflict and the Media*, 1: 1–18.

Cardwell, D. (2007) 'After Bell, Critics Want Mayor to Broaden Focus on Police', *New York Times*, 21 March.

Cavallero, J.J. and Plasketes, G. (2004) 'Gangsters, Fessos, Tricksters, and Sopranos: The Historical Roots of Italian American Stereotype Anxiety', *Journal of Popular Film and Television*, 32: 49–73.

Cawthra, G. (1993) *Policing South Africa: The SAP and the Transition from Apartheid*, London: Zed Books.

Chakraborti, N. (2007) 'Policing Muslim Communities', in Rowe, M. (ed.), *Policing Beyond Macpherson: Issues in Policing, Race and Society*, Cullompton: Willan Publishing, pp. 107–127.

Chakraborti, N. and Garland, J. (2003) 'An "Invisible" Problem? Uncovering the Nature of Racist Victimisation in Rural Suffolk', *International Review of Victimology*, 10: 1–17.

Chakraborti, N. and Garland, J. (2009) *Hate Crime: Impact, Causes and Responses*, London: Sage.

Cheliotis, L.K. and Liebling, A. (2006) 'Race Matters in British Prisons: Towards a Research Agenda', *British Journal of Criminology*, 46: 286–317.

Chibnall, S. (1977) *Law and Order News: An Analysis of Crime Reporting in the British Press*, London: Tavistock.

Chiricos, T. and Eschholz, S. (2002) 'The Racial and Ethnic Typification of Crime and the Criminal Typification of Race and Ethnicity in Local Television News', *Journal of Crime and Delinquency*, 39: 400–420.

Christie, N. (2000) *Crime Control as Industry: Towards GULAGS, Western Style*, London: Routledge.

Clancy, A., Hough, M., Aust, R. and Kershaw, C. (2001) *Crime, Policing and Justice – the Experience of Ethnic Minorities: Findings from the 2000 British Crime Survey*, Research Study 223. London: Home Office.

Clarke, J.W. (1998) 'Without Fear or Shame: Lynching, Capital Punishment and the Subculture of Violence in the American South', *British Journal of Political Science*, 28, 269–289.

Cloward, R. and Ohlin, L. (1960) *Delinquency and Opportunity: A Theory of Delinquent Gangs*, New York: Free Press.

Cohen, A. (1955) *Delinquent Boys: the Culture of the Gang*, New York: The Free Press.

Cohen, P. (1996) 'All White on the Night? Narratives of Nativism on the Isle of Dogs', in Butler, T. and Rustin, M. (eds), *Rising in the East? The Regeneration of East London*, London: Lawrence and Wishart.

Cohen, S. (1973) *Folk Devils and Moral Panics: The Creation of the Mods and Rockers*, London: Paladin.

Cohen, S. (2001) *States of Denial: Knowing about Atrocities and Suffering*, Cambridge: Polity Press.

Cole, B. (1999) 'Post-Colonial Systems', in Mawby, R. (ed.), *Policing across the World: Issues for the Twenty-First Century*, London: UCL Press, pp. 88–108.

Cole, D.P., Gittens, M., Tam, M., Williams, T., Ratushny, E. and Sri-Skanda-Rajah, S.G. (1995) *Report of the Commission on Systematic Racism in the Ontario Criminal Justice System*, Toronto: Queen's Printer for Ontario.

Coleman, R. (2004) *Reclaiming the Streets: Surveillance, Social Control and the City*, Cullompton: Willan Publishing.

Colls, R. (2002) *Identity of England*, Oxford: Oxford University Press.

Commission for Racial Equality (CRE) (1996) *Race and Equal Opportunities in the Police Service – a Programme for Action*, London: CRE.

Council of Europe (1994) *Formation de la Police Concernant les Relations avec les Migrants et les Groups Ethniques: Directives Pratiques*, Strasbourg: Les Editions du Conseil de L'Europe.

CPS (Crown Prosecution Service) (2001) *Report of an Independent Inquiry into Race Discrimination in the CPS*, London: Crown Prosecution Service.

CPS (Crown Prosecution Service) (2010a) *Crown Prosecution Service Single Equality Scheme 2006–2010*, London: Crown Prosecution Service.

CPS (Crown Prosecution Service) (2010b) *Workforce Diversity Data – Annual Report 2009–2010*, London: Crown Prosecution Service.

Cromby, J., Brown, S.D., Gross, H., Locke, A. and Patterson, A.E. (2010) 'Constructing Crime, Enacting Morality: Emotion, Crime and Anti-Social Behaviour in an Inner-City Community', *British Journal of Criminology*, 50: 873–895.

Cunneen, C., Luke, G. and Ralph, N. (2006) *Evaluation of the Aboriginal Over-Representation Strategy*, Sydney: Institute of Criminology.

Cunneen, C. and Schwartz, M. (2008) 'Funding Aboriginal and Torres Strait Islander Legal Services: Issues of Equity and Access', *Criminal Law Journal*, 32: 38–53.

Davie, N. (2005) Tracing the Criminal Brain: the Rise of Scientific Criminology in Britain, 1860–1918, Oxford: Bardwell Press.

Davies, J. (1989) 'From "Rookeries" to "Communities": Race, Poverty and Policing in London, 1850–1985', *History Workshop Journal*, 27: 66–79.

Davies, P., Francis, P. and Greer, C. (eds) (2007) *Victims, Crime and Society*, London: Sage.

Department of Corrections (2007) *Over-Representation of Māori in the Criminal Justice System: An Exploratory Report*, Wellington, NZ: Department of Corrections.

Dodd, V. (2011) 'Asian People 42 Times More Likely to be Held under Terror Law', *The Guardian*, 23 May, www.guardian.co.uk/uk/2011/may/23/counter-terror-stop-search-minorities.

Donohue, L.K. (2008) *The Cost of Counterterrorism: Power, Politics and Liberty*, Cambridge: Cambridge University Press.

Downes, D. and Rock, P. (2003) *Understanding Deviance* (4th edition), Oxford: Oxford University Press.

Doyle, A. (2003) *Arresting Images: Crime and Policing in Front of the Television Camera*, Toronto: University of Toronto Press.

du Bois, W.E.B. (1899) *The Philadelphia Negro*, Philadelphia, PA: University of Pennsylvania Press.

Durose, M.R., Langan, P.A., Smith, E.L. (2007) *Contacts Between Police and the Public, 2005*, Washington: Bureau of Justice Statistics.

ECRI (European Commission against Racism and Intolerance) (2002) *Second Report on Italy*, Strasbourg: Council of Europe.

Edward-Day, L. and Vandiver, M. (2000) 'Criminology and Genocide Studies: Notes on What Might Have Been and What Still Could Be', *Crime, Law and Social Change*, 34: 43–59.

EHRC (Equalities and Human Rights Commission) (2010) *Stop and Think: A Critical Review of the Use of Stop and Search Powers in England and Wales*, London: EHRC.

Emory Lyon, F. (1914/15) 'Race Betterment and the Crime Doctors', *Journal of the American Institute of Criminal Law and Criminology*, pp. 887–891.

Emsley, C. (1987) *Crime and Society in England, 1750–1900*, London: Longman.

Fattah, E. (ed.) (1986) *From Crime Policy to Victim Policy*, London: Macmillan.

Ferguson, R. (1998) *Representing 'Race': Ideology, Identity and the Media*, London: Arnold.

Ferrell, J., Hayward, K. and Young, J. (2008) *Cultural Criminology*, London: Sage.

Finn, M. (2006) 'Political Interface: The Banning of GTA III in Australia', in Garrelts, N. (ed.), *The Meaning and Culture of Grand Theft Auto: Critical Essays*, Jefferson, NC: McFarland Press, pp. 35–48.

Finn, R.L. (2011) 'Surveillant Staring: Race and the Everyday Surveillance of South Asian Women after 9/11', *Surveillance and Society*, 8: 413–426.

Fitzgerald, M. and Sibbitt, R. (1997) *Ethnic Monitoring in Police Forces: A Beginning*, Research Study 173. London: Home Office.

Free, M.D. (2002) 'Race and Pre-Sentencing Decisions in the United States: A Summary and Critique of the Research', *Criminal Justice Review*, 27(2): 203–232.

Frieburger, T.L., Marcum, C.D. and Pierce, M. (2010) 'The Impact of Race on the Pretrial Decision', *American Journal of Criminal Justice*, 35: 76–86.

Fryer, P. (1984) *Staying Power: The History of Black People in Britain*, London: Pluto Press.

Gabbidon, S.L. (2007) *Criminological Perspectives on Race and Crime*, New York: Routledge.

Gabbidon, S.L. and Taylor Greene, H. (2011) *Race and Crime: A Text/Reader*, London: Sage.

Garland, D. (1988) 'British Criminology before 1935', *British Journal of Criminology*, 28(2): 1–17.

Garland, D. (1994) 'Of Crimes and Criminals: The Development of Criminology in Britain', in Maguire, M., Morgan, R. and Reiner, R. (eds), *Oxford Handbook of Criminology*, Oxford: Oxford University Press, pp. 17–68.

Garland, D. (2001) *The Culture of Control: Crime and Social Order in Contemporary Society*, Oxford: Oxford University Press.

Garland, D. (2005) 'Penal Excess and Surplus Meaning: Public Torture Lynching in Twentieth-Century America', *Law and Society Review*, 39: 793–834.

Garland, J. and Chakraborti, N. (2006) 'Recognising and Responding to Victims of Rural Racism', *International Review of Victimology*, 13(1): 49–69.

Gilroy, P. (1987) *There Ain't No Black in the Union Jack: The Cultural Politics of Race and Nation*, London: Routledge.

Gilroy, P. (1993) *The Black Atlantic: Modernity and Double Consciousness*, London: Verso.

Gilroy, P. (2004) *After Empire: Melancholia or Convivial Culture?*, London: Taylor & Francis/Routledge.

Glass, R. (1960) *The Newcomers*, London: Centre for Urban Studies.

Glausser, W. (1990) 'Three Approaches to Locke and the Slave Trade', *Journal of the History of Ideas*, 51(2): 199–216.

Goddard, H. (1914) *Feeble-Mindedness: Its Causes and Consequences*, New York: The Macmillan Company.

Godfrey, B. and Dunstall, G. (eds) (2005) *Crime and Empire, 1840–1940: Criminal Justice in Local and Global Context*, Cullompton: Willan Publishing.

Goldberg, D.T. (1993) *Racist Culture: Philosophy and the Politics of Meaning*, Oxford: Blackwell.

Goldhagen, D.J. (1996) *Hitler's Willing Executioners: Ordinary Germans and the Holocaust*, London: Little, Brown.

Gordon, P. (1993) 'The Police and Racist Violence in Britain', in Björgo, T. and Witte, R. (eds) *Racist Violence in Europe*, Basingstoke: Macmillan Press, pp. 167–178.

Gordon, P. and Rosenberg, D. (1989) *Daily Racism: The Press and Black People in Britain*, London: The Runnymede Trust.

Gounev, P. and Bezlov, T. (2006) 'The Roma in Bulgaria's Criminal Justice System: From Ethnic Profiling to Imprisonment', *Critical Criminology*, 14: 313–338.

Greer, C., Ferrell, J. and Jewkes, J. (2007) 'It's the Image that Matters: Style, Substance and Critical Scholarship', *Crime Media and Culture*, 3: 5–10.

Greer, S. (2010) 'Anti-Terrorist Laws and the United Kingdom's "Suspect Muslim Community": A Reply to Pantazis and Pemberton', *British Journal of Criminology*, 50: 1171–1190.

Griffiths, P. (1971) *To Guard My People: The History of the Indian Police*, London: Ernest Benn Limited.

Grono, N. (2006) 'Darfur: The International Community's Failure to Protect', *African Affairs*, 105: 621–631.

Hagan, J. and Rymond-Richmond, W. (2009) *Darfur and the Crime of Genocide*, Cambridge: Cambridge University Press.

Hales, G., Lewis, C. and Silverstone, D. (2006) *Gun Crime: The Market in and Use of Illegal Firearms*, Research Study 298. London: Home Office.

Hales, J., Neville, C., Pudney, S. and Tipping, S. (2009) *Longitudinal Analysis of the Offending, Crime and Justice Survey 2003–06*, Research Report No. 19. London: Home Office.

Hall, N. (2005) *Hate Crime*, Cullompton: Willan Publishing.

Hall, S., Critcher, C., Jefferson, T., Clarke, J. and Roberts, B. (1978) *Policing the Crisis: Mugging, the State, and Law and Order*, London: Macmillan.

Hall, S., Winlow, S. and Ancrum, C. (2008) *Criminal Identities and Consumer Culture: Crime, Exclusion and the New Culture of Narcissism*, Cullompton: Willan Publishing.

Hallsworth, S. (2005) *Street Crime*, Cullompton: Willan Publishing.

Hallsworth, S. and Young, T. (2008) 'Gang Talk and Gang Talkers: A Critique', *Crime, Media, Culture*, 4: 175–195.

Hansard (2011) 'Counter-Terrorism Review', 26 January, col. 306–309.

Hartmann, P. and Husband, C. (1974) *Racism and the Mass Media*, London: Poytner-Davis.

Haveman, R. (2008) 'Doing Justice to Gacaca', in Smeulers, A. and Haveman, R. (eds), *Supranational Criminology: Towards a Criminology of International Crimes*, Antwerp: Intersentia, pp. 357–398.

Hayner, N.S. (1938) 'Social Factors in Oriental Crime', *American Journal of Sociology*, 43(6): 908–919.

Heer, G. and Atherton, S. (2008) '(In)Visible Barriers: The Experience of Asian Employees in the Probation Service', *The Howard Journal*, 47: 1–17.

Hentig, H. van (1948) *The Criminal and His Victim*, New Haven, CT: Yale University Press.

Her Majesty's Inspectorate of Constabulary (1996) *Developing Diversity in the Police Service*, London: Home Office.

Herrnstein, R. and Murray, C. (1994) *The Bell Curve: Intelligence and Class Structure in American Life*, New York: Free Press.

Hesse, B., Rai, D.K., Bennett, C. and McGilchrist, P. (1992) *Beneath the Surface: Racial Harassment*, Aldershot: Avebury.

Hill, R.S. (1986) *Policing the Colonial Frontier: The Theory and Practice of Coercive Social and Racial Control in New Zealand, 1767–1867*, Wellington, NZ: Department of Internal Affairs.

Hillyard, P. (1993) *Suspect Communities: People's Experience of the Prevention of Terrorism Acts in Britain*, London: Pluto Press.

Hogg, R. (2001) 'Penality and Modes of Regulating Indigenous Peoples in Australia', *Punishment and Society*, 3: 355–379.

Hogg, R. (2002) 'Criminology beyond the Nation State: Global Conflicts, Human Rights and the New World Disorder', in Carrington, K. and Hogg, R. (eds), *Critical Criminology: Issues, Debates, Challenges*, Cullompton: Willan Publishing, pp. 185–217.

Hogg, R.S., Druyts, E.F., Burris, S., Drucker, E. and Strathdee, S.A. (2008) 'Years of Life Lost to Prison: Racial and Gender Gradients in the United States of America', *Harm Reduction Journal*, 5(4).

Holdaway, S. (1996) *The Racialisation of British Policing*, Basingstoke: Macmillan.

Holdaway, S. and O'Neill, M. (2007) 'Black Police Associations and the Lawrence Report', in Rowe, M. (ed.) *Policing Beyond Macpherson: Issues in Policing, Race and Society*, Cullompton: Willan Publishing, pp. 88-106.

Home Office (1999) *Statistics on Race and the Criminal Justice System: A Home Office Publication under Section 95 of the Criminal Justice Act 1991*, London: Home Office.

Home Office (2000) *Statistics on Race and the Criminal Justice System: A Home Office Publication under Section 95 of the Criminal Justice Act 1991*, London: Home Office.

Home Office (2009) *Pursue, Prevent, Protect, Prepare: The United Kingdom's Strategy for Countering International Terrorism*, London: Home Office.

Home Office (2010a) *Crime in England and Wales 2009/10*, London: Home Office.

Home Office (2010b) *Operation of Police Powers under the Terrorism Act 2000 and Subsequent Legislation: Arrests, Outcomes and Stops & Searches, Quarterly Update to September 2009*, Statistical Bulletin 0410. London: Home Office.

Hood, R. (1992) *Race and Sentencing*, Oxford: Clarendon Press.

Hooton, E.A. (1939) *Crime and the Man*, Cambridge, MA: Harvard University Press.

Hopkins-Burke, R. (2001) *An Introduction to Criminological Theory*, Cullompton: Willan Publishing.

Hoskins, A. and O'Loughlin, B. (2009) 'Pre-Mediating Guilt: Radicalisation and Mediality in British News', *Critical Studies on Terrorism*, 2: 81–93.

House of Commons Communities and Local Government Committee (2010) *Preventing Violent Extremism: Sixth Report of Session 2009–10*, London: House of Commons.

House of Commons Home Affairs Committee (2007) *Young Black People and the Criminal Justice System*, London: The Stationery Office.

Howell, J. (2006) 'The Global War on Terror, Development and Civil Society', *Journal of International Development*, 18: 121–135.

Howell, J. and Lind, J. (2009) *Counter-Terrorism, Aid and Civil Society: Before and after the War on Terror*, Basingstoke: Palgrave Macmillan.

Hughes, G. (2007) *The Politics of Crime and Community*, London: Palgrave Macmillan.

Hughes, G. and Edwards, A. (eds) (2002) *Crime Control and Community: The New Politics of Public Safety*, Cullompton: Willan Publishing.

Human Rights Watch (2009) *'Wild Money': The Human Rights Consequences of Illegal Logging and Corruption in Indonesia's Forestry Sector*, New York: Human Rights Watch.

Hunte, J. (1965) *Nigger Hunting in England?* London: West Indian Standing Conference.

Hunter, J. (1914/15) 'Sterilization of Criminals', *Journal of the American Institute of Criminal Law and Criminology*: 514–539.

Huntington, S.P. (1997) *The Clash of Civilizations and the Remaking of World Order*, London: Simon & Schuster.

Iganski, P., Kielinger, V. and Patterson, S. (2005) *Hate Crimes against London's Jews*, London: Institute for Jewish Policy Research.

IRR (Institute of Race Relations) (1987) *Policing Against Black People*, London: Institute of Race Relations.

Jacobs, J.B. and Potter, K. (1998) *Hate Crimes: Criminal Law and Identity Politics*, New York: Oxford University Press.

James, Z. (2007) 'Policing Marginal Spaces: Controlling Gypsies and Travellers', *Criminology and Criminal Justice*, 7: 367–389.

Jansson, K. (2006) *Black and Minority Ethnic Groups' Experiences and Perceptions of Crime, Racially Motivated Crime and the Police: Findings from the 2004/05 British Crime Survey*, London: Home Office.

Jencks, C. (ed.) (1995) *Visual Culture*, London: Routledge.

Jenkinson, J. (1993) 'The 1919 Riots', in Panayi, P. (ed.), *Racial Violence in Britain, 1840–1950*, Leicester: Leicester University Press, pp. 92–111.

Jewkes, Y. (2004) *Media and Crime*, London: Sage.

Jewkes, Y. (2011) *Media and Crime*, second edition, London: Sage.

Johnston, L. (2006) 'Diversifying Police Recruitment? The Deployment of Police Community Support Officers in London', *The Howard Journal*, 45: 388–402.

Kaes, A. (2000) *M*, London: British Film Institute.

Kalra, V. and Rhodes, J. (2009) 'Local Events, National Implications: Riots in Oldham and Burnley 2001', in Waddington, D., Jobard, F. and King, M. (eds), *Rioting in the UK and France: A Comparative Analysis*, Cullompton: Willan Publishing, pp. 41–55.

Karmen, A. (1996) *Research into the Reasons Why the Murder Rate Has Dropped so Dramatically in New York City, 1994–95, Second Progress Report*, New York City: John Jay College of Criminal Justice.

Katz, J. (1988) *Seductions of Crime*, New York: Basic Books.

Keith, Justice (2006) *Report of the Zahid Mubarek Inquiry, Volumes 1 and 2*, London: The Stationery Office.

Keith, M. (1993) *Race, Riots and Policing – Lore and Disorder in a Multiracist Society*, London: UCL Press.

Kelman, H.C. (1973) 'Violence without Moral Restraint: Reflections on the Dehumanization of Victims and Victimizers', *Journal of Social Issues*, 29: 25–61.

Kerr, A. (2006) 'Spilling Hot Coffee? Grand Theft Auto as Contested Cultural Product', in Garrelts, N. (ed.), *The Meaning and Culture of Grand Theft Auto: Critical Essays*, Jefferson, NC: McFarland Press, pp. 17–34.

King, P. (2003) 'Moral Panics and Violent Street Crime, 1750–2000: A Comparative Perspective', in Godfrey, B., Emsley, C. and Dunstall, G. (eds), *Comparative Histories of Crime*, Cullompton: Willan Publishing.

King, R.D., Messner, S.F. and Baller, R.D. (2009) 'Contemporary Hate Crimes, Law Enforcement, and the Legacy of Racial Violence', *American Sociological Review*, 74: 291–315.

Lambert, R. (2008) 'Empowering Salafis and Islamists against Al-Qaeda: A London Counterterrorism Case Study', *Political Studies*, January: 31–35.

Larke, G.S. (2003) 'Organized Crime: Mafia Myths in Film and Television', in Mason, P. (ed.), *Criminal Visions: Media Representations of Crime and Justice*, Cullompton: Willan Publishing, pp. 116–132.

Law, I. (2002) *Race in the News*, Basingstoke: Palgrave.

Law, I. (2010) *Racism and Ethnicity: Global Debates, Dilemmas, Directions*, London: Pearson Education

Lea, R. and Chambers, G. (2007) 'Monoamine Oxidase, Addiction, and the "Warrior" Gene Hypothesis', *New Zealand Medical Journal*, Vol. 120, No. 1250.

Lee, M. (2007) *Inventing Fear of Crime: Criminology and the Politics of Anxiety*, Cullompton: Willan Publishing.

Leonard, D. (2006) 'Virtual Gangstas, Coming to a Suburban House Near You: Demonization, Commodification and Policing Blackness', in Garrelts, N. (ed.), *The Meaning and Culture of Grand Theft Auto: Critical Essays*, Jefferson, NC: McFarland Press, pp. 49–69.

Lewis, S. (2009) 'The Probation Service and Race Equality', in Bhui, H.S. (ed.), *Race and Criminal Justice*, London: Sage, pp. 102–121.

Loader, I. (2000) 'Plural Policing and Democratic Governance', *Social and Legal Studies*, 9: 323–345.

Loader, I. and Mulcahy, A. (2003) *Policing and the Condition of England – Memory, Politics and Culture*, Oxford: Oxford University Press.

Loader, I. and Walker, N. (2007) *Civilizing Security*, Cambridge: Cambridge University Press.

Macpherson, Sir W. (1999) *The Stephen Lawrence Inquiry – Report of an Inquiry by Sir William Macpherson of Cluny*, CM 4262-1, London: HMSO.

Maier-Katkin, D., Mears, D.P. and Bernard, T.J. (2009) 'Towards a Criminology of Crimes Against Humanity', *Theoretical Criminology*, 13: 227–255.

Malik, K. (1996) *The Meaning of Race: Race, History and Culture in Western Society*, London: Macmillan.

Malik, S. (2002) *Representing Black Britain: Black and Asian Images on Television*, London: Sage.

Malleson, K. (2009) 'Diversity in the Judiciary: The Case for Positive Action', *Journal of Law and Society*, 36: 376–402.

Maneri, M. (2011) 'Media Discourse on Immigration: Control Practices and the Language We Live', in Palidda, S. (ed.), *Racial Criminalization of Migrants in the 21st Century*, Farnham: Ashgate, pp. 77–93.

Mannheim, H. (1965) *Comparative Criminology: A Text Book*, London: Routledge and Kegan Paul.

Mantouvalou, V. (2006) 'Anti-Terrorism Measures Fall Short of European Standards', in Bunyan, T. (ed.), *The War on Freedom and Democracy: Essays on Civil Liberties in Europe*, Nottingham: Spokesman Books, pp. 161–166.

Matsueda, R.L. (2006) 'Differential Social Organization, Collective Action, and Crime', *Crime, Law, and Social Change*, 46: 3–33.

Mazerolle, L. and Ransley, J. (2005) *Third Party Policing*, Cambridge: Cambridge University Press.

McClintock, A. (1995) *Imperial Leather – Race, Gender and Sexuality in the Colonial Contest*, London: Routledge.

McCulloch, J. and Pickering, S. (2005) 'Suppressing the Financing of Terrorism: Proliferating State Crime, Eroding Censure and Extending Neo-Colonialism', *British Journal of Criminology*, 45: 470–486.

McDevitt, J., Levin, J. and Bennett, S. (2002) 'Hate Crime Offenders: An Expanded Typology', *Journal of Social Issues*, 58: 303–317.

McGhee, D. (2008) *The End of Multiculturalism? Terrorism, Integration and Human Rights*, Maidenhead: Open University Press.

McLaughlin, E. (1991) 'Police Accountability and Black People: into the 1990s', in Cashmore, E. and McLaughlin, E. (eds), *Out of Order? Policing Black People*, London: Routledge, pp. 109–133.

McLaughlin, E. (2007) *The New Policing*, London: Sage.

McMahon, W. and Roberts, R. (2011) 'Truth and Lies about "Race" and "Crime"', *Criminal Justice Matters*, 83: 20–21.

Meer, N. and Modood, T. (2011) 'The Racialisation of Muslims', in Sayyid, S. and Karim Vakil, A. (eds), *Thinking Through Islamaphobia: Global Perspectives*, London: C. Hurst and Co., pp. 69–83.

Melossi, D. (2008) *Controlling Crime, Controlling Society: Thinking about Crime in Europe and America*, Cambridge: Polity Press.

Michael, J. and Adler, M. (1933) *Crime, Law and Social Science*, New York: Harcourt, Brace Jovanovich.

Miles, R. (1989) *Racism*, London: Routledge.

Miles, R. (1993) *Racism after 'Race Relations'*, London: Routledge.

Miller, K. (2007) 'Jacking the Dial: Radio, Race and Place in *Grand Theft Auto*', *Ethnomusicology*, 51: 402–438.

Ministry of Justice (2010) *Statistics on Race and the Criminal Justice System 2008/09*, London: Ministry of Justice.

Modood, T. (2007) *Multiculturalism: A Civic Idea*, London: Polity Press.

Modood, T. and Ahmad, F. (2007) 'British Muslim Perspectives on Multiculturalism', *Theory Culture Society*, 24: 187–213.

Montagu, A. (1972) *Statement on Race*, Oxford: Oxford University Press.

Mooney, J. and Young, J. (2000) 'Policing Ethnic Minorities: Stop and Search in North London', in Marlow, A. and Loveday, B. (eds), *After Macpherson: Policing after the Stephen Lawrence Inquiry*, Lyme Regis: Russell House Publishing, pp. 73–87.

Morgan, R. (2006) 'Race, Probation and Inspections', in Lewis, S., Raynor, P., Smith, D. and Wardak, A. (eds), *Race and Probation*, Cullompton: Willan Publishing, pp. 41–57.

Morris, L. (1994) *Dangerous Classes: The Underclass and Social Citizenship*, London: Routledge.

Morrison, B. (2009) *Identifying and Responding to Bias in the Criminal Justice System: A Review of International and New Zealand Research*, Wellington, NZ: Ministry of Justice.

Morsch, J. (1991) 'The Problem of Motive in Hate Crime: The Argument against the Presumption of Racial Motivation', *Journal of Criminal Law and Criminology*, 82: 659–689.

Mossman, E., Mayhew, P., Jordan, J. and Rowe, M. (2008) *Literature Reviews about the Barriers to Recruiting a Diverse Workforce*, Wellington: New Zealand Police.

Mullard, M. and Cole, B. (2007) 'Introduction', in Mullard, M. and Cole, B. (eds), *Globalisation, Citizenship and the War on Terror*, Cheltenham: Edward Elgar, pp. 1–12.

Mullins, C. (2009) '"We Are Going to Rape You and Taste Tutsi Women": Rape during the 1994 Rwandan Genocide', *British Journal of Criminology*, 49: 719–735.

Muncie, J. (1996) 'The Construction and Deconstruction of Crime', in Muncie, J. and McLaughlin, E. (eds), *The Problem of Crime*, London: Open University Press, pp. 5–64.

Muncie, J. (2004) *Youth and Crime*, London: Sage.

Murji, K. (2002) 'It's Not a Black Thing', *Criminal Justice Matters*, 47: 32–33.

Murji, K. and Solomos, J. (eds) (2005) *Racialization: Studies in Theory and Practice*, Oxford: Oxford University Press.

Murray, C. (1984) *Losing Ground: American Social Policy: 1950–1980*, New York: Basic Books.

Murray, S. (2005) 'High Art/Low Life: The Art of Playing *Grand Theft Auto*', *Performing Arts Journal*, 27: 91–98.

Mustard, D. (2001) 'Racial, Ethnic and Gender Disparities in Sentencing: Evidence from the US Federal Courts', *The Journal of Law and Economics*, 19: 285–314.

MVA and Miller, J. (2000) *Profiling Populations Available for Stops and Searches*, Police Research Series Paper 131. London: Home Office.

Mythen, G., Walklate, S. and Khan, F. (2009) '"I'm a Muslim, but I'm not a Terrorist": Victimization, Risky Identities and the Performance of Safety', *British Journal of Criminology*, 49(6): 736–754.

Newburn, T. (2007) *Criminology*, Cullompton: Willan Publishing.

NOMS (National Offender Management Service) (2011) *Annual Staff Diversity Review: 2009/10*, London: Ministry of Justice.

Norris, C., Fielding, N., Kemp, C. and Fielding, J. (1992) 'Black and Blue: An Analysis of the Influence of Race on Being Stopped by the Police', *British Journal of Sociology*, 43: 207–223.

Nott, J.C. and Gliddon, G.R. (1854) *Types of Mankind: Or Ethnological Researches*, Philadelphia, PA: Lippincott.

Oakley, G. (1976) *The Devil's Music: A History of the Blues*, London: BBC Books.

Oliver, M.B. (1994) 'Portrayals of Crime, Race, and Aggression in Reality-Based Police Shows: A Content Analysis', *Journal of Broadcast and Electronic Media*, 38: 179–192.

O'Malley, P. (1973) 'The Amplification of Māori Crime: Cultural and Economic Barriers to Equal Justice in New Zealand', *Race*, 15(1): 47–57.

Oriola, T. (2009) 'Counter-Terrorism and Alien Justice: The Case of Security Certificates in Canada', *Critical Studies on Terrorism*, 2: 257–274.

OSJI (Open Society Justice Initiative) (2009) *Ethnic Profiling in the European Union: Pervasive, Ineffective and Discriminatory*, New York: OSJI.

Pager, D. (2008) 'The Republican Ideal?: National Minorities and the Criminal Justice System in Contemporary France', *Punishment and Society*, 10: 375–400.

Pantazis, C. and Pemberton, S. (2009) 'From the "Old" to the "New" Suspect Community: Examining the Impacts of Recent UK Counter-Terrorist Legislation', *British Journal of Criminology*, 49: 646–666.

Park, R. and Burgess, E. (1925/1967) *The City*, Chicago: University of Chicago Press.

Pearson, G. (1983) *Hooligan – A History of Respectable Fears*, London: Macmillan.

Perry, B. (2001) *In the Name of Hate: Understanding Hate Crime*, New York: Routledge.

Petersen, J.B. (2009) 'Corner-Boy Masculinity: Intersections of Inner-City Manhood', in Potter, T. and Marshall, C.W. (eds), *The Wire: Urban Decay and American Television*, New York: Continuum, pp. 107–121.

Pitts, J. (2008) *Reluctant Gangsters: The Changing Face of Youth Crime*, Cullompton: Willan Publishing.

Police Review (2001) 'Diversity Drive "Not Motivated" by Human Rights', *Police Review*, 27 April, p. 14.

Potter, T. and Marshall, C.W. (eds) (2009) *The Wire: Urban Decay and American Television*, New York: Continuum.

Pratt, J. (2008) 'When Penal Populism Stops: Legitimacy, Scandal and the Power to Punish in New Zealand', *Australian and New Zealand Journal of Criminology*, 41: 364–383.

Prenzler, T. (2009) *Ethics and Accountability in Criminal Justice: Towards a Universal Standard*, Bowen Hills, Queensland: Australian Academic Press.

Prunier, G. (2007) *Darfur: The Ambiguous Genocide*, London: C. Hurst and Co.

Pryce, K. (1979) *Endless Pressure: A Study of West Indian Lifestyles in Bristol*, Bristol: Bristol Classical Press.

Radzinowicz, L. (1966) *Ideology and Crime: A Study of Crime in its Social and Historical Context*, London: Heinemann Educational.

Rafter, N. (1992) 'Criminal Anthropology in the United States', *Criminology*, 30: 525–545.

Rafter, N. (2004) 'Earnest A. Hooton and the Biological Tradition in American Criminology', *Criminology*, 42: 735–773.

Rafter, N. (2006) *Shots in the Mirror: Crime Films and Society*, New York: Oxford University Press.

Rafter, N. (2008) *The Criminal Brain: Understanding Biological Theories of Crime*, New York: New York University Press.

Rafter, N. (2008) 'Criminology's Darkest Hour: Biocriminology in Nazi Germany', *Australian and New Zealand Journal of Criminology*, 41(2): 287–306.

Ramirez, D.A., Hoopes, J. and Quinlan, T.L. (2003) 'Defining Racial Profiling in a Post-September 11 World', *American Criminal Law Review*, 40: 1195–1233.

Rattansi, A. and Westwood, S. (1994) 'Modern Racisms, Racialised Identities', in Rattansi, A. and Westwood, S. (eds), *Racism, Modernity and Identity on the Western Front*, Oxford: Polity Press, pp. 1–12.

Raumati Hook, G. (2009) '"Warrior Genes" and the Disease of Being Māori', *MAI Review*, 2. www.review.mai.ac.nz

Ray, L., Smith, D. and Wastell, L. (2004) 'Shame, Rage and Racist Violence', *British Journal of Criminology*, 44: 350–368.

Reiner, R. (1993) 'Race, Crime and Justice: Models of Interpretation', in Gelsthorpe, L. and McWilliam, W. (eds), *Minority Ethnic Groups and the Criminal Justice System*, Cambridge: Cambridge University Institute of Criminology.

Reiner, R. (2007) *Law and Order: An Honest Citizen's Guide to Crime and Control*, Cambridge: Polity Press.

Rex, J. (1970) *Race Relations in Sociological Theory*, London: Weidenfeld and Nicolson.

Rex, J. (1986) *Race and Ethnicity*, Milton Keynes: Open University Press.

Rex, J. and Moore, R. (1967) *Race, Community and Conflict*, London: Oxford University Press.

Richards, A. (2011) 'The Problem with "Radicalization": The Remit of "Prevent" and the Need to Refocus on Terrorism in the UK', *International Affairs*, 87: 143–152.

Richards, G. (1997) *Race, Racism and Psychology: Towards a Reflexive History*, London: Routledge.

Richards, K. (2007) *Juveniles' Contact with the Criminal Justice System in Australia*, Canberra: Australian Institute of Criminology.

Roberg, R., Novak, K. and Cordner, G. (2005) *Police and Society*, Los Angeles, CA: Roxbury Publishing Company.

Roberts, C. and Innes, M. (2009) 'The "Death" of Dixon?: Policing Gun Crime and the End of the Generalist Police Constable in England and Wales', *Criminology and Criminal Justice*, 9: 337–357.

Roberts, J. and Gabor, T. (1990) 'Lombrosian Wine in a New Bottle: Research on Crime and Race', *Canadian Journal of Criminology*, 32: 291–313.

Robertson, G. (2006) *Crimes Against Humanity: The Struggle for Global Justice* (3rd edition), London: Penguin.

Rock, P. (ed.) (1994) *History of Criminology*, Aldershot: Dartmouth.

Rock, P. (2007) 'Caesare Lombroso as a Signal Criminologist', *Criminology and Criminal Justice*, 7(2): 117–133.

Rowe, M. (1998) *The Racialization of Disorder in Twentieth Century Britain*, Aldershot: Ashgate.

Rowe, M. (2004) *Policing, Race and Racism*, Cullompton: Willan Publishing.

Rowe, M. and Garland, J. (2007) 'Police Diversity Training: A Silver Bullet Tarnished?', in Rowe, M. (ed.), *Policing beyond Macpherson: Issues in Policing, Race, and Society*, Cullompton: Willan Publishing, pp. 43–65.

Rummel, R.J. (1994) *Death by Government*, New Brunswick, NJ: Transaction Publishers.

Rushton, J. Philippe (1990) 'Race and Crime: A Reply to Roberts and Gabor', *Canadian Journal of Criminology*, 32: 315–319.

Sabine, G.H. (1960) *A History of Political Theory*, London: George G. Harrap and Co. Ltd.

Saggar, S. (1992) *Race and Politics in Britain*, London: Harvester Wheatsheaf.

Sampson, A. and Phillips, C. (1992) *Multiple Victimisation: Racial Attacks on an East London Estate*, Crime Prevention Unit Series Paper 56. London: Home Office.

Sampson, R. and Wilson, W.J. (1995) 'Toward a Theory of Race, Crime, and Urban Inequality', in Hagan, J. and Peterson, R. (eds), *Crime and Inequality*, Palo Alto, CA: Stanford University Press.

Savelsberg, J.J. (2010) *Crime and Human Rights*, London: Sage.

Scally, R.J. (1995) *The End of Hidden Ireland: Rebellion, Famine and Emigration*, Oxford: Oxford University Press.

Scarman, Lord (1981) *The Brixton Disorders: 10–12 April 1981 – Report of an Inquiry by the Rt Hon Lord Scarman, OBE*, London: HMSO.

Scottish Government (2011) *Crime and Justice Series: Racist Incidents Recorded by the Police in Scotland, 2009–10*, Edinburgh: Scottish Government.

Seawell, P.D. (2005) 'Rape as a Social Construct: A Comparative Analysis of Rape in the Bosnian and Rwandan Genocides and U.S. Domestic Law', *National Black Law Journal*, 18: 180–200.

Sharp, C. and Budd, T. (2005) *Minority Ethnic Groups and Crime: Findings from the Offending, Crime and Justice Survey 2003*, Online Report 33/05. London: Home Office.

Shaw, C.R. and Mackay, H.D. (1942) *Juvenile Delinquency and Urban Areas*, Chicago: Chicago University Press.

Shaw, M. (2003) *War and Genocide*, Cambridge: Polity Press.

Shihadeh, E. and Shrum, W. (2004) 'Serious Crime in Urban Neighbourhoods: Is There a Race Effect?', *Sociological Spectrum*, 24(4): 507–533.

Sibbitt, R. (1997) *The Perpetrators of Racial Harassment and Racial Violence*, Home Office Research Study 176. London: Home Office.

Siemens, D. (2009) 'Explaining Crime: Berlin Newspapers and the Construction of the Criminal in Weimar Germany', *Journal of European Studies*, 39(3): 336–352.

Sim, J. (1982) 'Scarman: The Police Counter-Attack', in Eve, M. and Musson, D. (eds), *The Socialist Register 1982*, pp. 57–77.

Simon, D. (2000) 'Corporate Environmental Crimes and Social Inequality: New Directions for Environmental Justice Research', *American Behavioral Scientist*, 43: 633–645.

Simon, J. (2007) *Governing Through Crime: How the War on Crime Transformed American Democracy and Created a Culture of Fear*, Oxford: Oxford University Press.

Sivanandan, A. (2006) 'Race, Terror and Civil Society', *Race and Class*, 47: 1–8.

Skinns, L. (2010) *Police Custody: Governance, Legitimacy and Reform in the Criminal Justice Process*, Cullompton: Willan Publishing.

Small, S. (1994) *Racialised Barriers: The Black Experience in the United States and England in the 1980s*, London: Routledge.

Smeulers, A. and Hoex, L. (2010) 'Studying the Microdynamics of the Rwandan Genocide', *British Journal of Criminology*, 50: 435–454.

Smith, D.J. (1994) 'Race, Crime and Criminal Justice', in Maguier, M., Reiner, R. and Morgan, R. (eds), *The Oxford Handbook of Criminology*, Oxford: Clarendon Press, pp. 1041–1117.

Smith, K., Flatley, J., Coleman, K., Osborne, S., Kaiza, P. and Roe, S. (2010) *Homicides, Firearm Offences and Intimate Violence 2008/09*, Statistical Bulletin 01/10. London: Home Office.

Snowball, L. and Weatherburn, D. (2007) 'Does Racial Bias in Sentencing Contribute to Indigenous Overrepresentation in Prison?', *Australian and New Zealand Journal of Criminology*, 40: 272–290.

Solinge, T.B. van (2010) 'Deforestation Crimes and Conflicts in the Amazon', *Critical Criminology*, 18: 263–277.

Solomos, J. (1988) *Black Youth, Racism and the State: The Politics of Ideology and Policy*, Cambridge; Cambridge University Press.

Solomos, J. and Back, L. (1996) *Racism and Society*, London: Macmillan.

South, N. (2010) 'The Ecocidal Tendencies of Late Modernity: Transnational Crime, Social Exclusion, Victims and Rights', in White, R. (ed.), *Global Environmental Harm: Criminological Perspectives*, Cullompton: Willan Publishing, pp. 228–247.

Spalek, B. (ed.) (2002) *Islam, Crime and Criminal Justice*, Cullompton: Willan Publishing.

Spalek, B. and Lambert, R. (2008) 'Muslim Communities, Counter-Terrorism and Counter-Radicalisation: A Critically Reflective Approach to Engagement', *International Journal of Law, Crime and Justice*, 36: 257–270.

Spalek, B., Lambert, R. and Baker, A.H. (2009) 'Minority Muslim Communities and Criminal Justice: Stigmatized UK Faith Identities post- 9/11 and 7/7', in Bhui, H.S. (ed.), *Race and Criminal Justice*, London: Sage, pp. 170–187.

Spalek, B. and McDonald, L.Z. (2009) 'Terror Crime Prevention: Constructing Muslim Practices and Beliefs as "Anti-Social" and "Extreme" through CONTEST 2', *Social Policy and Society*, 9: 123–132.

Spohn, C.C. (2000) 'Thirty Years of Sentencing Reform: The Quest for a Racially Neutral Sentencing Process', *Criminal Justice*, 3: 427–501.

Stanley, E. (2007) 'Towards a Criminology for Human Rights', in Barton, A., Corteen, K., Scott, D. and Whyte, D. (eds), *Expanding the Criminological Imagination: Critical Readings in Criminology*, Cullompton: Willan Publishing, pp. 168–197.

Stanley, E. (2009) *Torture, Truth and Justice: The Case of Timor-Leste*, London: Routledge.

Steen, S., Engen, R. and Gainey, R. (2005) 'Images of Danger: Racial Stereotyping, Case Processing and Criminal Sentencing', *Criminology*, 43: 435–468.

Stevens, P. and Willis, C. (1979) *Race, Crime and Arrests*, London: Home Office.

Stone, V. and Tuffin, R. (2000) *Attitudes of People from Minority Ethnic Communities towards a Career in the Police Service*, Police Research Series Paper 136. London: Home Office.

Sutherland, E. (1949) *White Collar Crime*, New York: Holt, Rinehart & Winston.

Sykes, G.M. and Matza, D. (1957) 'Techniques of Neutralization: A Theory of Delinquency', *American Sociological* Review, 22: 664–670.

Tamang, R. (2009) 'Portrayal of Crime in Televised News in Canada: Distortion and Privileges', *The Journal of the Institute of Justice and International Studies*, 9: 193–199.

Tamkin, P., Aston, J., Cummings, J., Hooker, H., Pollard, E., Rick, J., Sheppard, E. and Tackey, N.D. (2003) *A Review of Training in Racism Awareness and Valuing Cultural Diversity*, London: Institute for Employment Studies.

Taylor, I., Walton, P. and Young, J. (1973) *The New Criminology: For a Social Theory of Deviance*, London: Routledge and Kegan Paul.

Taylor, N. (2007) *Juveniles in Detention in Australia, 1981–2007*, Canberra: Australian Institute of Criminology.

Taylor, S. (2009) 'The Crown Prosecution Service and Race Equality', in Bhui, H.S. (ed.), *Race and the Criminal Justice System*, London: Sage, pp. 66–82.

Tilley, N. (2008) 'Broken Windows', in Newburn, T. and Neyroud, P. (eds), *Dictionary of Policing*, Cullompton: Willan Publishing, pp. 20–22.

Turk, A. (1969) *Criminality and the Social Order*, Chicago: Rand-McNally.

Valentino, B.A. (2004) *Final Solutions: Mass Killing and Genocide in the 20th Century*, Ithaca, NY and London: Cornell University Press.

Van Dijk, T. (1991) *Racism and the Press*, London: Routledge.

Vanstone, M. (2006) 'Room for Improvement: A History of the Probation Service's Response to Race', in Lewis, S., Raynor, P., Smith, D. and Wardak, A. (eds), *Race and Probation*, Cullompton: Willan Publishing, pp. 13–24.

Vold, G. and Bernard, T. (1986) *Theoretical Criminology* (3rd edition), New York: Oxford University Press.

Wacquant, L. (2000) 'The New "Peculiar Institution": On the Prison as Surrogate Ghetto', *Theoretical Criminology*, 4: 377–389.

Wacquant, L. (2001) 'Deadly Symbiosis: When Ghetto and Prison Meet and Mesh', *Punishment and Society*, 3: 95–134.

Wacquant, L. (2009) *Punishing the Poor: The Neoliberal Government of Social Insecurity*, Durham, NC: Duke University Press.

Waddington, P.A.J., Stenson, K. and Don, D. (2004) 'In Proportion: Race and Police Stop and Search', *British Journal of Criminology*, 44: 889–914.

Walker, C. (2007) 'Keeping Control of Terrorists without Losing Control of Constitutionalism', *Stanford Law Review*, 59: 1395–1463.

Walker, C. (2009) 'Neighbor Terrorism and the All-Risks Policing of Terrorism', *Journal of National Security Law and Policy*, 3: 121–168.

Walker, M.A. (1989) 'The Court Disposal and Remands of White, Afro-Caribbean, and Asian Men, London 1983', *British Journal of Criminology*, 29: 353–367.

Walmsley, R. (2009) *World Prison Population List* (8th edition), London: King's College, International Centre for Prison Studies.

Walsh, A. and Beaver, K.M. (eds) (2009) *Biosocial Criminology: New Directions in Theory and Research*, New York: Routledge.

Walters, R. (2009) 'The State, Knowledge Production and Criminology', in Sim, J., Tombs, S. and Whyte, D. (eds), *State, Power, Crime: Readings in Critical Criminology*, London: Sage, pp. 200–213.

Ward, G., Farrell, A. and Rousseau, D. (2009) 'Does Racial Balance in Workforce Representation Yield Equal Justice? Race Relations of Sentencing in Federal Court Organizations', *Law & Society Review*, 43: 757–805.

Webster, C. (2003) 'Race, Space and Fear: Imagined Geographies of Racism, Crime, Violence and Disorder in Northern England', *Capital and Class*, 80: 95–122.

Webster, C. (2007) *Understanding Race and Crime*, Maidenhead: Open University Press.

Webster, C. (in press, 2012) 'The Discourse on "Race" in Criminological Theory', in Hall, S. and Winlow, S. (eds), *New Directions in Criminological Theory*, London: Routledge.

West, H. and Sobel, W. (2009) *Prison Inmates at Mid-Year 2008*, Washington, DC: Bureau of Justice Statistics.

Westmarland, L. (2002) *Gender and Policing: Sex, Power and Police Culture*, Cullompton: Willan Publishing.

Wetzell, R.F. (2000) *Inventing the Criminal: A History of German Criminology, 1880–1945*, Chapel Hill, NC: University of North Carolina Press.

White, R. (2008) *Crimes Against Nature: Environmental Criminology and Ecological Justice*, Cullompton: Willan Publishing.

White, R. (2010) 'Globalisation and Environmental Harm', in White, R. (ed.), *Global Environmental Harm: Criminological Perspectives*, Cullompton: Willan Publishing, pp. 3–19.

White, R. (2011) *Transnational Environmental Crime: Towards an Eco-Global Criminology*, London: Routledge.

Whitfield, J. (2004) *Unhappy Dialogue: The Metropolitan Police and Black Londoners in Post-War Britain*, Cullompton: Willan Publishing.

Wilkins, L. (1964) *Social Deviance*, London: Tavistock.

Willetts, T. (2007) 'People Have Started Carrying Guns Personalised in Different Colours', *The Guardian*, 3 August.

Willis, C. (1983) *The Use, Effectiveness and Impact of Police Stop and Search Powers*, London: Home Office.

Wilson, J.Q. and Herrnstein, R. (1985) *Crime and Human Nature*, New York: Simon & Schuster.

Wilson, J.Q. and Kelling, G. (1982) 'Broken Windows', *Atlantic Monthly*, 249(3): 29–36, 38.

Wilson, W.J. (1987) *The Truly Disadvantaged: The Inner City, the Underclass, and Public Policy*, Chicago: University of Chicago Press.

Wood, J. and Shearing, C. (2007) *Imaging Security*, Cullompton: Willan Publishing.

Wright, J.P. (2009) 'Inconvenient Truths: Science, Race and Crime', in Walsh, A. and Beaver, K.M. (eds), *Biosocial Criminology: New Directions in Theory and Research*, New York: Routledge, pp. 137–153.

Wynn, N. (2004) 'Counselling the Mafia: The Sopranos', *Journal of American Studies*, 38: 127–132.

Young, J. (2011) *The Criminological Imagination*, Cambridge: Polity Press.

Young, R.J.C. (1995) *Colonial Desire – Hybridity in Theory, Culture and Race*, London: Routledge.

Zedner, L. (2002) 'Victims', in Maguire, M., Morgan, R. and Reiner, R. (eds), *Oxford Handbook of Criminology* (3rd edition), Oxford: Oxford University Press, pp. 419–456.

Zimring, F.E. (2003) *The Contradictions of American Capital Punishment*, New York: Oxford University Press.

Index

213